Canadian Environmental
Assessment in Transition

Canadian Environmental Assessment in Transition

edited by
A. John Sinclair

Department of Geography Publication Series

Series Editor   Bruce Mitchell
Editorial Assistant   Kate Evans
Cover Design   Kathy Lawson
Printing   M & T Insta-Print (K-W) Ltd.

Cover Photos by Barrett and Mackay Photography Inc.

Canadian Association of Geographers

Public Issues Committee
General Editor   Jean Andrey
Publication Number 5

Canadian Cataloguing in Publication Data

Main entry under title:

Canadian Cataloguing in Publication Data

Main entry under title:

Canadian environmental assessment in transition

Department of Geography publication series, ISSN 0843-7378
; 49)
ISBN 0-921083-57-2

1. Environmental impact analysis - Canada. I. Sinclair, A. John.
II. University of Waterloo. Dept. of Geography.
III. Series.

GE160.C3C34 1997   333.7'14'0971   C97-931549-2

Preface

The Canadian Association of Geographers' (CAG) Environment and Resources Study Group was formed in response to the growing number of people in the geographic community with both teaching and research interests in these areas. As part of its current mission the group works to facilitate a network among Canadian geographers who are interested in environment and resource studies and who are affiliated with government agencies, the private sector, non-government organizations, universities and other organizations. The purpose of the network is to encourage work or activities and the sharing of interests in this area. Among other activities, the study group has organized special sessions at the annual meetings of the CAG to fulfill this mission.

The current book is based, in large part, on papers presented during a series of special sessions organized by the study group for the 1996 annual meetings of the CAG in Saskatoon, Saskatchewan. In the original call for papers the net was cast widely around the focus - "Canadian Environmental Assessment in Transition". Authors were asked to direct their papers to recent developments - conceptual, methodological, institutional - and their application or demonstration in Canadian case studies of any aspect of environmental assessment.

To present the works as clearly as possible, the eleven refereed papers included in this book have been divided into three sections which find their link in common questions relating to environmental assessment (EA) process and procedure. The three sections deal with: Issues of Public Involvement in EA; Methodological Approaches to EA Components and Processes; and, Contextual Considerations for Environmental Assessment. Canadian case studies are used to illuminate the arguments presented in the papers. In this way the project adds considerably to previous works on EA by geographers, such as Whitney and MacLaren's (1985) *Environmental Impact Assessment: The Canadian Experience.*

The book is the fifth to be published in the CAG Public Issues series. The Public Issues Study Group (formerly Committee) was formed in the late 1980s to promote understanding and stimulate geographical research on matters of public importance. All of the monographs in this series are based, at least in part, on papers presented at annual meetings of the Canadian Association of Geographers.

Acknowledgements

I would first like to thank Jean Andrey for encouraging me to take on this project and for helping out right from step one - drafting the call for papers. The reviewers are owed special thanks for the time and effort required to read and comment on *all* of the papers submitted. The assistance and support of the series editor, Bruce Mitchell, was also greatly appreciated. Alan Diduck not only provided valued input, but also offered assistance with other pursuits allowing me to finish this project in a timely fashion, for which I am indebted.

Lastly, I owe a great deal to Kate Evans, and her two assistants Molly and Maggie, for their efforts in producing this manuscript and for always keeping me on my toes by "never being wrong".

Table of Contents

List of Figures

List of Tables

Introduction

Canadian Environmental Assessment in Transition:
What Does the Future Hold?

A. John Sinclair
University of Manitoba

I t is less than thirty years since the United States Congress introduced the world to the first legislated environmental assessment (EA) process under the enabling provisions of the National Environmental Policy Act (1969). As Nikiforuk (1997:4) notes, it is quite a remarkable feat that in this time nearly 100 countries around the world have adopted similar public policies - "even institutions as big as the World Bank now endorse EA". It is also true that during this time EA processes and provisions have remained in an almost constant state of transition as we have learned more about the strengths and weaknesses of existing EA theory and practice.

Many identify the basic underpinnings of EA as being quite simple. Meredith (1991), for example, describes EA as a form of "minimum regret planning"; through assessment we ensure that externalities are identified, evaluated and incorporated into the decision-making process. Wood (1995), views EA as the evaluation of the effects likely to arise from a major project (or other action) significantly affecting the natural and human environment. Northey (1997:2), author of the 761 page "guide" to the Canadian Environmental Assessment Act, says that "after weighing the impacts and costs to creatures, plants and human communities, an EA gives a public agency or public representatives all the evidence they need to make an informed decision: a go or no go. That's it. It's no more compelling than that".

Out of these seemingly simple roots have grown complicated Acts and regulations that attempt to guide EA decision making. Along with this, a whole host of ideas and concepts of what a "proper" EA should include, and through
what methods it should be carried out, have evolved. As
well, we are slowly gaining insight into the true nature of
EA. Beattie (1995) offers three truths: EAs are not science -
although they often use the results and techniques of science; EAs always contain unexamined and unexplained
value assumptions; and, EAs are and will always be political. The last of these has caused, perhaps, the most controversy in the evolution of "proper" EA and is the least acceptable to most EA practitioners.

Considerable human and financial resources regularly
are devoted to individual assessments, and there is a steady
and growing stream of papers in both the gray and scholar-
ly literature into new areas of concern, such as gender-
impact assessment (Verloo and Roggeband, 1996), strategic
perspectives analysis (Dale and Lane, 1994) and strategic
environmental assessment (Partidário, 1996). In spite of
this, and perhaps as a result, debates continue to flourish
at the conceptual, regulatory, institutional and applied levels. In Canada there is growing concern over the efficiency
and integrity of EA as it has evolved in this country.
According to Smith (1993:1), "Despite two decades of evolution and a myriad of techniques, present practice appears
unable to help in preventing environmental disasters...or
poor resource management...". He suggests that these problems have not occurred because developments were
unplanned or their impacts unforeseen, but rather because
EA has been flawed conceptually.

In a highly critical report, Nikiforuk (1997:i), describes the EA process at the federal level in Canada as follows:

Environmental assessment has become a cynical, irrational and highly discretionary federal public policy in Canada. What should be a coherent and democratic filter to ensure that ecological and economic follies do not ruin Canada's natural riches has become a bureaucratic exercise that is neither cost-effective nor conservation-minded.

Gibson (1992), Delicaet (1995) and others, have detailed the deficiencies of the new federal EA legislation in Canada and have compared it to the process it replaced, the Environmental Assessment Review Process (EARP). Currently, the federal EA agency in Canada is scrambling to find ways to make the EA process more efficient and cost-effective. In addition to these problems, the public perception of Ottawa's political will regarding EA suffered a further blow with the federal agreement to sell CANDU nuclear reactors to China with no precondition of an EA.

Uncertainty and controversy also plague provincial EA processes and shared federal and provincial EA cases in Canada. The environmental community in the Atlantic provinces complains that projects in economically depressed areas seem to go ahead regardless of impact. In Newfoundland there is continued and vigorous debate over the initiation of separate EAs for Voisey's Bay mining and smelting activities, as well as the amount of intervener funding available in the case. Comments by the Prime Minister caused the early adjournment of the first day of public hearings into the proposed Sable Island gas project in April of 1997. In Ontario, the adoption of new EA and public participation legislation in 1996 makes virtually all decisions at the discretion of the Minister responsible. In Alberta court cases continue against the federal government in the Sunpine Forest Products logging road case, and controversy persists over the constitution of the joint federal-provincial EA hearing panel in the Cheviot mine case. Reports out of the Northwest Territories indicate that the EA of the BHP diamond mine was "fundamentally flawed; the process was neither rigorous, comprehensive, nor fair" (O'Reilly, 1996:4).

Questions are also being raised about the integration of sustainable development into EA process design. Lawrence (1997), notes that although EA is well recognized as a means of achieving sustainability, the latter is not well integrated into EA theory and practice. Among other things, he argues that sustainability should be incorporated into EA at the legislative, policy and institutional levels. In Manitoba, attempts over the last two years to integrate the two concepts at the legislative level were met with significant opposition, primarily because the new legislation was seen as being "unabashedly pro development". Partly as a result of this opposition, the assessment components of the new legislation were shelved in early 1997.

The CAG Project

Recent conceptual and methodological debates surrounding EA process and design in Canada, such as those noted above, provided a backdrop for this project. The many issues surrounding the current evolution or transition of EA in Canada led to the decision by the Canadian Association of Geographers' (CAG), Environment and Resources Study Group to hold special sessions on EA at the 1996 annual meetings of the CAG in Saskatoon. The mission of the study group is to facilitate a network among Canadian geographers who are interested in environment and resource studies and who are affiliated with government agencies, the private sector, non-government organizations, universities and other organizations. The purpose of the network is to encourage work or activities and the sharing of interests in this area. EA has always been a central consideration of study group members.

A call for papers was circulated to geographers and other practitioners with a concern for EA. Since not all with interest in the project could attend the CAG meetings in Saskatoon, individuals were also offered the opportunity to submit a paper for this volume. In the original call for papers the net was cast widely around the session theme - "Canadian Environmental Assessment in Transition". Authors were asked to direct their papers to recent developments - conceptual, methodological, institutional, etc. - and their application or demonstration in Canadian case studies of any aspect of environmental assessment.

Overview of this Volume

The chapters contained in this book are a refereed selection of those papers presented at the CAG meetings and submitted to the study group. To present the works as clearly as possible, the eleven chapters have been divided into three sections which find their link in common questions relating to EA process and procedure. The three sections deal with: Issues of Public Involvement in EA; Methodological Approaches to EA Components and Processes; and, Contextual Considerations for EA. Inevitably, the issues considered in some of the chapters overlap with other sections, but the sections provide groupings of the common central themes of each chapter.

Issues of Public Involvement in EA

Although public involvement is well recognized as an essential element of EA, it has attracted a fair amount of controversy. Many of the current criticisms of EA stem from ineffective public participation and the lack of integration of public positions into the decision-making process. The first section of the book addresses these issues; it offers four chapters that consider the role of, and methodological and conceptual approaches to, public involvement.

The first chapter, by Richard Kuhn, "Public Participation in the Hearings on the Nuclear Fuel Waste Disposal Concept", focuses on the contentious review of a proposal to construct an underground nuclear waste disposal facility in the Canadian Shield. Kuhn critically assesses the process for involving the public and other stakeholders in the EA by looking at the minutes of assessment hearings and surveying the participants in the hearing process. By commenting on the adequacy of the public involvement components, Kuhn establishes the competing rationalities and agendas brought forward by proponents and opponents, and examines these in light of the political and procedural processes initiated to assess proposals.

The second chapter, by Mark Prystupa, Don Hine, Craig Summers and John Lewko, looks further at participants in the EA process through characterizing the representativeness of those involved in the EA hearings regarding the decommissioning of the Elliot Lake Uranium Mine Tailings Areas in Ontario. Employing survey research results, the authors indicate that select interest groups and government agencies dominated the hearings and outline that there was minimal participation from individual citizens. The authors also demonstrate that, through attempts to be an open process, the hearings actually exacerbated elite interests. Participants both within and outside the hearings process indicate that the main hindrances to more representative participation were the technical and adversarial nature of the hearings.

Education, information dissemination and social learning, in the context of public involvement in EA, are new areas gaining attention in the literature (e.g., Sinclair and Diduck, 1995; Webler et al., 1995; Sullivan et al., 1996 and, Regnier and Penna, 1996). In the third chapter in this section, Diduck and Sinclair examine the effectiveness of education techniques employed in EA public involvement processes. To clarify the role that education can potentially play in the EA process, the theories of critical pedagogy, environmental adult transformation and social learning are considered and it is shown how they lead to the concept of critical EA education, which encompasses both "education about" and "education through EA". The authors find empirical support for critical EA education by considering a recent Manitoba EA case involving the Pembina Valley Water Supply System. They conclude that critical EA education has the potential to clarify the role of education in the context of public involvement and that it has the potential to increase the effectiveness of EA by helping participants present credible and forceful counter-hegemonic discourses.

The section is rounded out by Thomas Meredith in a chapter that considers another aspect of making public involvement in EA more effective. Although Meredith acknowledges that the mechanisms for achieving effective participation are unclear, he argues that multi-stakeholder participation in EA is a duel (or lottery). The duel is played out with information and communication tools, since knowledge and the ability to access and control information are power. The chapter examines issues of information flow, characterizes limitations on information flow and assesses means of overcoming the limitations. Issues addressed include: the lack of knowledge about information sources; technical limits on data management; lack of paradigms for data interrelation; and, problems with data presentation, among others. The chapter ends by considering solutions to many of the problems presented through techniques such as non-obtrusive links with the research community.

Methodological Approaches to EA Components and Processes

The four chapters in Section II focus on methodological considerations of the EA process, especially in terms of: "follow-up" or audit activities; EA of non-project events; social impact assessment; and, strategic environmental assessment.

Locke and Storey lead off the section by providing an empirically rich account of current EA audit methodols as illustrated in the case of the Hibernia offshore oil platform construction project. Until recently there has been little concern with "follow-up" activities, or audits, designed to evaluate the accuracy of impact predictions, the effectiveness of impact management strategies or, more generally, the role of EA in decision making. Locke and Storey found that, of the audits done in Canada, United States and other jurisdictions, most have been limited to an examination of bio-physical issues. The authors raise a number of issues concerning the way in which the original impact predictions were made in the Hibernia case and the quality of the monitoring data available for audit purposes. They also question the value of the audit methodology itself.

Spaling and MacDonald's discussion of the "Environmental Assessment of Non-Project Activities" establishes an approach for undertakings that may cause environmental problems but are not considered project events. The EA of a single non-project event such as land drainage or fertilizer application is generally deemed insignificant, but the incremental impacts of numerous events may accumulate over time and across space. Their case study focuses on agriculture. The chapter is based on the development of an indicator to assess the risk of water contamination. Using a budget approach, the indicator determines the amount of surplus moisture, nutrients and pesticides that are potentially available and could cause contamination. With this approach the authors establish a method for analyzing and assessing the inherent cumulative effects of non-project activities.

The assessment of policies, and policy decisions, continues to be conceptually abstract for most decision makers. Strategic environmental assessment (SEA), which involves systematic and full integration of environmental issues in the early stages of decisions made at the policy, planning and program levels, is in its infancy in Canada. In the third chapter of the section, Novakowski and Wellar apply principles for SEA to the National Capital Commission's Plan for Canada's Capital. Their work raises important concerns and questions that need to be addressed within SEA at the needs/justification, scoping, prediction and policy alternatives levels.

In the last chapter of the section, Haque considers aspects of the planning process followed when demands for new service provisions in rural communities on the Canadian prairies are deliberated. The author employs a case study of the Pembina Valley Water Supply Project to examine the relationship between regional economic impact assessment (REIA) and social impact assessment (SIA). The approach taken is to consider the limitations of the REIA process, usually used in service-provision decision making, through a survey of both farm and non-farm households in the Rural Municipalities of Macdonald and Rhineland, Manitoba. By applying an SIA approach, the chapter illuminates important questions not included in the regional economic growth issues investigated as part of REIA.

Contextual Considerations for Environmental Assessment

The chapters in section III of the book step back and reflect on the context in which EA is being carried out and evaluated, and offer theoretical considerations for moving forward.

In the first chapter of the section, David Lawrence explores the fertile middle ground between those advocating a standardized EA process, suited to any and all situations, and those who believe that each EA planning process should be unique. In this chapter, EA process design, at both the regulatory and applied levels, is addressed.

Through identifying a series of contextual categories, such as proposal type, proponent type, and setting type, attention is given to how the boundaries among these categories might be spanned and then integrated by means of transcending frameworks. The chapter offers an approach to EA practitioners, at both the regulatory and applied levels, for guiding and undertaking EA in a structured yet flexible manner.

Juliet Rowlson asserts that, although many appraisals of EA processes have been undertaken in Canada in an effort to make them more inclusive and open, social scientists have often couched these appraisals in scientific discourse. She questions this stance by arguing that it has undesirable political implications. Through a case study of the EARP process used in the Vancouver Airport EA, Rowlson illustrates how, in practice, participants' voices have been rendered marginal in appraisals of EA processes. She argues that the use of a scientific evaluative framework has ensured that evaluations of EA process have unintentionally silenced the voices of EA participants who are unable to engage with its rhetoric. She examines the opportunities provided by a more 'situated' approach in which appraisals of EA can be reworked.

In the final chapter of the book, Greer-Wootten confronts the contextual framing of issues surrounding the production of knowledge in EA. He views this issue in two primary ways: theoretically - the distinction between positivist and post-positivist; and practically - the distinction between the frameworks of practice and the work of practitioners. He establishes that the linkage between these two aspects of context is seen in the largely technocratic work of practitioners that feeds into the administrative structure of EA. Further, he examines the literature on EA, including writings on the trend to more broad-based and anticipatory EA, as opposed to the narrow, technocratic, disciplinary approach. He argues that a basis for change in EA, allowing for a shift from the current technocratic "straightjacket", can be found in Habermas' Critical Theory.

Conclusions

If EA is to survive as a major tool in the shift to sustainability, it must continue to evolve as has been the case in the years since the first assessments were conducted. While our understanding of EA process and design has improved, new questions continue to challenge conventional wisdom as development decisions are made. Each section of this book suggests sound directions for the transition of EA in Canada, and taken together the chapters identify ways of improving current EA practice and thinking in Canada.

In the first section of the book, for example, the authors provide direction in regard to public involvement, an essential and always controversial aspect of EA. The representativeness of the participants in public hearings, as well as the adequacy of involvement components, is questioned and new approaches to encourage the involvement of non-participants are offered. The essential foundations of involvement, knowledge and information are also queried. Specific direction is offered by way of "critical EA education", which is suggested as a means of encouraging community participation in EA and critical debate about pro-development discourses. As well, new techniques for improving the information flow among participants are illuminated.

New directions are also established on the methodological front. In terms of "follow-up" audit activities, it is concluded that impact predictions need careful consideration with respect to how they are developed and presented if auditing is to take place. It is suggested that, in making predictions rather than focusing on the demands that the project will place upon the various components of the environment - the 'unknowns', it might be appropriate to emphasize the 'known' existing capacities of these environmental components. This would result in the emphasis of EA moving from impact prediction to impact management. New approaches for assessing the impact of non-project activities on the environment are also delineated by way of an indicator model, which utilizes existing data bases and GIS technology. In addition, the issue of policy assessment, or SEA, is tackled and a framework for this activity is created and successfully tested.

Aspects of EA's context are explored in the last section of the book. It is established, for example, that in questioning and designing an EA process, social scientists must be cognizant of the EA participants who may be unintentionally silenced by rhetoric. A 'situated' approach that would see the views of participants solicited and presented in a clear and transparent fashion provides a direction for EA process evaluation and design in the future. The difficult task of respecting and yet transcending contextual differences in planning process, design and execution is also addressed. It is argued that through bottom-up and lateral communication, and through the identification of core EA principles, balancing the competing needs of differentiation and integration in EA design can be achieved.

Given the nature of this project, not all aspects or current controversies in EA process and design have been addressed - nor could they be in a single volume. The volume does, however, further the issues raised in previous works by geographers such as MacLaren and Whitney (1985), Whitney and MacLaren (1985) and Smith (1993), and it is hoped that it will also stimulate the reader and encourage more discussion and interest in EA among geographers and others, as have these previous volumes. Conflict and uncertainty regarding EA will continue, and in Canada we are currently at a critical point in determining future directions for EA. It is hoped that this project and this volume, in some modest way, illuminate the future course and help ensure "minimum regret planning" for this and future generations.

References

Beattie, R.B. (1995) "Everything you already know about EIA (but don't often admit)," *Environmental Impact Assessment Review*, 15: 109-114.

Dale, A.P. and Lane, M.B. (1994) "Strategic perspectives analysis: a procedure for participatory and political social impact assessment," *Society and Natural Resources*, 7: 253-267.

Delicaet, A. (1995) "The new Canadian environmental assessment act: a comparison with the environmental assessment review process," *Environmental Impact Assessment Review*, 15: 497-505.

Gibson, R.B. (1992) "The new Canadian environmental assessment act: possible responses to its main deficiencies," *Journal of Environmental Law and Practice*, 2: 223-255.

Lawrence, D. P. (1997) "Integrating sustainability and environmental impact assessment," *Environmental Management*, 21: 23-42.

MacLaren, V.W. and Whitney, J.B. (eds.) (1985) *New Directions in Environmental Impact Assessment in Canada*, Toronto, ON: Methuen.

Meredith, T. (1991) "Environmental impact assessment and monitoring," in Mitchell, B. (ed.), *Resources Management and Development*, London, UK: Oxford Press, 224-245.

Nikiforuk, A. (1997) *"The Nasty Game:" The Failure of Environmental Assessment in Canada*, Toronto, ON:

Report prepared for the Walter and Duncan Gordon Foundation.

Northey, R. (1997) as referenced in *"The Nasty Game:" The Failure of Environmental Assessment in Canada*, A. Nikiforuk, Toronto, ON: Report prepared for the Walter and Duncan Gordon Foundation, Toronto.

O'Reilly, K. (1996) "Diamond mining and the demise of environmental assessment in the north," *Northern Perspectives*, 24: 1-4.

Partidário, M.R. (1996) "Strategic environmental assessment: key issues emerging from recent practice," *Environmental Impact Assessment Review*, 16: 31-55.

Regnier, R. and Penna, P. (1996) "The limits of empowerment in anti-nuclear advocacy: a case study of adult education for technological literacy," *The Canadian Journal For the Study of Adult Education*, 10(2): 35-57.

Smith, L.G. (1993) *Impact Assessment and Sustainable Resource Management*, Essex, UK: Longman Scientific and Technical Ltd.

Sinclair, A.J. and Diduck, A. (1995) "Public education: an undervalued component of the environmental assessment public involvement process," *Environmental Impact Assessment Review*, 15: 219-240.

Sullivan, W.C., Kuo, F. and Prabhu, M. (1996) "Assessing the impact of environmental impact statements on citizens," *Environmental Impact Assessment Review*, 16: 171-182.

Verloo, M. and Roggeband, C. (1996) "Gender impact assessment: the development of a new instrument in the Netherlands," *Impact Assessment*, 14: 3-20.

Webler, T., Kastenholz, H. and Renn, O. (1995) "Public participation in impact assessment: a social learning perspective," *Environmental Impact Assessment Review*, 15: 443-463.

Whitney, J.B. and MacLaren, V.W. (1985) *Environmental Impact Assessment: The Canadian Experience*, Toronto, ON: University of Toronto Press.

Wood, C. (1995) *Environmental Impact Assessment: A Comparative Review*, Essex, UK: Longman Scientific and Technical.

Winnipeg, Manitoba
August 1997

Section 1

Issues in Public Involvement in Environmental Assessment

Chapter 1

Public Participation in the Hearings on the Canadian Nuclear Fuel Waste Disposal Concept

Richard G. Kuhn
University of Guelph

Although many countries use and rely on nuclear power, to date, none have constructed a facility to dispose of high-level nuclear fuel waste (IAEA, 1993). The problems associated with nuclear fuel waste management are complex and significantly more involved than just the development of sound technology. Public acceptance of proposed initiatives and the political dynamic of the decision-making process are also key elements (Openshaw et al., 1989; Jacob, 1990). Of particular importance has been the emergence of broad public participation in siting perceived hazardous facilities. The involvement of the public introduces social and political dimensions into a process that was once the sole domain of the technocrat. In many instances, public hostility develops against any proposals to situate perceived hazardous facilities, particularly those related to the nuclear industry (Armour, 1992). Hostility and distrust are not confined to the proposed facility. Kemp and O'Riordan (1988: 37), for example, note that "public distrust over radioactive waste spills over into the distrust of the organizations responsible for disposal plans, and dissatisfaction with the decision making processes employed."

This chapter will provide a critical review of the hearing process undertaken by the Canadian Environmental Assessment Agency on the Canadian Nuclear Fuel Waste Management and Disposal Concept. The focus will be on the hearing process itself, rather than on the specific issues raised in the hearings concerning the technical adequacy of the concept. It is maintained that the primacy given to the technical aspects of the concept by the federal government and the project proponents, and the structure of the hearing process, effectively alienate those constituencies most likely to be affected by the siting of the facility if it is deemed to be feasible and eventually constructed.

Background

Nuclear power currently generates approximately 15% of the electricity in Canada. The vast majority is produced in the Province of Ontario where nuclear energy accounts for more than half of all electricity generation. For the last thirty years, Canadian nuclear utilities have managed a fuel waste volume of about 16,000 tons through wet and dry interim storage methods (AECL, 1994). While both have proven safe, the federal government has mandated that a disposal facility be constructed to remove the management burden from future generations. Determining the technical requirements and feasibility of this option was initiated in 1978 (Aikin et al., 1977).

The proposed Canadian nuclear fuel waste (NFW) disposal concept consists of deep geologic burial in plutonic rock formations in the Canadian Shield. Transport shafts will be excavated down 500 to 1,000 metres connecting with a series of tunnels and leading to a network of disposal rooms. The disposal area will consist of approximately two square kilometres and have a storage capacity of 191,000 tonnes. Spent fuel will be transported in sealed corrosion-resistant canisters to the disposal facility, and then emplaced in bored holes. A sand/clay sealing material will surround the emplaced canisters to prevent movement of water into or out of the canister. As rooms are filled to capacity, final backfilling with the sand/clay material will continue until the entire network is exhausted and all vaults sealed (AECL, 1994). Field research has been carried out in an underground research laboratory in Whiteshell, Manitoba.

The federal government is currently reviewing the technical feasibility of the geologic option under federal environmental assessment legislation. The environmental assessment (EA) of the NFW facility consists of two distinct stages: 1) a generic appraisal of the construction and closure technology, and 2) detailed site selection and facility construction. The first stage began in 1986 and should be completed in 1997. The review process and public hearings are being administered by the Canadian Environmental Assessment Agency (CEAA).

Atomic Energy of Canada Limited (AECL) and Ontario Hydro (both Crown corporations) submitted an environmental impact statement (EIS) on the pre- and post-closure disposal technology in September 1994. A series of meetings was held in 1990 to allow for public input into the definition of the EIS's scope. The meetings were conducted by an Environmental Assessment Panel, who gathered input from government experts and interested stakeholders (FEARO, 1991). On the basis of these submissions, guidelines were prepared for the requirements of the EIS. Submissions by the public and interested stakeholders regarding the adequacy of the EIS in the context of the guidelines were subsequently received in 1995 (FEARO, 1995). The Environmental Assessment Panel deemed that the guidelines were met sufficiently to allow the process to continue (EA Panel, 1995a). A second round of public hearings began in early 1996 concerning the EIS document itself. Once completed, a ministerial decision will then be made on whether or not to accept the EIS and disposal technology. If deep geologic burial receives approval, the second stage of site selection will commence. The siting process is expected to last 20 years.

That prospective plans initiated by governments and energy agencies to design and construct a facility to dispose of high-level nuclear fuel waste are fraught with controversy is evident in a number of countries (Jacob, 1990; Kemp, 1992; IAEA, 1993). Although scientific claims as to the safety and long-term reliability of the proposed facilitates abound, public and interest group opposition has thwarted recent attempts in the United States (US) and the United Kingdom (UK) to begin construction (Kunreuther et al., 1993). In Canada, public concern is also affecting the NFW management program:

> Social and environmental considerations have slowed the Canadian program. Many communities that were approached for permission to carry out local geologic studies were opposed to such investigations (Auditor General of Canada, 1995: 3-15).

Constituencies

The controversy surrounding issues related to nuclear waste disposal can in part be explained by the different perspectives or "rationalities" used by various stakeholders to assess the viability of management initiatives. As Kemp (1990: 1249) maintains:

> Scientific knowledge of radioactive decay, waste arisings, geologic formations, and the economics of packaging and disposal are brought together in a technically rational process to inform policy choices. However, the public and political reception of those choices does not always occur within a similar framework of technical rationality. Rather, a process of 'practical rationality' is at work. This is the realm of value judgements and political choices.

The rules and standards governing the process of decision making are major influences on practical rationality. If decisions are arrived at openly, fairly and in a comprehensible manner, then there is a greater chance of gaining public agreement through a more practically rational, political decision-making process (Kemp, 1990). Strict adherence to technically rational arguments and evidence in promoting NFW disposal technology to the public to the exclusion of value-laden and "softer" considerations often results in public rejection. Both perspectives are vital to successful project implementation and sound and democratic decision making. The seeming incompatibility of these two rationalities is at the heart of much of the debate surrounding the nuclear industry generally, and nuclear fuel waste management specifically.

Conflicts that emerge in the process of nuclear fuel waste disposal reflect the different formulations of procedure, and the legitimacy of the proponents and the rationality they bring to the issue. This is reinforced by the reliance on risk analysis. It is well known that a wide gulf exists in the perception and measurement of risk between those in the nuclear establishment and those who are not (Carter, 1987; Eiser et al., 1995; Slovic, 1987). Leiss and Chociolko (1994) provide an insightful analysis. They maintain that there are three "risk constituencies", each with its own distinctive outlook. The first is the corporate/government constituency representing the primary innovators and promoters of involuntary risk through their advocacy of industrial development. Those responsible for promoting risk activities are for the most part insulated from personal exposure to the most hazardous materials used in industry. The power of this constituency is further noted by Parenteau (1988) who argues that major corporations, by virtue of their ability to shape the economic and political environment, can influence government decision making as well as participate in it directly.

The second constituency includes labour and local communities, who usually bear a disproportionate share of the identifiable loses from projects. For example, occupational risk exposure levels almost always exceed general population exposure levels for the same materials. For local communities, involuntary risks associated with risk producing facilities are always place-specific rather than spread uniformly throughout the natural and social environment. The unequal distribution of risks and benefits is the prevailing concept for both labour and risk bearing communities. The third group is described by Leiss and Chociolko (1994) as the public interest constituency, composed largely of environmental and consumer groups with broad organizational mandates and membership bases. These groups usually do not have a direct stake in risk controversies, although their involvement brings the consideration of aspects that would otherwise be deemed outside the decision-making purview (e.g. protection of endangered wildlife species). These groups generally adopt risk adverse positions as a matter of course.

The corporate/government and public interest constituencies occupy two ends of a spectrum of acceptable risk, while the labour/local constituency occupies the middle ground (Leiss and Chociolko, 1994). The significance and importance of these constituencies are that their framework for assessing risks and impacts of proposed projects are fundamentally different and often intractable. These differences extend beyond the assessment of potential risks and benefits to fundamental disagreements about project evaluation and information requirements. This in turn is indicative of competing rationalities (i.e. technical vs. practical). Finding common ground for these groups to participate meaningfully and equitably in decision-making processes becomes a major challenge for regulators and project proponents.

Trust and Legitimacy

Trust in project proponents and the perceived legitimacy brought to bear in facility-siting decisions are fundamental to project acceptance and eventual siting (Armour, 1992; Kemp et al., 1984; Slovic et al., 1991). Jacob (1990) identifies trust and legitimacy as two of the main issues at the core of conflict surrounding NFW disposal. These two issues relate to access to, control of, and confidence in the expertise used to establish the scientific credibility of a solution, and general acceptance of the political process used to define the problem and identify and implement a solution. The reason that the US-proposed NFW disposal facility at Yucca Mountain in Nevada is in "shambles" (Slovic et al., 1991) is because the trust and legitimacy of the nuclear establishment (corporate/government constituency) was severely undermined in the eyes of that constituency most affected (Nevada residents) and advocates on their behalf (public interest groups). The predominant focus on technically rational arguments and evidence failed to convince the general public that the solution was safe and acceptable.

According to Shelley et al. (1988), decentralized democratic procedures that emphasize public participation have the strongest potential for conflict resolution. To a large extent, resolving conflict, such as in cases involving siting perceived hazardous facilities, involves placating local opposition to siting proposals. However, the methods by which agencies set agendas and the perceptions of the decision-making process by participants and sponsors are vital. Fiorino (1990) maintains that the standard approaches for defining and eventually solving "risk problems" are more technocratic than democratic in their orientation. This may or may not be a problem insofar as there is consensus that the issue is purely a technical one. For most, if not all, major development projects, this is not the case. Fiorino (1990: 227) provides three arguments against the adoption of a strictly technocratic approach. The first is that lay judgements about risk are as sound, or more so, than technical experts'. Second, he argues that a technocratic orientation in inherently undemocratic in that the "value dimension" of a project proposal is often ignored or not given a legitimate place in the decision-making process. Finally, effective lay participation in risk decisions makes them more legitimate and leads to better results. From these premises, Fiorino (1990) claims that decision-making processes involving perceived hazardous facilities should have four key characteristics: 1) there should be direct participation by the unaffiliated general public and non-aligned groups; 2) the general public must share in collective decision making; 3) there must be face-to-face discussions between the project proponent and the general public over a period of time; and 4) there must be opportunity for citizens to participate on some basis of equity with administrative officials and technical experts. Specifically, the process should allow citizens to define issues, question technical experts, dispute evidence and shape the agenda. In other words, the approach to decision making should not be defined by the proponent as a purely technical one without some broad base of consent from constituencies most likely to be affected. As well, power must be granted to local and public constituencies if the trust and legitimacy of the implementing organization and the decision process generally are to be maintained. If these issues are not addressed in the assessment process, the majority of participants will likely adopt a negative attitude from the outset.

The difficulty in the EA process is ensuring that amenity groups and the general public (the "public interest constituency") have real power. It has to be recognized that amenity groups can only be effective if the local government has the power to determine policy rather than have major policy decisions imposed upon them from more powerful governments and agencies. Local power is constrained by a number of factors. It can only operate within the framework set by the social, economic and political structures of society as a whole and, with most major projects and initiatives, planning systems have mechanisms built into them to allow central governments to intervene to bring decisions into line with national policy (Rees, 1990). Many analysts agree that environmental groups have less influence with government than do the major economic interests (Paehlke, 1989; Rees, 1990). They have fewer resources, lack the ability to enact powerful sanctions, and are not of central importance to the effective performance of government, the economy or various sectors of production. Indeed, the general public and environmental groups can be regarded as largely irrelevant to the overall direction of policy. As noted by Rees (1990: 412), "from a structuralist perspective, the political debate is largely a charade and the actors party to it have little significance. Rather, effective policy is determined by economic interests which the apparatus of the state is designed to support."

Rees' (1990) critique culminates in her contention that the inclusion of environmental groups and the general public in decision-making processes is merely a ploy to invoke "non-decisions". This essentially means that central governments that move to promote public participation or facilitate environmental mediation at the local level simply act to divert environmental pressure away from fundamental policies such as industrial growth, energy development, and the like. Active environmental groups become "institutionalized" and subsequently become less able to openly challenge policy while the promoters of technocratic resource development and regulation agencies thwart interests challenging established policies and practices. This latter ploy is possible as government departments and agencies are able to monopolize information, and the technical knowledge and experience required to challenge meaningfully large-scale initiatives is unlikely to be had by the public. Issues where the public can have meaningful input (e.g., risk perceptions, local knowledge) are relegated as secondary or outside the mandate of the decision process.

The next section will examine in some detail two aspects of the Environmental Assessment process: the 1990 Scoping Meeting presentations and input to the preparation of guidelines for the EIS, and the 1995 public submissions concerning the adequacy of the EIS submitted by the Atomic Energy of Canada Ltd. and Ontario Hydro. These data are supplemented with some results from a questionnaire survey undertaken in January 1995 with participants in the 1990 hearings.

1990 Scoping Meetings

The Federal Environmental Assessment Review Office (now the Canadian Environmental Assessment Agency) established an Environmental Assessment Panel in 1989. The panel held public meetings in five provinces in October and November 1990. The purpose of the meetings was "to undertake a review of Atomic Energy of Canada Ltd.'s (AECL) concept of geologic disposal of nuclear fuel wastes in Canada along with a broad range of nuclear fuel waste management issues" (Ministry of the Environment, 1989:1). As further noted, the results obtained by the panel "will be used to make recommendations to assist the governments of Canada and Ontario in reaching decisions on the acceptability of the disposal concept and on the steps that must be taken to ensure the safe management of nuclear fuel wastes in Canada" (Ministry of the Environment, 1989:1). The specific goal was to provide detailed guidelines of the requirements for the EIS to be prepared by the AECL and Ontario Hydro. Although alternatives to geologic disposal could be considered, emphasis on the Canadian deep disposal option was stressed. Siting considerations were to be limited to reviewing methodologies to characterize sites and the potential availability of sites in Canada.

The Panel's mandate explicitly discounted a number of nuclear-related issues from consideration at the 1990 public hearings. Specifically:

The energy policies of Canada and the provinces; the role of nuclear energy with these policies, including the construction, operation and safety of new or existing nuclear power plants; fuel reprocessing as an energy policy; and military applications of nuclear technology are issues outside the Panel's mandate and should not be addressed during the review" (Ministry of the Environment, 1989: 4).

Content Analysis

A total of 175 submissions were made to the Panel: 72 oral submissions and 103 written submissions. As expected, many issues were raised. Ontario Hydro (1991) identified 29 distinct issues in 10 general categories including public health and safety, the effectiveness of disposal technology, monitoring and retrievability, alternative disposal methods and the public participation process. From this list and from a review of the Ontario Hydro synopsis, a misleading picture emerges. While a full range of issues was raised at the scoping meetings, the prevalence and emphasis of certain issues over others becomes lost. In order to obtain a clearer notion of the relative importance of certain issues raised by stakeholders, a content analysis of the scoping meeting presentations was undertaken. The purpose of the content analysis was to identify the relative importance placed on various components of the nuclear fuel waste issue, particularly in the context of the scoping meetings. There was some overlap between the oral and written presentation. To avoid double counting, only the results from the written submissions will be presented. In total, 103 written submissions were analysed. In keeping with the aim of this chapter, the discussion will focus on the submissions related to the hearing process rather that on the substantive issues raised concerning the disposal concept.

Each written submission was examined 1) to identify the position as to the support for or opposition to the Canadian disposal concept and to identify the affiliation of each submitter; and 2) to classify the major focus or foci of each submission. Only the major issues raised in each submission were noted.

Position and Affiliation

The vast majority of submissions expressed opposition to the disposal concept (42.7%) or did not provide a definitive position (39.8%). Less than one-fifth (17.5%) endorsed the concept. The largest group of submissions came from private citizens (37.9%). Environmental and community groups and consulting and professional organizations comprised the other major group. Government representatives and native representatives each had less than 10% of the submissions.

A breakdown of respondents' affiliations and support for or opposition to the disposal concept is provided in Table 1.1. The majority of government, professional and consulting groups supported the disposal concept while the majority of environmental and community organizations, private citizens, and First Nations was opposed.

Table 1.1
1990 Scoping Meeting Participants and Support for the
Canadian NFW Disposal Concept

	Position Towards CNFWDC		
Representatives	**Support**	**Oppose**	**Neutral**
Government	4	1	4
Environmental and Community Groups	0	19	10
Aboriginal Groups	0	3	4
Private Citizens	8	20	11
Consulting and Professional Organizations	6	1	12
Total	**18**	**44**	**41**

Scoping Meeting Focus

The major focus of each submission was recorded. In total, 28 categories were found. These related to risk assessment, health impacts, energy policy, economic implications, environmental concerns, social consequences, technological issues, and the hearing process and procedure. These categories were subsequently collapsed into five general categories to facilitate analysis and to isolate those that were directed towards the hearing process. Of particular importance to this paper were the submissions that either focussed exclusively on the hearing process or included, as a primary focus, the hearing process and some other aspect of the disposal concept.

As noted by Ontario Hydro (1991: 1-1) in its review of the hearing submissions, "a large number of participants complained that the terms of reference of the review were too narrow and restrictive". A review of the written submissions attests to this. Over 10% of the submissions criticised the hearing process, while an additional 55% criticised the process and provided some other input regarding the disposal concept. Collectively, 66% of the submissions made explicit reference to perceived flaws in the scoping meetings or the Environmental Assessment Panel.

The most contentious aspect of the hearings was that the terms of reference given to the Panel were too restrictive. Indeed, 42 written submissions made reference to this. Other issues raised concerning the process included lack of confidence in the Panel (27 submissions), intervenor funding was too low (15), not enough preparation time was provided (15), and the scoping meetings were not adequately advertised (10). Importantly, the vast majority of submitters who were opposed to the disposal concept focused on the review process. Of the 44 submissions that expressed clear opposition to the disposal concept, 39 also expressed dissatisfaction with the hearing process (Table 1.2). In other words, those stakeholders who most need to be convinced of the merits of the disposal concept and the viability of the technology are arguably those who are the most alienated. It is worth noting that 11 of the 18 submissions explicitly in favour of the proposal also were critical of the process, while 18 of the 41 "neutral/unclear" submissions focused on the process.

The hearing process conducted by FEARO (now the CEAA) was designed to allow for meaningful input from a diversity of stakeholders. While fulfilling that goal, the process may in fact have alienated a substantial number of presenters and representatives. In this context, the hearings may have been counter-productive. To explore this issue in greater detail, a questionnaire survey was designed and mailed to participants of the scoping meetings. The survey instrument was part of a larger project related to the siting and management of a proposed nuclear fuel waste disposal facility (Ballard and Kuhn, 1996; Kuhn, 1996). A series of questions was included regarding the presenter's perceptions of the hearings.

Table 1.2
**1990 Scoping Meeting Focus and Support for the Canadian
NFW Disposal Concept**

	Position Towards CNFWDC		
Submission Focus	**Support**	**Oppose**	**Neutral**
Technical	1	0	7
Non-Technical	3	4	12
Technical/Non-Technical	3	1	4
Hearing Process	0	8	3
Hearing Process and Other	11	31	15
Total	**18**	**44**	**41**

Survey Administration and Analysis

Stakeholders and experts who made written or oral submissions to the 1990 Environmental Assessment Panel's scoping meetings for the Canadian NFW disposal concept comprised the respondent population. No accurate records were kept of participants' addresses. However, 143 addresses were confirmed from lists obtained from CEAA and AECL. Unfortunately, many respondents had moved in the last five years and new addresses were unattainable. The available population (those respondents with a proper address) was 129 individuals.

A questionnaire survey was mailed to these 129 potential respondents in January 1995. The survey package consisted of an introductory letter, a questionnaire, and a prepaid return envelope. A reminder card was mailed to each respondent two weeks following the initial mailing and follow-up phone calls were made one week after that. The questionnaire yielded responses from 47 individuals for a response rate of 36%. This group accounts for 23.5% of the total number of participants involved in the Environmental Assessment hearings.

The specialised nature of the research subject meant that the respondent population was atypical in terms of sex and education when compared to a normal Canadian community. There was an unequal gender representation in the sample with 80% of respondents being male. The sample was also exceptionally well educated; half of the respondents had completed post-graduate degrees, and another third had completed a university degree. Seven distinct stakeholder groups were represented. Private citizens and environmental groups comprised the largest categories (32% and 21%, respectively). Responses were also received from members of professional societies (15%), community interest groups (13%), government agencies (13%), consulting agencies (4%) and a First Nation organization (2%).

The representation of groups in the sample corresponds well with those who participated in the EA hearings. A review of the hearing proceedings reveals that private citizens made approximately 38% of the submissions, and 28% of the submissions were made by environmental and community organizations. One-fifth of submissions were made by professional societies and consulting organizations while government (9%) and First Nations (7%) had the lowest rates of participation. Thus, the respondents to the survey represent accurately those who participated in the EA hearings. These individuals can be considered to be the active public; those who were involved, and likely to stay involved, in the assessment process. The results, however, may not necessarily reflect the sentiments of the public at large.

With a sample size of 47 respondents, data analysis was limited to descriptive and non-parametric statistics. A Shapiro-Wilk's W Test was run and confirmed that the data were not normally distributed. A Kruskal-Wallis analysis of variance was the non-parametric test used. This test is the non-parametric equivalent to ANOVA and is used to compare three or more independent random sample mean ranks for differences. Relationships are assumed to be statistically significant when p < 0.05.

Stakeholder Perceptions of the Hearing Process

Support for the Canadian NFW Disposal Concept

Respondents were initially requested to state whether, during the Scoping Meetings, they supported the Canadian NFW disposal concept. Just under one-third supported the concept (30%; n=14) while over half were opposed (53%; n=25). The remaining respondents did not reply to this question (17%; n=8). These respondents were not excluded, as a non-response may have indicated a "neutral" or "undecided" position that was not provided for in the questionnaire. This category of respondents was labelled "neutral" to retain the robustness of subsequent analysis and to include them in the discussion.

Respondents' affiliation at the time of their presentation to the EA Panel and their stated position towards the Canadian NFW disposal concept are presented in Table 1.3. To avoid data fragmentation, affiliation was collapsed into four categories from the initial seven (government representatives, professional societies and consulting groups, environmental and community organizations, and private citizens). As shown, the majority of those opposed to the disposal concept were representatives from environmental and community organizations and private citizens. No government representatives were opposed. Support for the disposal concept was evident from all four groups. These results are generally in keeping with those found in the written submissions to the scoping meetings.

Table 1.3
Questionnaire Respondents: Affiliation and Position Towards the Canadian NFW Disposal Concept (CNFWDC)

Affiliation	Position Towards CNFWDC		
	Support	Oppose	Neutral
Government	3	0	3
Environmental and Community Organizations	2	14	1
Private Citizens	4	9	2
Consulting and Professional Organizations	5	2	2
Total	14	25	8

Scoping Meetings

Respondents were asked how satisfied they were with the Panel's Final Guidelines for the Preparation of an Environmental Impact Statement. Approximately half were "satisfied" or "completely satisfied". A Kruskal-Wallis analysis of ranks was undertaken to determine if there were differences between respondents' position towards the disposal concept and their stated level of satisfaction. A statistically significant difference was found. Specifically, those who supported or were neutral towards the proposal were significantly more likely to be satisfied with the final guidelines (H= 22.24, p< 0.0000). Alternatively, those opposed to the disposal concept were almost uniformly unsatisfied. More detailed questions were posed regarding the level of satisfaction with the resultant guidelines, the role of the proponents in the scoping hearings, and the limitations placed on the scoping hearings.

Satisfaction with Scoping Process

Respondents were asked to indicate their level of agreement with six statements regarding their involvement and satisfaction with the scoping process. A five-point scale was provided ranging from "strongly disagree" (1) to "strongly agree" (5). A Kruskal-Wallis analysis of ranks was used to identify areas of divergence amongst the groups supporting, opposed to, or neutral towards the Canadian NFW disposal concept (Table 1.4). Statistically significant differences for three of the six statements were found. Specifically, respondents who supported the disposal concept agreed that their concerns were reflected in the final guidelines document and that the Environmental Panel members listened carefully to their input. Those respondents opposed to the disposal concept did not agree that their concerns were reflected in the Final guidelines and felt they had minimal influence in the panel members' decisions. Generally, all respondents agreed that there were better ways to register their concerns and, despite this, they were able to participate effectively in the hearings. In fact, all participants felt that they had some influence on the decision-making process. Collectively, these results demonstrate that the participants at the hearings believed that they were involved in a worthwhile endeavour, and although their concerns may not have been included in the final guidelines document, their role in the hearings was meaningful and acknowledged.

Role of Hearing Proponents

The purpose of these questions was to uncover respondents' level of satisfaction with the role played by participants in the Scoping Hearings who were either the proponents or administrators. A five-point scale was provided ranging from "strongly disagree" (1) to "strongly agree" (5). A Kruskal-Wallis analysis of ranks was conducted to identify areas of difference among the groups supporting, opposed to, or neutral toward the disposal concept. As depicted in Table 1.5, statistically significant differences were found among the three groups for all six statements. In all cases, those in favour of the disposal concept were supportive of government actions, the role of the AECL and the panel members.

Those respondents opposed to the disposal concept strongly disagreed. In all cases, respondents in the neutral category had median scores between the extreme groups.

Table 1.4
Satisfaction with the Scoping Meetings

Statement[1]	Position Towards the CNFWDC (Group Medians)			H	p
	Support	Oppose	Neutral		
Your concerns were reflected in the Final Guidelines	4	2	3.5	26.48	0.0000
Panel members listened carefully to your input	4	3	3.5	9.77	0.0076
You felt you influenced panel members' decisions	3	2	3.5	13.92	0.0009
You felt powerless, with no influence on decisions	2	2	2.5	2.82	ns
You participated effectively in the scoping meetings	4	3	3.5	5.61	ns
You felt there were better ways of registering your concerns	3	4	3	4.00	ns

[1]Responses ranged from 1 (strongly disagree) to 5 (strongly agree).
ns = not statistically significant.

These results portend to potentially severe difficulties in the entire EA process. Confidence, trust and perceived legitimacy of the project proponent and regulator are of fundamental importance in ensuring project approval and eventual siting. These qualities are perceived in the AECL and government by only those already in favour of the disposal concept. For those respondents opposed or neutral to the disposal option, trust in government and the AECL is very low. Further, the competence of the EA Panel and the AECL is questioned. As these represent a significant constituency in the overall process (i.e., the public interest and labour

and local communities), the results take on added significance. As has been demonstrated in the US and UK, if these
elements are not present among the majority of potentially
affected stakeholders (and advocates on their behalf) the
entire siting process is in jeopardy.

Table 1.5
**Satisfaction with Scoping Meeting Proponents and
Administrators**

Statement[1]	Position Towards the CNFWDC (Group Medians)			H	p
	Support	Oppose	Neutral		
Government actions to date have demonstrated the trust necessary to locate a facility	4	1	2	27.27	0.0000
You felt confident all government agencies are committed to protecting public health and safety	4	1	2	20.60	0.0000
You felt government agencies were competent of assessing the technical feasibility of permanent geologic disposal	4.5	1	2.5	22.58	0.0000
You felt there should be an independent technical review by other countries	2	4	2.5	8.83	0.0151
You have confidence in the AECL	4	1	1.5	23.07	0.0000
You have confidence in the appointed panel members	4	2	3	11.68	0.0029

[1]Responses ranged from 1 (strongly disagree) to 5 (strongly agree).

Scoping Hearing Limitations

As noted earlier, limitations were placed on the Scoping
Panel by the terms of reference provided by government.
The purpose of this section of the questionnaire was to
determine respondents' perceptions of these limitations. A

five-point scale was provided (strongly disagree (1) to strongly agree (5)) and the results were subjected to a Kruskal-Wallis analysis of ranks to uncover potential differences among the three groups (Table 1.6). Statistically significant differences were again uncovered. Those respondents opposed to the disposal concept strongly agreed that the hearing process was too limited and that a substantially wider range of issues should have been debated and included in the inquiry. Those respondents in favour of the facility tended to disagree.

These results are in keeping with those uncovered from the scoping hearing transcripts. Limitations imposed on the EA process are seen by a sizable proportion of stakeholders as undermining the credibility and legitimacy of the project proponents and regulators. Of particular importance is the closure of debate, at this stage, of related issues of nuclear power and the eventual siting of a NFW facility. Defining the management of NFW as a predominately technical issue (which in part it is) isolates a substantial proportion of societal views as irrelevant, or at best, not fundamental to the decision-making process. This is an error as experience elsewhere has shown. To have one agency or stakeholder group (i.e., the nuclear establishment) define the problem and its feasible solution, and to control the readily available machinery of administrative action and policy implementation, is to attempt to evade ideological conflicts over the goals of energy and nuclear policies. For many stakeholders, this is not acceptable.

1995 Comments on the Adequacy of the EIS

The public and interested stakeholders were invited by the Environmental Assessment Panel to submit written comments on the adequacy of the EIS submitted by the AECL and Ontario Hydro. A total of 51 submissions was received from the general public and various interest groups. Additional invited submissions were received from the

Scientific Review Group, the OECD Nuclear Energy Agency, the Royal Society of Canada as well as from a number of government agencies (e.g., Transport Canada, Atomic Energy Control Board, Environment Canada). In total, 65 submissions were received (EA Panel, 1995b).

Table 1.6
Satisfaction with Limitations on Scoping Meetings

Statement[1]	PositionTowards the CNFWDC (Group Medians)			H	p
	Support	Oppose	Neutral		
All nuclear-related issues needed to be debated	2	5	4	18.22	0.0001
Siting issues and community concerns needed to be debated	3	5	4	17.79	0.0001
The potential of compensation becoming a means of economic bribery needed to be debated	2	5	3.5	14.79	0.0006
The ethics of using nuclear power needed to be debated	2	5	4	14.02	0.0009
The possibility of a disposal facility encouraging nuclear power expansion needed to be debated	2	5	4	11.39	0.0034

[1]Responses ranged from 1 (strongly disagree) to 5 (strongly agree).

The majority of the submissions made by the general public and interest groups was critical of the EIS. In fact, 27 of the 51 submissions (53%) categorically stated that the document was so deficient with respect to the Guidelines document that it would be premature to continue with further public hearings. Just over one-fifth of the submissions provided support for the EIS and urged for the continuance of the next phase of public hearings, while the remaining 13 submissions did not provide a categorical position. However, a total of 41 submissions noted deficiencies in the EIS document (EA Panel, 1995b). Many of the deficiencies noted were in relation to the AECL's and Ontario Hydro's failure to adhere strictly to the *Guidelines for the Preparation of an EIS*, which was the focus of the first round of public hearings. Specific issues raised included the problem of a generic assessment, lack of suitable attention given to alternatives to geologic burial, inadequate funding provided to intervenor groups, failure to address the potential consequences of catastrophic failure and release of radioactive materials, and inadequate attention given to First Nations' concerns of land use and land claims.

The invited submissions from the Scientific Review Group, the Canadian Geoscience Council, the OECD Nuclear Energy Agency Review Group were generally positive and at times enthusiastic about the EIS and the need to press on with the hearing process. Although some technical deficiencies were noted, no major problems were articulated. A review of these submissions gives the impression that the process has been going on for long enough, that the scientific and technical bases for proceeding are sufficiently advanced, and any delay is pointless and counter-productive.

In December 1995, the EA Panel concluded that "sufficient information is now or will be available from the AECL and other sources in time to allow public hearings to begin in March [1996]" (EA Panel, 1995a:1). This decision was based on a review of the EIS itself and the submissions received from government departments and agencies, associations, non-governmental organizations and individuals. Thus, despite the fact that the majority of the submissions categorically stated that the hearings should not proceed, the Panel deigned to press ahead, citing "its obligation ... to present to government in a timely fashion its best advice on the long-term management of nuclear fuel waste".

The public did influence the nature and structure of the next round of public hearings which consisted of three phases focussing on : 1) broad societal issues related to the long-term management of NFW; 2) technical sessions on the long-term safety of the disposal concept from scientific and engineering viewpoints; and 3) fora for participants to provide their final opinions and views on the safety and acceptability of the disposal concept and any other issues relevant to the Panel's mandate (EA Panel, 1996).

Conclusions

There has been a significant shift in Canada in the management of resources and the assessment of major projects. This shift has been described as a move from paternalistic forms of decision making to a more active participatory style of politics (O'Riordan and O'Riordan, 1993). While paternalism was tolerated two decades ago, public perceptions over the legitimacy of closed decision-making procedures, the sanctity of experts, and the exclusion of meaningful public participation have rendered it obsolete (Hadden, 1991). The process of decision making has become as important as the final outcome of those decisions.

The inclusion of a range of participants in formal decision-making structures such as the Environmental Assessment of the Canadian NFW disposal concept as required by the Canadian Environmental Assessment Act guarantees that the public interest and labour and local constituencies have access to funds and the opportunity to present their views. There have been many meetings and opportunities for the presentation of views. However, the impact of these on the proponent and actual decision-making body is far from clear. Submissions reveal that there is substantial lack of trust in the expertise used to establish the scientific and technical credibility of the proposal, and that the process to find a solution is flawed and too narrowly defined. These are attributes noted by Jacob (1990) as being

the primary stumbling block to the acceptance of the proposed NFW disposal facility proposed for Yucca Mountain,
Nevada.

The initial definition of the issue as a purely technical
one is perceived as an injustice by many hearing participants and may be viewed as an attempt by the project proponent to evade ideological debates and conflict over the
goals of the nuclear industry and energy policy generally.
This focus on the technical aspects of the concept have a
distinct impact on how policy is shaped and ultimately
implemented. Issues and objections raised in the 1990
Scoping Meetings were often deemed outside the mandate of
the EA Panel or beyond the scope of the inquiry but were
vehemently put forward as central concerns by local citizens
and environmental organizations (e.g., debate on the impact
of a disposal facility on future Canadian energy policy; fear
of catastrophic accidents etc.). Having the EA divided into
two distinct stages also removed the immediate threat to
potential host communities and rendered the initial phase
geographically innocuous, at least to the extent that no specific community on the Canadian Shield was under direct
consideration. The broader issue of regional equity of having
a non-nuclear producing region accept the wastes of the
nuclear generating regions (mainly southern Ontario) was
also skirted by the initial definition of a feasible solution. A
more blatant denial of public input was the decision to proceed with the 1996 hearings on the adequacy of the EIS
submitted by the AECL and Ontario Hydro despite the fact
that the majority of submitters claimed that the EIS documents did not sufficiently address the issues specified in the
EIS Guidelines.

The opportunity to participate in the EA process cannot
be equated with the ability to influence the decision-making
process. Commitment to power sharing is required. By
shaping the definition of the problem and its feasible solution (geological burial in the Canadian Shield), and control-

ling the apparatus of information and research, both the public interest constituency and the local and labour constituency are left in positions of relative powerlessness. At a minimum, the definition of the terms of reference of the EA should be open to public scrutiny and debate. This would go some way to avoiding the cynicism and distrust that develop in a supposedly open process.

It is too early to tell what the effect of the 1996 hearings will be. The formal inclusion of a series of hearings on the social aspects of the disposal concept leaves room for optimism. This is clearly a progressive step, and in the longer term a necessary one towards overcoming problems of legitimacy and trust. Inclusion of a broader range of issues as legitimate concerns reflects the continuing evolution of the EA process in Canada from initially considering only the economic and technical aspects of development proposals. The EA process, as noted by Novek (1995), has also become a forum for democratic debate and education. Pressure to devolve decision-making responsibility will likely continue as environmental awareness increases and as the range and interests of stakeholders expands.

Note: Financial support for this research was provided by the Social Sciences and Humanities Research Council of Canada.

References

Aikin, A.M., Harrison, J.M. and Hare, F.K. (Chairman) (1977) *The Management of Canada's Nuclear Fuel Wastes: Report of a Study prepared under Contract for the Ministry of Energy, Mines and Resources*, Ottawa, ON: Ministry of Supply and Services, Report EP 77-6.

Armour, A.M. (1992) "The cooperative process: facility siting the democratic way," *Plan Canada*, March: 29-34.

Atomic Energy of Canada Limited (AECL) (1994) *Environmental Impact Statement on the Concept for Disposal of Canada's Nuclear Fuel Waste*, Pinawa, MB: AECL-10711.

Auditor General of Canada (1995) "Federal radioactive waste management," in *Report of the Auditor General of Canada to the House of Commons*, Ottawa, ON: Minister of Supply and Services, 3-1 - 3-33.

Ballard, K.R. and Kuhn, R.G. (1996) "Developing and testing a facility location model for Canadian nuclear fuel waste," *Risk Analysis*, 16: 821-832.

Carter, L.J. (1987) *Nuclear Imperatives and Public Trust: Dealing with Radioactive Waste*, Washington, DC: Resources for the Future.

Eiser, R.J., Van Der Pligt, J. and Spears, R. (1995) *Nuclear Neighbourhoods: Community Responses to Reactor Siting*, Exeter, UK: University of Exeter Press.

Environmental Assessment Panel (1995a) *News Release December 12, 1995*, Ottawa, ON: Government of Canada.

_____ (1995b) *Compendium of Comments Received on the*

Adequacy of the Environmental Impact Statement on the Nuclear Fuel Waste Management and Disposal Concept, 2 vols., Ottawa, ON: Nuclear Fuel Waste disposal Concept Environmental Assessment Panel.

_____ (1996) *News Release February 1, 1996*, Ottawa, ON: Government of Canada.

Federal Environmental Assessment Review Office (FEARO) (1991) *Hearings by the Environmental Assessment Review Office on the Nuclear Fuel Waste Management and Disposal Concept: Scoping meetings, October 1990*, Hull, PQ: FEARO.

_____ (1995) *Compendium of Comments Received on the Adequacy of the Environmental Impact Statement on the Nuclear Fuel Waste Management and Disposal Concept,* Hull, PQ: Nuclear Fuel Waste Disposal Concept Environmental Assessment Panel.

Fiorino, D.J. (1990) "Citizen participation and environmental risk: a survey of institutional mechanisms," *Science, Technology, and Human Values*, 15: 226-243.

Hadden, S.G. (1991) "Public perception of hazardous waste," *Risk Analysis*, 11: 47-57.

International Atomic Energy Agency (IAEA) (1993) *Report on Radioactive Waste Disposal*, Vienna, Austria: IAEA Technical Report No. 34.

Jacob, G. (1990) *Site Unseen: The Politics of Siting a Nuclear Waste Repository*, Pittsburgh, PA: University of Pittsburgh Press.

Kemp, R. (1990) "Why not in my backyard? A radical interpretation of public opposition to the deep disposal of radioactive waste in the U.K.," *Environment and*

Planning A, 22: 1239-1258.

_____ (1992) *The Politics of Radioactive Waste Disposal*, Manchester, UK: Manchester University Press.

Kemp, R. and O'Riordan, T. (1988) "Planning for radioactive waste disposal: some central considerations," *Land Use Policy*, 5: 37-44.

Kemp, R., O'Riordan, T. and Purdue, M. (1984) "Investigation as legitimacy: the maturing of the big public inquiry," *Geoforum*, 15: 477-488.

Kuhn, R.G. (1996) "Siting a nuclear fuel waste disposal facility in Canada: a view from the public," in *International Conference on Deep Geological Disposal and Radioactive Waste: Conference Proceedings*, Winnipeg, MN: Canadian Nuclear Society, 10-45 - 10-54.

Kunreuther, H., Fitzgerald, K. and Aarts, T.D. (1993) "Siting noxious facilities: a test of the facility siting credo," *Risk Analysis*, 13: 301-318.

Leiss, W. and Chociolko, C. (1994) *Risk and Responsibility*, Montreal, PQ: McGill-Queen's University Press.

Ministry of the Environment, Canada (1989) *Terms of Reference for the Nuclear Fuel Waste Management and Disposal Concept Environmental Assessment Panel*, Ottawa, ON: Federal Environmental Assessment Review Office.

Novek, J. (1995) "Environmental impact assessment and sustainable development: case studies of environmental conflict," *Society and Natural Resources*, 8: 145-159.

Ontario Hydro (1991) *Federal Environmental Assessment of*

Nuclear Fuel Waste Management and Disposal: Summary of Scoping Meetings Issues, Toronto, ON.

Openshaw, S., Carver, S. and Fernie, J. (1989) *Britain's Nuclear Waste: Safety and Siting*, London, UK: Belhaven Press.

O'Riordan, T. and O'Riordan, J. (1993) "On evaluating public examination of controversial projects," in H.D. Foster (ed.), *Advances in Resource Management: Tributes to W.R. Derrick Sewell*, London, UK: Belhaven Press, 19-52.

Paehlke, R. (1989) *Environmentalism and the Future of Progressive Politics*, New Haven, CT: Yale University Press.

Parenteau, R. (1988) *Public Participation in Environmental Decision Making*, Ottawa, ON: Federal Environmental Assessment Review Office.

Rees, J. (1990) *Natural Resources: Allocation, Economic and Policy*, 2nd ed., London, UK: Routledge.

Shelley, F.M., Solomon, B.D., Pasqualetti, M.J. and Murauskas, G.T. (1988) "Locational conflict and the siting of nuclear disposal repositories: an international appraisal," *Environment and Planning C*, 6: 323-333.

Slovic, P. (1987) "Perception of risk," *Science*, 236: 280-285.

Slovic, P., Layman, M., Kraus, N., Flynn, J., Chalmers, J., and Gesell, G. (1991) "Perceived risk, stigma, and potential economic impacts of a high-level nuclear waste repository in Nevada," *Risk Analysis*, 11: 683-700.

Chapter 2

The Representativeness of the Elliot Lake Uranium Mine Tailings Areas EARP Public Hearings

Mark Prystupa, Laurentian University;
Don Hine, University of New England;
Craig Summers, Laurentian University and
John Lewko, Laurentian University

Public participation refers to activities that seek to involve those affected by a decision so that they may have input into it. Demand for more open decision-making processes began in the late 1960s as interest groups sought to mobilize their rapidly increasing membership. Through the 1970s and 1980s, public hearings became the primary procedure for representing public interests in policy matters. For example, Checkoway (1981) has called the hearing the most traditional method for public participation. Smith (1984) suggests that hearings have become so commonplace that they have often been considered synonymous with public participation. Today, all federal and provincial environmental assessment processes in Canada contain provisions for public hearings.

A perceived failing of the public hearing has been their inability to involve a balanced range of stakeholders. According to Gundry and Heberlein (1984:175):

> The belief that the people involved, as well as the opinions gathered, in public meetings are not representative of the client public has been stated so often that it is now generally accepted.

Several authors (Sewell and O'Riordan, 1976; Cupps, 1977; Reed, 1984; Kihl, 1985; Westman, 1985; Boothroyd, 1990; Smith, 1993) have identified representativeness as a fundamental prerequisite for effective and equitable public participation. The concern is that, instead of overcoming political inequality, public hearings may exacerbate it by allowing an elite minority to sway the hearings in its favour (Solandt, 1975; Sewell and O'Riordan, 1976). Thus, if participants in hearings are not representative of the public, there should be a movement away from this technique of citizen participation to one that can involve a balanced range of interests.

Despite the prevalent belief that public hearings are unrepresentative, it has yet to be demonstrated empirically. The lone systematic evaluation on the subject was completed by Gundry and Heberlein (1984) in their investigation of three series of hearings in Wisconsin. These authors found that opinions on policy preferences were similar between those who participated in hearings and the local population, despite some differences in demographic characteristics and a larger variance of opinions among participants.

Given that Gundry and Heberlein's findings are over a decade old, represent only one geographic area and set of institutional arrangements, it is not clear how well they will generalise to other settings. Thus, the purpose of this study is to provide additional empirical data on the representativeness of public hearings. The focus of this investigation is on the hearings held to review the decommissioning of four uranium mine tailings areas near Elliot Lake, Ontario under the Environmental Assessment and Review Process (EARP). To set the context, a description is provided of the EARP public hearing process and details on the Elliot Lake public hearings. These sections are followed by an explanation of the methodology; an assessment on how representative the public hearings were, a discussion of the relationships among the various participant subgroups and their implications for future public hearing practise under the Canadian Environmental Assessment Act (CEAA).

Public Hearings in the Environmental Assessment and Review Process

EARP was established by a Federal Cabinet decision on December 20, 1973 (Couch, 1988). In 1984 a Guidelines Order strengthened and updated the process. The Guidelines Order outlines two stages within the process: an initial assessment and a panel review. The vast majority of projects (i.e., > 95%) never move beyond the first stage of initial assessment or screening and, therefore, do not require public hearings (Prystupa, 1994). When an initial assessment decision concludes that a proposal has potentially significant adverse environmental and/or directly related socio-economic impacts, or public concern is great, the Minister of the initiating department may recommend that the Minister of the Environment conduct a panel review. These reviews may differ in type and focus, but two elements are always present (FEARO, 1987:3):

- the proposal undergoes detailed examination by an independent panel, with opportunity for public involvement, including comment on the review documents and participation in public hearings;

- each panel has a specific mandate, describing the nature and scope of the review. The scope of a public review may include, at the direction of the initiating Minister and the Environment Minister, such matters as the general socio-economic effects, assessment of technology, and the need for the proposal.

All public hearings, under EARP, are non-judicial and held in areas where there is expected to be significant stakeholder interest. Those wanting to make a presentation are encouraged to preregister to the Panel Secretariat and supply a written text, but are not required to do so. Questioning is allowed with a focus on clarification and not cross-examination. Representation by legal counsel is rare and is discouraged. All material received by the Panel, from either the proponent or the public, is made available for viewing. Transcripts of the hearings are also made available to the public within a reasonable period.

Over the past several years, hearings have typically taken place over two stages. The first stage is called scoping sessions. The goal of this stage of citizen participation is to provide an opportunity for the public to identify their concerns and matters of interest about the project. If their concerns are judged to be significant and within the scope of the Panel's terms of references, the Panel will include them in a list of information requirements for the proponent to include in its Environmental Impact Statement (EIS). The second stage of hearings is held after the proponent completes the EIS. If the Panel judges the EIS, with the aid of written submissions from the public, to be adequate it will give notice of the scheduling of public hearings. Time is allowed for prospective participants to review the proponent's documents and provide a critical examination of the project details and its options. Following the review the Panel will write an advisory report indicating if the project should be approved, not approved, or approved under certain specified conditions. The Ministers of the Environment and the initiating department have final decision-making authority.

In January 1995 the Canadian Environmental Assessment Act (CEAA) replaced EARP as the federal environmental assessment legislation in Canada. Since the review of the decommissioning of the uranium mine tailings in the Elliot Lake area began before the new Act came into force it was completed under EARP; however, all new panel reviews begun after January 1995 will be subject to the new procedures. Public hearings held under CEAA are similar to those held under EARP (Regulatory Advisory Committee, 1996). The hearings will remain non-judicial although there are provisions for witnesses to be subpoenaed. As an alternative, or in addition, to public hearings under CEAA the Minister of the Environment may refer the assessment to a mediator. As was the case with EARP, the vast majority of proposals under CEAA are screened and do not go to a panel review or comprehensive study, and, therefore, provide limited opportunities for public input (CEAA, 1996a).

The Elliot Lake Hearings

The Elliot Lake hearings focussed on the decommissioning of four uranium mine tailings areas (i.e., Quirke 1 and 2, Panel, Denison, and Stanrock) by two proponents (Rio Algom Limited and Denison Mines Limited) near Elliot Lake (Figure 2.1). Earlier the mining companies had received licences for the decommissioning of the mines and mills. There was considerable environmental and public concern, however, over the decommissioning of the tailings management areas. Consequently, the agency with regulatory authority, the Atomic Energy Control Board, referred the tailings decommissioning proposals for review by an Environmental Assessment Panel under EARP. In September 1993 the Federal Environmental Assessment Review Office, now the Canadian Environmental Assessment Agency, established a three-member panel.

Scoping sessions were held on five days in December, 1993 in Elliot Lake, Sudbury and the Serpent River First Nation Reserve. Intervenor funding totaling $61,600 was provided to six groups to help them prepare their submissions. Many presentations were critical of the Panel's terms of reference that precluded the investigation of several other tailings areas closed before the requirement to obtain a license for decommissioning. Subsequently, in August of 1994 the Minister of the Environment revised the terms of reference to include the contribution of the four mines

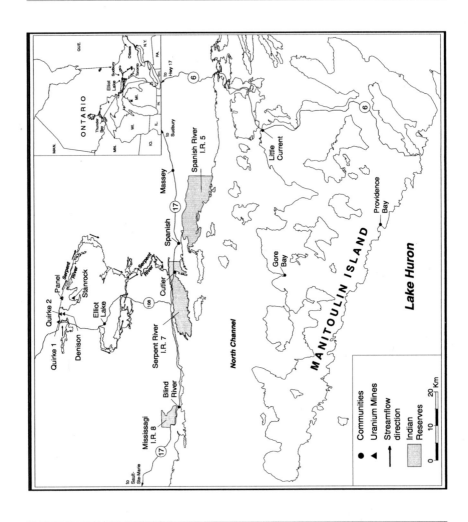

Figure 2.1

**Uranium Mine
Tailings Areas Under
EARP Review in the
Elliot Lake Region**

under review to the cumulative environmental impact resulting from several decades of uranium mining in the region. The Panel released its EIS Guidelines to the proponents later in the same month.

In December of 1994 a further $61,600 was awarded in intervenor funding, this time for the public hearings. Two groups received the bulk of the funding. Northwatch, a coalition of environmental groups across Northern Ontario, received $25,000, and the Serpent River First Nation received $30,100. The proponents submitted their EISs in May of 1995. After requesting and receiving additional information from the proponents, the Panel announced the timing of the hearings on October 6, 1995 to commence on November 14, 1995. Three types of hearings were held (EARP Panel, 1995a:1-2):

- Community Sessions — to encourage full and open participation of people living in or adjacent to the study area. Priority was given to people living in or adjacent to the study area.

- General Sessions — to provide the opportunity for all interested persons to make presentations to the panel on both technical and non-technical subjects.

- Technical Sessions — to provide an opportunity for interested persons to give a presentation on specific technical issues.

Table 2.1 shows the timing and location of the public hearings. The sessions in Elliot Lake and Sudbury were televised in Elliot Lake on the local cable channel. The Report of the Environmental Assessment Panel was released in June 1996 (CEAA, 1996b).

Table 2.1
Public Hearing Details

Date	Times	Session Type	Location
Nov. 14	9:00 - 12:00 13:30 - 17:00	General Community	Elliot Lake
Nov. 15	13:30 - 17:00 19:00 - 22:00	Technical Technical	Elliot Lake
Nov. 16	9:00 - 12:00 13:30 - 17:00 19:00-22:00	Technical Technical General	Elliot Lake
Nov. 17	9:00 - 12:00 13:30 - 17:00	Technical Technical	Elliot Lake
Nov. 18	9:00 - 12:00 13:30 - 17:00	Technical Technical	Elliot Lake
Nov. 27	9:00 - 12:00 13:30 - 17:00	General General	Sudbury
Jan. 23	14:00 - 21:00	Community	Serpent River
Jan. 26	13:30 - 17:00	General	Elliot Lake

Who Participated?

Table 2.2 displays the affiliation of those who participated in
the public hearings. The numbers in the columns differ
because several people may have been involved in one presentation or a person or a group may have made multiple-
presentations. Interest groups were most prevalent,
accounting for 39% of the total submissions. Most of these
submissions were critical of the proponents' proposals. The
two mining companies made 22% of the presentations, predominantly to explain and justify their desired options.
Submissions by Non-Native individuals, 9% of the total,
dealt with a wide range of issues from concern for the environment and the economy of Elliot Lake, to the need for an
ongoing public role in monitoring and mitigation. Native

individuals contributed 10% of the submissions, predominately expressing concerns about the environment, their health, and the way mining activity has disrupted their traditional lifestyle. Government agency representatives (13%) and academics (6%) rounded out the submissions dealing chiefly with technical matters. Attendance at the hearings by the public was generally low (i.e., typically about 20-25 people) with the exception of the Hearing held on the Serpent River First Nation Reserve (i.e., approximately 70 people).

Table 2.2
Participation by Affiliation

	Number of Groups		Number of Individuals		Number of Submissions	
	Number	%	Number	%	Number	%
Interest Groups	8	25.8	18	30.5	26	38.8
Proponents	2	6.5	9	15.3	15	22.4
Governments	5	16.1	10	16.9	9	13.4
Academics	4	12.9	4	6.8	4	6.0
Natives	7	22.6	10	16.9	7	10.4
Individuals	5	16.1	8	13.6	6	9.0
Total	31		59		67	

Methods

Sample and Questionnaire

Methods were established to compare the representativeness of those who participated in the public hearings versus those who did not. From April to June 1996, 51 of the 59 people who participated (those people who made a presentation) in the public hearings completed a questionnaire. Since several of the presentations comprised more than one person, and some people presented more than once, this sample had representation from 65 of the 67 submissions made at the hearings. Table 2.3 displays the sample sizes and response rates of the various participant subgroups used in the analysis of the data. Respondents in these groups were compared to 176 (response rate 63%) Non-Native regional residents from the City of Elliot Lake and the Township of the North Shore (pop. 15,000) and 18 (response rate 90%) Native residents of the Serpent River First Nation Reserve (pop. 300). These areas (Figure 2.1) were selected for case study because they are expected to experience the greatest environmental, social, and economic effects stemming from the tailings decommissioning process (CEAA, 1996b).

Table 2.3
Questionnaire Samples Sizes and Response Rates

Subgroup	Number Sampled	Total Number of Participants in the Hearings	Response rate (%)
Proponents	5	9	56
Academics/ Government	13	14	93
Interest Groups	16	18	89
Individuals	8	8	100
Natives	9	10	90
Total	51	59	86

Hearings participants were identified by using the public hearing transcripts. Non-participants were randomly sampled from local telephone listings. All Non-Natives were administered the questionnaire over the phone. Native participants sampled were interviewed in-person by a member of their community.

Questionnaire

To assess the representativeness of the Elliot Lake hearings, participants in the public hearings were compared with local residents who did not participate in the hearings on three demographic variables (age, education level, and financial security) and three cognitive-affective variables (satisfaction with the decommissioning process, perceived risks of the tailings from the decommissioned mines, and emotional responses).

The three demographic measures (age, education level, and financial security) were each measured by single items. For age, respondents were asked to report their birth date, from which their age was computed. Education level was measured by a scale ranging from 1 (less than high school) to 5 (postgraduate degree). Financial security was assessed by an item that asked "How well does your present income cover monthly expenses" (1 = does not cover expenses, 5 = covers all expenses and allows for very good savings).

Satisfaction with the decommissioning was measured by a single 5-point Likert scale item which asked: "How satisfied are you with the current decommissioning (or closure) process for the uranium mines and tailings in Elliot Lake" (1 = very unsatisfied, 5 = very satisfied).

Emotional responses to the decommissioning process were measured using a procedure similar to that employed by Peters and Slovic (1995), and Slovic, Flynn, and Layman (1991). Respondents were asked to list three thoughts or images that immediately come to mind in response to the phrase "mine closures and mine decommissioning in Elliot Lake." They were then asked to rate each thought or image on a scale ranging from 1 (very negative) to 5 (very positive). These ratings were averaged to form a single measure of emotion. Cronbach's α for this measure was .78, indicating adequate internal consistency.

Risk perceptions were assessed by 12 items addressing various health risks associated with the containment of the uranium mine tailings from the decommissioned mines (e.g., radon gas, radiation, acid mine drainage, contaminated vegetation, contaminated water, etc.). Each risk was rated on a 11-point scale ranging from 0 (no risk) to 10 (strong likelihood of high fatalities). A risk perception score was computed by averaging the original items. Cronbach's alpha associated with this measure was .97.

Representativeness of Participants

Descriptive Statistics of the Questionnaire Respondents

Respondents' ages ranged from 14 to 83, with a mean of 49.16 (SD = 15.60). Education levels ranged from less than high school (19%) to postgraduate professional degree (12%). The modal response for education level was high school (34%). In response to the financial security item, 27% of respondents indicated that their present income does not usually cover all of their expenses or just barely covers their expenses, 46% indicated their income adequately covers their expenses, and 26% indicated that their income covers all expenses and allows for some savings or very good savings.

Approximately one-fifth (22%) of the sample indicated that they were very unsatisfied or unsatisfied with the Elliot Lake decommissioning process, whereas 37% indicated they were neutral and 40% indicated they were satisfied or very satisfied. The mean satisfaction score was 3.13 (SD = 1.00).

Scores on the risk perception measure covered the full range of the scale (0 to 10). The mean risk score was 3.21

(SD = 2.59), suggesting that, on average, respondents believed that the uranium tailings from the decommissioned mines posed only minimal risks to human lives.

In terms of the emotions measure, respondents generated a wide range of thoughts and images to the stimulus cue "mine closures and mine decommissioning at Elliot Lake." Among the most common responses were: loss of work, threats to health, and threats to the environment. A complete listing of responses is available from the first author. Seventy-three percent of the images generated by the respondents were rated as negative or very negative, whereas only 14% were rated as positive or very positive. The average rating across all thoughts and images was 2.15 (SD = .84), reflecting a moderately negative emotional association with the decommissioning process.

Representativeness of the Elliot Lake Hearings

MANOVA was employed to investigate whether individuals who participated at the Elliot Lake hearings differed significantly from non-participants on the cognitive-affective and demographic variables described earlier. Separate analyses were conducted for Non-Native and Natives because of the significant differences in responses for the two samples. The results of these analyses are presented in Table 2.4.

Non-Native respondents who participated in the hearings differed significantly from Non-Native non-participants on two of the cognitive-affective variables, and two of the demographic variables. Relative to non-participants, participators tended to be more educated, more financially secure, less satisfied with the decommissioning process, and have a more positive emotional association with mine decommissioning in Elliot Lake. For Native participants and Native non-participants, no statistical differences were found on any of the dependent variables.

Table 2.4

Summary of MANOVA Contrasting Public Hearing Participants and Non-Participants

Dependent Variables	Non-Natives			Natives[a]		
	Participants	Non-Participants	Univariate Significance Test and Effects Sizes[b]	Participants	Non-Participants	Univariate Significance Test and Effects Sizes[b]
Demographic						
Age	48.3(14.31)	49.7(15.65)	$F_{(1,203)}=.22, r=-.3$	45.2(17.91)	47.3(16.70)	$F_{(1,26)}=.09, r=-.06$
Education	4.03(1.29)	2.39(1.00)	$F_{(1,204)}=67.59^{**}, r=.50$	2.22(1.20)	2.06(1.30)	$F_{(1,26)}=.10, r=.06$
Financial Security	3.41(.95)	2.92(.86)	$F_{(1,197)}=7.84^{**}, r=.20$	2.57(.98)	2.86(1.10)	$F_{(1,20)}=.34, r=-.13$
Cognitive-Affective						
Satisfaction	3.00(1.45)	3.36(.74)	$F_{(1,216)}=5.08^{*}, r=-.15$	1.78(.67)	1.88(.81)	$F_{(1,24)}=.09, r=-.06$
Emotion	2.61(1.05)	2.01(.058)	$F_{(1,213)}=25.17^{**}, r=.33$	2.63(1.61)	2.25(1.46)	$F_{(1,25)}=.36, r=.12$
Perceived Risk	3.14(2.56)	2.51(1.88)	$F_{(1,209)}=3.08, r=.12$	8.41(1.63)	7.53(1.90)	$F_{(1,25)}=1.38, r=.23$

$^{*}p < .05$, $^{**}p < .01$. Cell entries are means with standard deviations in parantheses. Wilks' λ for the multivariates tests were .67 [$F_{(6,179)}$ = 14.78, p < .001] for the Non-Natives and .86 [$F_{(6,13)}$ = .35, p is not significant for the Natives.

[a] Normally the univariate significance tests and effect sizes are not interpreted if the multivariate test is not significant, however, because of limited power for this analysis they are reported here to confirm the similarity between Native Participants and Native Non-Participants.

[b] To minimize the effect of missing data, the univariate tests from the MANOVA were replaced by tests conducted on each dependent variable separately. Both sets of univariate analyses produced inevitably the same results. However, the F-values and means for the reported analyses we thought better represented the 'true' differences between groups.

Given that there was considerable variability in the responses provided by the Non-Native participants, a second MANOVA was conducted to assess the representativeness of specific subgroups who made submissions at the hearings (i.e., Proponents, Interest Groups, Academics/ Government, and unaffiliated Individuals). Table 2.3 displays the sample size and the total number of hearing participants for each category. The same dependent variables were used as in the previous MANOVA.

The results of this analysis, which are summarised in Table 2.5, indicate that unaffiliated Individuals most closely resembled the non-participants, sharing statistically similar values for age, financial security, emotional response to mine decommissioning, and perceived risk. The data also revealed the close association between: 1) the Proponents and Academics/Government, and 2) the Interest Groups and Individuals. Both pairs of participant groups shared statistically similar results for all six variables studied. The two pairings were also similar to each other on demographic characteristics, but the Proponents and Academics/ Government tended to be more satisfied with the decommissioning process and have more positive associations.

Relationships Between Participant Subgroups

Local stakeholders have frequently objected to outsiders influencing project determinations since the decisions taken are going to affect them primarily. This conviction was evident in the environmental assessment review process for Elliot Lake. Judith Stevens, for instance, told the Panel in the scoping sessions that:

> Once you have gone back to your respective homes and communities, we remain, along with the decommissioning problems and the growing tailings areas. The impact of your recommendations will ultimately affect my two small children . . . Therefore, I urge

Table 2.5
Summary of MANOVA Contrasting Non-Native Participant Subgroups and Non-Native Non-Participants

Dependent Variables	Proponents	Academics/Government	Interest Groups	Individuals	Non-Participants	Univariate Significance Test $F_{(4,181)}$
Demographic						
Age	53.40[a](11.50)	51.86[a](13.82)	43.58[a](14.50)	49.00[a](16.66)	49.66[a](15.64)	0.52
Education	4.20[a,b](0.45)	4.88[b](0.35)	3.77[a](1.59)	3.43[a](1.40)	2.39[c](1.00)	16.26**
Financial Security	3.80[a](1.10)	3.83[a](0.98)	3.27[a,b](0.90)	3.00[a,b](0.82)	2.92[b](0.86)	3.13*
Cognitive-Affective						
Satisfaction	4.20[a](1.79)	3.77[a,b](1.09)	2.33[c](1.18)	2.25[c](1.28)	3.36[b](0.74)	8.27**
Emotion	3.40[a](0.72)	3.10[a](0.96)	2.24[b](0.98)	2.00[b](0.93)	2.01[b](0.58)	6.93**
Perceived Risk	1.95[a](2.79)	1.94[a](1.94)	4.39[b](2.81)	3.65[a,b](1.93)	2.51[a](1.88)	5.83**

*p<.05, **p<.01. Wilks' λ for the multivariate test was .52 [$F_{(24,615)}$ = 5.29, p < .001]. Cell entries are means with standard deviations in parentheses. Focused contrasts were conducted using Duncan's multiple range test. Entries that share the same superscript are not significantly different.

you to remember these impacts once you are safely removed from this area (EARP Panel, 1993b:7).

Similarly, Earl Commanda, the Chief of the Serpent River First Nation, stated in the public hearing held on the Reserve that:

Our community has been living in the Serpent River Watershed for some 10,000 years . . . and we intend to live here . . . for another 10,000 years (EARP Panel, 1996:129).

Participation that is unrepresentative of regional interests can occur when either the local people who are involved do not match the views of the broader community, or external interests overshadow local ones. Unbalanced representation by regional interests may be more of a concern because Panels may look to community members as spokespeople, particularly with respect to social and economic issues. The Chair showed that the Panel was looking to use local participants' submissions when he said:

It is individuals who come in to express their personal views and concerns that very often give us the most enlightening insights into the preoccupations, the concerns that people have about the issues that this Panel has been set up to review (EARP Panel, 1993a:2).

The EARP report also responded to local intervenor's concerns about an ongoing role in the monitoring of the tailings areas in recommending the establishment of a community based organisation to oversee this function.

The analysis in this paper compared Non-Native and Native participants in the hearings to Non-Native and Native non-participants on three demographic and three cognitive-affective variables. The data revealed that Native participants represented Native non-participants, but the same did not hold true for the Non-Native comparison. This finding might have been expected for two reasons. First, all Natives who participated were from the Serpent River First Nation, whereas many Non-Native participants were not from the regional area (i.e., 32 of 49). Second, the hearing format on the Reserve was more conducive to having community members take part. The meeting on the Reserve was co-chaired by a respected member of the community, was less formal, and included a feast. This session of the hearings was the most successful at getting local people to participate, both as presenters and in asking questions. For example, the Serpent River public hearing session had the greatest number of local people presenting (12 compared to the next highest of 7) and the greatest number of people who asked questions during the session (10 compared to the next highest of 8) of any of the hearings.

As reported earlier, it was the Individuals subgroup that most closely resembled the non-participants in Non-Native analysis. Everyone in this category, like the Native participants, was from the Elliot Lake region. However, there were some differences between the two groups. Individuals were more likely to have a greater level of formal education than non-participants, perhaps making them feel more qualified and comfortable to take part in the hearings. The two subgroups also differed in their satisfaction of the EARP process. This departure may have resulted from a decline in the Individuals' ratings after their involvement. The dissatisfaction may have resulted from the hearings being intimidating and technical no matter whether they were general, technical, or community sessions. For example, George Farkouh, the Mayor of Elliot Lake remarked that:

> This process is intimidating to most people and many, if not all of us, lack the technical and legal expertise to make adequate presentations to this Panel (EARP Panel, 1995b:197).

Another individual presenter remarked about having difficulty understanding all the technical terms that came up at the hearing:

When the term "Becquerel" was mentioned, I thought maybe that was a subspecies of pickerel and I was wondering where I could catch one. I went home . . . feeling something like the ore in the crusher, you know, I was being beaten smaller and smaller (EARP Panel, 1995d:84).

A minority of people from the Interest Groups, 8 out of 18, were from the Elliot Lake region. Like the Individuals, Interest Groups differed from the Non-Native non-participants in having a higher education and lower satisfaction with the EARP process. However, Interest Groups additionally had a heightened perception of risk. The majority, 14 of 19 who made submissions representing Interest Groups, were associated with environmental organisations. These people are likely to have more of a concern for the natural environment than other Non-Native participants who are not members of such groups, probably accounting for their greater level of perceived risk. In the hearings the Interest Groups were prominent in challenging the proponents' plans, scientific methods and results, with greater technical vigour than most individuals would be able to. In so doing these environmental organisations may aid in an area where the skills of a community and its residents may be deficient. Therefore, as Berger (1976:5) stated, interest groups "do not represent the public interest, but it is in the public interest that they participate."

The Proponents and Academics/Government groups maintained a higher educational attainment, were more financially secure, and had a more positive emotional response to tailings decommissioning than the non-participants. The Proponents additionally had a higher degree of satisfaction with the EARP process. The differences with respect to emotional response and satisfaction with EARP may result from the professionals having a greater familiarity with tailings and environmental assessment procedures. Interestingly, non-participants' risk perception was statistically similar to the Proponents and Academics/ Government. This occurrence may be due to the proponents public education efforts. For example, Rio Algom Limited published a newsletter, offered mine tours, and maintained an open house display in the main mall in Elliot Lake. The Academics/Government subgroup critically analysed the proponents' technical data and brought forward additional information to aid decision making. The mining companies' presentations were largely to explain and clarify their proposals.

Responses to the cognitive-affective variables were not dependent on the demographic variables of age, education, and financial security. For example, Interest Groups had all three demographic variables statistically similar to the Proponents but differed on all cognitive-affective variables. The Native Non-Native demographic, however, was very influential in affecting risk perception, with Natives perceiving a much greater level of risk than any of the other groups. The Serpent River First Nation had been particularly affected by the uranium mining industry in the past, being downstream of several tailings management areas before there were as many environmental controls in the 1950s and 1960s. At one time people were told not to drink the water or consume beyond a certain limit of fish from the Serpent River. This experience may account for the Native's greater environmental and health concerns with respect to the tailings.

Conclusion

The analysis found that public hearing participants in the EARP review of the decommissioning of uranium mine tailings areas in the Elliot Lake area were not representative of non-participants in the regional area. However, local Native and Non-Native participants were representative. Since the Environmental Assessment Panel looked to these people to represent local preferences, the concern that local interests were being overshadowed by non-regional interests did not appear to be a problem in this case. On technical issues concerning the protection of the environment or health, other participating subgroups could engage one another in a sound debate fostering more informed decisions. Thus, these other subgroups may not have represented regional residents but they were better equipped to handle more scientific matters that aided in protecting local people.

The issue of whether public hearings represent regional residents has not been settled. Our findings disagree with the Gundry and Heberlein (1984) study referred to in the introduction where they found participants were representative. The Elliot Lake hearings were different from most in that rather than reviewing a project development they assessed a project decommissioning. The more difficult issue of which groups are most successful at influencing decisions has yet to be fully explored (see Chapter 1). Individual participants were found to be the most representative but their numbers are often small in public hearing formats, making balanced participation more fragile. In order to help ensure that participation is balanced, the public hearing procedures under the CEAA should be altered so that they are more conducive to participation by the local public. This may involve more actively soliciting the involvement of community members through such methods as open houses or round table discussions. One presenter, Art Young, had his own suggestion on how the Elliot Lake Environmental Assessment Panel could hear more what local people thought of the decommissioning of the uranium mine tailings areas in encouraging its members to:

> . . . go to the Renaissance Centre. You will get a cheap lunch...and you will be able to talk to some seniors. Don't take my word for how they feel, go and ask on your lunch hour . . . (EARP Panel, 1995c:311).

Additionally, the provisions for mediation in CEAA should only be employed when there is sufficient local representation that reflects the variety of viewpoints held in the regional area of the development.

Acknowledgements

We would like to thank all the people who completed the questionnaire. Funding was provided by the Centre for Resource Studies, Queen's University. The map was prepared by Léo Larivière, Technologist for the Department of Geography, Laurentian University.

References

Berger, T.R. (1976) "The Mackenzie Valley pipeline inquiry," *Queens Quarterly*, Vol. 83: 1-12.

Boothroyd, P. (1990) "On using environmental assessment to promote fair sustainable development," in Jacobs, P. and Sadler, B. (eds.), *Sustainable Development and Environmental Assessment: Perspective on Planning for a Common Future*, Hull, PQ: Canadian Environmental Assessment Research Council.

CEAA (1996a) *Annual Report, 1995-1996*, Hull, PQ: Canadian Environmental Assessment Agency.

_____ (1996b) *Decommissioning of Uranium Mine Tailings*

Management Areas in the Elliot Lake Area, Hull, PQ: Canadian Environmental Assessment Agency.

Couch, W.J. (1988) *Environmental Assessment in Canada: 1988 Summary of Current Practice*, Ottawa, ON: Canadian Council of Resource and Environment Ministers.

Cupps, D.S. (1977) "Emerging problems of citizen participation," *Public Administration Review*, 57: 478-487.

Checkoway, B. (1981) "The politics of public hearings," *Journal of Behavioural Science*, 17: 566-582.

EARP Panel (1993a) *Environmental Assessment Panel Reviewing Decommissioning Proposals for Elliot Lake Uranium Mine Tailings Management Areas*, Transcript of the Scoping Session Held in Elliot Lake on 9 December, Hull, PQ: Canadian Environmental Assessment Agency.

_____ (1993b) *Environmental Assessment Panel Reviewing Decommissioning Proposals for Elliot Lake Uranium Mine Tailings Management Areas*, Transcript of the Scoping Session Held in Elliot Lake on 11 December, Hull, PQ: Canadian Environmental Assessment Agency.

_____ (1995a) *Procedures for Public Hearings: Environmental Assessment Panel Reviewing Decommissioning Proposals for Elliot Lake Uranium Mine Tailings Management Areas*, Hull, PQ: Canadian Environmental Assessment Agency.

_____ (1995b) *Environmental Assessment Panel Reviewing Decommissioning Proposals for Elliot Lake Uranium Mine Tailings Management Areas*, Transcript of the Public Hearing Held in Elliot Lake on 15 November, Hull, PQ: Canadian Environmental Assessment Agency.

_____ (1995c) *Environmental Assessment Panel Reviewing Decommissioning Proposals for Elliot Lake Uranium Mine Tailings Management Areas*, Transcript of the Public Hearing Held in Elliot Lake on 16 November, Hull, PQ: Canadian Environmental Assessment Agency.

_____ (1995d) *Environmental Assessment Panel Reviewing Decommissioning Proposals for Elliot Lake Uranium Mine Tailings Management Areas*, Transcript of the Public Hearing Held in Elliot Lake on 18 November, Hull, PQ: Canadian Environmental Assessment Agency.

_____ (1996) *Environmental Assessment Panel Reviewing Decommissioning Proposals for Elliot Lake Uranium Mine Tailings Management Areas*, Transcript of the Public Hearing Held on the Serpent River First Nation Reserve on 23 January, Hull, PQ: Canadian Environmental Assessment Agency.

FEARO (1987) *The Federal Environmental Assessment and Review Process*, Hull, PQ: Federal Environmental Assessment and Review Office.

Gundry, K.G. and Heberlein, T.A. (1984) "Do public meetings represent the public?," *American Planning Association Journal*, 50: 175-182.

Kihl, M. (1985) "The viability of public hearings in transportation planning," *The Journal of Applied Behavioral Sciences*, 21: 185-200.

Peters, E. and Slovic, P. (1995) "The role of affect and worldviews as orienting dispositions in the perception and acceptance of nuclear power," *Decision Research Report*, No. 95-1.

Prystupa, M.V. (1994) *An Evaluation of Yukon Environmental Assessment Interest Representation*, London, ON: Ph.D.

Thesis, Department of Geography, University of Western Ontario.

Reed, M. (1984) *Citizen Participation and Public Hearings: Evaluating Northern Experience*, Cornett Occasional Paper No. 4, Victoria, BC: Department of Geography, University of Victoria.

Regulatory Advisory Committee (1996) *Procedures for an Assessment by a Review Panel: Canadian Environmental Assessment Act*, Hull, PQ: Prepared for the Canadian Environmental Assessment Agency.

Sewell, W.R. and O'Riordan, T. (1976) "The culture of participation in environmental decisionmaking," *Natural Resources Journal*, 16: 1-22.

Slovic, P., Flynn, J.H. and Layman, M. (1991) "Perceived risk, trust, and the politics of nuclear waste," *Science*, 254: 1603-1607.

Smith, L.G. (1984) "Public participation in policy making," *Geoforum*, 15: 253-259.

_____ (1993) *Impact Assessment and Sustainable Resource Management*, London, UK: Longman.

Solandt, O.M. (1975) *Report of the Solandt Commission*, Toronto, ON: Government of Ontario.

Westman, W.E. (1985) *Ecology, Impact Assessment and Environmental Planning*, New York, NY: John Wiley and Sons.

Chapter 3

Testing the Concept of Critical Environmental Assessment (EA) Education[1]

Alan P. Diduck
Community Legal Education Association (Manitoba)
and
A. John Sinclair
University of Manitoba

In the years since the passage of the National Environmental Policy Act in 1969, environmental assessment practitioners have continued to encourage increased involvement of the public in EA procedures. In fact, it is recognized by some that a significant source of enlightenment within the EA process comes from the public involvement component. However, while a large literature exists regarding the nature of and rationale for public involvement, such programs can at best be described as tentative.

Schibuola and Byer (1991) argue that public involvement is frequently inadequate because of a lack of knowledge: "public groups often lack the knowledge to adequately critique a document or the financial resources to retain an expert to do so". This is supported by Sullivan et al. (1996), who discovered that citizens' understanding of the project description portion of an EIS was "atrocious". On two measures of understanding (understanding the gist of the project and understanding potential environmental effects), 70% of the 113 participants answered correctly at a level no better than blind guessing. Earlier commentaries have also recognized that education (or the lack thereof) is an important public involvement issue (e.g., Grima, 1985 and Bush, 1990).

Education creates an awareness of the process and facilitates an understanding of substantive environmental, economic and social issues. It forms the foundation for fair, effective and meaningful participation (Praxis, 1988). Further, *critical EA education* has the potential to improve planning and assessment of development activities by helping introduce counter-hegemonic discourses that work to reverse current trends of unsustainable resource exploitation.

This chapter explores the role of education in EA, identifies the range of techniques used to conduct EA education, and develops a rationale for the concept of critical EA education. Through consideration of the nature of public involvement in EA, the theories of critical pedagogy and transformative learning, and selected principles of environmental education, the concept of critical EA education is developed as one approach to improving public involvement in EA. The concept is then applied to the environmental assessment case of the Pembina Valley Water Supply System, from southwestern Manitoba. The education techniques used in the case are analyzed in the context of critical education theory. Knowledge of the case, held by the participants involved, is assessed, including a rudimentary evaluation of critical consciousness.

Public Involvement in EA

There is a significant and growing literature on theoretical and practical dimensions of public participation (see, for example *The Journal of Public Participation*). There is also a significant literature on the specific area of public participation in EA. This literature is reviewed in some detail by Sinclair and Diduck (1995) and by Diduck (1995). In addition to the first two chapters of this book, a considerable effort in the area of public involvement in EA has been waged by geographers. For example, Smith (1993), considers 'interest representation' as critical to impact assessment in resources management and identifies public involvement steps, and Storey et al. (1991) consider the importance and role of public involvement in social impact assessments. Further, Meredith (1992) establishes that environmental impact assessment must be made 'pertinent' to be successful through establishing community-based impact assessments that directly involve those affected.

Education as an Element of Public Involvement

Through reviewing the literature and considering the Canadian experience with EA, Sinclair and Diduck (1995) identify 40 distinct education techniques that are available for use in EA. The authors note that "together these techniques not only represent a consensus of the existing literature, they provide a useful and interesting checklist of the potential activities that could be undertaken in facilitating EA education. The list runs the gamut from rudimentary, information dissemination techniques such as newspaper advertising to sophisticated pedagogical techniques such as participatory drama" (Sinclair and Diduck, 1995: 230).

Further consideration of the experience of selected EA practitioners, EA legislation in three Canadian jurisdictions, and the role of various media in other environmental contexts leads to the identification of a further 13 education techniques, bringing the total to 53, as shown in Table 3.1 (Diduck, 1995).

Through this research, Sinclair and Diduck (1995) argue that the literature clearly indicates that education is an integral component of public involvement. They note, however, that education, as it is conceived above, is largely restricted to information dissemination and communication practices. In this paper therefore, it is argued that education

Table 3.1
Education Techniques Categorized According to Format

- audio/visual/electronic

slide presentations	film presentations
computerized participation	videotape
-knowledge-based systems	
-electronic publishing	
-information retrieval systems	
-interactive computer software	

- traditional publishing (printed) (verbal)

publications	brochures
newspaper inserts	notices
feature articles	position papers
reports	newsletters
information kits	central depositories
decisions and reasons	translation
plain language legislation	posters
photonovel	manuals

- direct/individualized

direct mail	phone lines
field offices	technical assistance
direct e-mail	

- media

public service announcements	news releases
news conferences	advertising
call-in television	talk radio
coverage of hearings	interviews

- public presentations/events

workshops	conferences
panels	open houses
exhibits/displays	contests
simulation exercises	- song contests
meetings	town hall meetings
dialogues/coffee klatches	brainstorming
speakers bureau	special event days
discussion group conferencing	

- formal education

integration into existing curricula
discussion in literacy programs

Identified from the EA literature, the legislation of selected jurisdictions and the literature from other environmental contexts.

can become an even more important element of the EA public involvement process, when it is conceived in terms of critical pedagogy and related concepts.

Critical Pedagogy

A Brief Overview

The particular form of education explored in this research is critical EA education. At its foundation is Paulo Freire's (1970) theory, critical pedagogy. This theory, presenting a kind of "secular liberation theology" (Aronowitz, 1993:12), is based on the conviction that every human being is capable of critically engaging the world in a dialogical encounter with others. The theory accepts the transformative possibilities of willed human action, both on an individual and a social level.

Critical pedagogy defines education as a locus where the individual and society are constructed, a social interaction which can either empower or domesticate the pupil (Shor, 1993). A premium is placed on democratic dialogue which shifts the center of the learning process from the teacher to the student. This shift signifies a change in traditional power relationships, not only in the classroom but in the broader social order (Aronowitz, 1993). Although Aronowitz (1993:10) argues that Freire's theories present a "truly revolutionary pedagogy" and should not be domesticated into mere methodology, the instructional implications of Freire's work should not be ignored. Nor should Freire's explicit analysis of countervailing methodological approaches. In Chapter two of *Pedagogy of the Oppressed*, he describes the banking method of instruction. To this he counterposes a different approach namely, problem-posing, dialogical education.

According to Shor (1993), in the banking approach students are viewed as empty vessels to be filled with facts from an official syllabus. In Freire's words, such education becomes:

> "...an act of depositing, in which the students are
> the depositories and the teacher is the depositor.
> Instead of communicating, the teacher issues com-
> muniqués and makes deposits which the students
> patiently receive, memorize and repeat. The more
> students work at storing the deposits entrusted to
> them, the less they develop the critical conscious-
> ness which would result from their intervention in
> the world as transformers of that world" (Freire,
> 1970:58).

In contrast to the banking approach, Freire offers problem-posing, dialogical education. In this approach the
teacher poses critical problems for inquiry which relate to
important features of student experience. This allows the
students to see their thought and language reflected in the
course of study. That is, academic material is integrated
into student life and thought. The dialogical approach
invites students to think critically about the course subject
matter and doctrines, the learning process itself and society.
It also challenges students and teachers to empower themselves for social change and to advance democracy and
equality (Freire, 1970; Shor, 1993).

Shor (1993) identifies 10 descriptors of critical pedagogy:

- participatory - students participate in making their education;
- situated - the course subject matter is situated in student thought and language;
- critical - discussion encourages self-reflection and
  social reflection;
- democratic - discourse is constructed mutually by students and teacher;
- dialogical - the basic format is dialogue around prob-

lems posed in class;
- desocializational - students are desocialized from passivity in the classroom;
- multicultural - cultural diversity of society is recognized and accepted;
- research oriented - the teacher does research into the speech, behaviour, and cognitive development of the students while the students research problems posed by the teacher;
- activist - the classroom is active and interactive; and,
- affective - the dialogue is interested in a broad development of human feeling.

Applying the Principles in the Context of EA

The principles of critical pedagogy have been applied not only in the formal classroom but also in the field of adult education (e.g., Kirkwood and Kirkwood, 1989 and Lankshear, 1993). In addition, the methodological implications of critical pedagogy are entirely consistent with well-accepted guidelines for working with adult learners. For example, Knowles (1980, 1984) promotes the concept of learner-centered instruction because it views learners as mutual partners in the education process. This view is supported by Apps (1991) who discusses the benefits of incorporating learner input into course design. Pratt (1988) adds that even if learners require both support and direction, they can still be involved in designing and directing their learning in meaningful ways. Imel (1993) advocates participatory instructional methodologies such as small group work. She also suggests that instructors should support opportunities for individual problem solving by learners.

Critical pedagogy is also congruent with the adult education theory of transformative learning. Transformative learning describes how adult learners construe, validate and reformulate the meaning of their experiences (Mezirow, 1991). As in Freirean theory, transformative learning is concerned with emancipation and the development of critical consciousness (Mezirow, 1990). A recent treatment of the subject is offered by Cranton (1994). In presenting practical strategies for facilitating and maintaining the transformative process, the author discusses a range of techniques including dialogical and participatory methods such as various questioning techniques, journal-writing exercises and diverse experiential activities.

Usang (1992) suggests the relevance of Freirean theory to environmental education. She introduces the concept of green literacy, defined as "...the skill of transmitting and receiving information in an intelligible manner with sustainable environmental elements built in" (Usang, 1992:51). She argues that three main strategies exist that can be used separately or together to enhance green literacy: the Freirean method; the functional method; and, the organic method. By using the Freirean approach, adults can begin to question the condition of their environment and to find answers to their problems. "Questions like why do we have poor harvest and worsening soil erosion? What can we do to cut down our family size? Where can we get help? How can we go about it?" (Usang, 1992:51).

Criticisms

A revealing application of Freirean theory in a Canadian EA case is reported by Regnier and Penna (1996). The authors examine the work of the Inter-Church Uranium Committee Education Cooperative (ICUCEC) during the environmental assessment of three proposed uranium mines in Saskatchewan. ICUCEC organized public participation and conducted various forms of public education using a critical education approach. Despite some measure of success, ICUCEC's efforts failed to "alter the corporate power structure" or the technologies advocated by the project proponents. The authors analyze these events in terms of critical education and technological literacy and identify what they describe as limitations to the development of citizen empowerment through critical adult education.

Another criticism of critical pedagogy is the sexism of Freire's language and his androcentric concept of liberation. It is interesting to note, however, that bell hooks (sic), a well-known Feminist theoretician, has defended Freire's writings by placing them within an historical perspective and by stressing the importance of his work for people of colour and other traditionally marginalized groups (hooks, 1993). Freire himself has responded to the criticism by stressing the substance of his views rather than the form. He argues that his position has always been that a pedagogy of liberation must be based on an equal partnership among men and women free of hierarchical control and patriarchal assumptions (Freire, 1993).

Freire's theories have also been criticized by structuralists, who propose the fallacy of humanism (Aronowitz, 1993). For his part, Freire responds by positing that the main body of his work is in line with critical post-modern thought. He argues that many aspects of his work can be appropriated into and extended by critical post-modernist thought. Moreover, he counters by criticizing post modernism's lack of political will and its failure to value human narratives of liberation and social justice (Freire, 1993).

In spite of the limitations and criticisms of critical education, a fairly convincing rationale can be presented for the application of critical education concepts to public involvement in EA.

The Foundation of Critical EA Education

There are two main elements to the rationale for applying critical education to environmental assessment: i) critical education contributes to human liberation and fundamental democratic principles; and, ii) critical EA education has potentially far reaching and profound benefits for the planning and assessment of development activities.

Democratic Precepts

Adult education, including critical education, has direct links to human liberation and precepts of democracy. The entire Freirean approach to education constitutes "pedagogical politics of conversion" in which passive objects of history reinvent themselves as active subjects capable of profoundly changing the quality of their lives (West, 1993). Freire (1985) goes so far as to argue that the primary purpose of education is to further human liberation. He also argues that the centerpiece of the struggle for human liberation is the struggle for democracy (Freire, 1993).

Further support can be discerned in the literature on the rationale for public legal education. This body of literature is relevant because education about EA is, at least partly, a form of public legal education, inasmuch as it deals with EA legislation and regulations, government policy, public hearings, and administrative proceedings. The theoretical rationale for public legal education has been explored by a number of writers, for example, by Alderson (1992) in a paper commissioned by the Department of Justice Canada. In a document prepared for The Manitoba Law Foundation, Thompson (1989) summarized the literature in the following manner:

- legal awareness creates a more orderly and law abiding society;
- legal knowledge facilitates recognition of legal problems when and if they occur, which permits individuals to seek appropriate professional assistance;
- citizens' knowledge of law and access to legal services are critical to the administration of justice and to the functioning of an equitable and democratic society; and,
- awareness of law empowers citizens who are socially and economically disadvantaged, allowing them to take

a more active part in the political process.

The Freirean triad of education, liberation and democracy is further supported by findings from a recent study on learning in citizens' groups (Alexander, 1994). Participant observation and interviews were used to reveal what members of citizens' groups learn and how they learn it. This was done in the context of a land-use planning exercise. The resultant findings were put in the form of 25 propositions. Within this set, seven subcategories were identified, one of which, "What is Learned? Empowerment", pertains to the education-liberation-democracy connection. According to Alexander (1994), group members developed "citizenship skills" which meant that for them democracy ceased to be an abstraction. They discovered not only the merits of social activism, but also their ability to effect change. As well, group members sometimes became interested in fostering these values in others. Finally, members of citizens' groups developed an appreciation for the complexities of issues and the validity of other points of view.

Improved Planning

Critical EA education fosters critical consciousness, which, in turn, enables members of the public to evaluate dominant discourses and present credible and forceful counter discourses. This challenges the status quo and can make EA a truly effective planning mechanism to help reverse current trends of unsustainable resource exploitation. The potential for positive gains increases when EA is truly open, broad and anticipatory, and members of the public are given the opportunity to influence fundamental issues such as need, purpose and alternatives.

Discourse analysis of the type conducted by Richardson et al. (1993) is helpful in presenting the argument. Social power is created and justified through discourse, both verbal and symbolic (Anderson, 1988, cited in Richardson et al., 1993). Discourse also supplements force, often obviating the need for coercive force and transforming simple power into legitimate authority (Lincoln, 1989, cited in Richardson et al., 1993).

In the EA context there is a significant power imbalance between project proponents (and an often supportive local or regional government) on one hand and members of the public on the other hand. Proponents and governments present the dominant discourses of big business, the democratic state and the scientific establishment. Members of the public present counter discourses, often motivated by environmental protection, transformation of the political process and community control over matters of development (Richardson et al., 1993).

A number of techniques are available for critiquing dominant discourses, including the deconstruction of binary oppositions. A binary opposition is a device that places two ideas or things in a hierarchy to ensure that one is favoured over another. A typical pro-development binary opposition is *jobs v. the environment*. Richardson et al. (1993) suggest that breaking through the dichotomies presented in typical pro-development binary oppositions opens up environmental issues to greater scrutiny. Doing so redefines the debate by bringing new and often nontraditional issues into the discussion. What follows are three examples of nontraditional issues and approaches that challenge ideologies and principles at the very foundation of Western pro-development philosophies.

Cooperation

Pro-development, dominant discourse is often founded on an individualistic and competitive view of human nature. This view holds that resource users cannot cooperate toward their common interests, i.e., collective action to escape a social trap is impossible. A social trap is any situation in which short-term local reinforcements affecting an individual are inconsistent with the long-term global best interest of the individual and society (Costanza, 1987). However, recent theoretical developments, supported by case study research, challenge the conventional view. Berkes (1989) cites numerous examples of societies around the world in which natural resources are used in a sustainable, adaptive and cooperative manner. As well, the work of Axelrod and Hamilton (1981) and Peck and Feldman (1986) provide the basis for a credible theory on the evolution of cooperation.

Counter-hegemonic discourses can be developed based on this recent research and critical EA education can facilitate the development of such counter discourses by fostering critical consciousness in resource communities.

Ecological Economics

An extension of Western society's bias towards individualism and competition is its reliance on neoclassical economic theory. Neoclassical analysis is often at the heart of dominant discourses offered in EA. However, since environmental mismanagement and resource exploitation can be justified under neoclassicism (Goodland et al., 1989), it is obvious that effective counter discourses are required. A growing literature on alternative economic models provides the foundation for such discourses. One such alternative to neoclassical analysis is the paradigm of ecological economics. Key characteristics which define the ecological economics approach are summarized by Berkes (1993): a holistic view of the nature-economy relationship; treating the economic system as a subset of the whole environment; a primary concern with natural capital; and, accounting for a greater diversity of values than those normally considered by economists. Traditional economic theory treats natural resources as "free gifts of nature" (Grima and Berkes, 1989). Ecological economics rejects this position and gives natural resources the same status as human-made capital (Berkes, 1993).

Ecological economics aims for sustainable development by expanding the dimensions found in conventional economics and conventional ecology (Costanza, 1991). For those involved in EA, ecological economics presents an innovative and fascinating alternative to the dominant economic discourse.

Traditional Ecological Knowledge

Another of the basic elements of dominant discourse in EA is conventional Western science, which is based on a dualistic world view in which humans are viewed as being apart from and above the natural world. The ideals of science are generally reductionist in focus and have led to a disintegration of the unity of the Western world's theoretical knowledge and intellectual framework. According to Kockelmans (1979:146), this "dangerous fragmentation of our entire epistemological domain" has contributed to a crises in Western society. He argues that there is a tension between the world which our sciences describe and the world in which we actually live. This tension is evident in the difficulties that modern science has had in furthering human understanding and manipulation of complex ecological systems. According to Gadgil et al. (1993), science-based societies have tended to over-use and simplify complex systems, resulting in resource depletion and environmental degradation. It is increasingly apparent that counter discourses offering alternatives to Western resource management systems are necessary.

Fuel for such counter discourses is offered by traditional ecological knowledge (TEK). TEK, according to Gadgil et al. (1993), is a cumulative body of knowledge and beliefs about the relationship of living beings with one another and with their environment handed down through generations by cultural transmissions. TEK is usually intricately linked to a belief system which stresses respect for the natural world. The belief system often takes a holistic perspective which recognizes the place of humans within the natural system. TEK has potential to contribute to Holling and Bocking's (1990) "constant foundations of sustainable development" and, hence, can be a valuable tool when developing alternatives to Western resource management systems.

Critical EA Education

Critical EA education encompasses both "education about EA" and "education through EA". In metaphorical terms, education about EA serves as an on-ramp to the public involvement process. Education about EA is necessary to bring public participants up to speed before they enter the main flow of the involvement process. Within the participatory framework provided by critical pedagogy, a range of methods of instruction should be used to provide education about EA. The content should cover both process and substance issues and may include matters such as:

- the engineering aspects of a project;
- ecological, economic and social analyses of proposed project alternatives;
- how communities and ecosystems work;
- how status quo decision-making processes and project decisions can be challenged; and,
- how members of the public can work together to define and pursue their own goals.

Once in the main flow, members of the public can critically engage the EA world and challenge the status quo in a more-informed manner.

Education through EA occurs when participation in the main flow reinforces critical consciousness and, at a more macro level, becomes an educational process in itself. Participants gain experience in making presentations. They learn how to file an appeal. They are introduced to lobbying and advocacy. They gain confidence in their interactions with "experts". Education through EA provides the means of developing informed, critical, social activists capable of engaging their communities in meaningful and critical dialogue and of mounting efforts for real social change.

Education about EA and education through EA are inter-dependent. The former provides the foundation for the latter, while the latter gives substance and real meaning to the former. Taken together, education about EA and education through EA compose critical EA education whose main goal should be empowerment and social action.

Support for the notion that environmental education can lead to social activism can be found in Ibikunle-Johnson's (1989:14) study of grassroots participation and community action in central Africa: "knowledge, awareness, attitude and perceptions of grassroots people can be mobilized and transformed through participatory environmental education to generate motivations and skills for effective environmental management."

Further support can be found in Finger's (1989) theory of environmental adult transformation. Finger reports on a study from Switzerland which examined the histories of seven individuals in an attempt to discover what, where and how adults learn about the environment, and where the learning process leads them. He takes an approach comparable to that of Paulo Freire's in describing the concept of environmental adult transformation. Environmental adult transformation functions to lead the individual to environmental concern and potentially to act on sociopolitical commitment to protect the environment. The process is generated by three basic generative themes:

i)   fundamental motivations (either social or individual);
ii) sensitization contexts (again, this can either stem from society or from the individual); and,
iii) environmental life experiences (either institutional or non-formal).

The author distinguishes environmental adult transformation from environmental adult learning. The latter is generated by knowledge and information. It is mainly cognitive in nature, leading to understanding of specific environmental issues. The two main functions of environmental adult learning are to make the individual feel safer and more secure and to provide some degree of social and political emancipation. "Environmental adult learning is certainly part of the process of environmental adult transformation, though the precise relation between the two has not yet been established. It draws its energy, its motivations and even its main learning contexts from the latter" (Finger, 1989:31). Further research is required but it may be that education about EA leads to environmental adult learning while education through EA leads to environmental adult transformation.

Yet further support for the general dynamics and overall goal of critical EA education can be found in social learning theory. Using a case study of the siting of a waste disposal facility in Switzerland, Webler et al. (1995) examine how group communication processes can influence the development of a social contract on collective action to solve a mutual problem. The authors take an interdisciplinary approach to social learning, focusing on both psychological and sociological dimensions. They recognize two general components to social learning: cognitive enhancement (the acquisition of knowledge) and moral development (growth in the ability to make judgments about right and wrong). Among other things, the authors argue that the "crystallization point" of public participation planning exercises ..."is when the group transforms from a collection of individuals pursuing their private interests to a collectivity which defines and is oriented toward shared interests" Webler et al. (1995:460).

Alexander's (1994) research in the area of social learning is also supportive. He used interviews and participant observation during a land use planning exercise to address the questions of what citizens' groups learn and how the learning takes place. His findings, expressed in the form of propositions, are congruent with the basic characteristics of Freirean methodology:

- members of citizens' groups learn through a variety of methods but "hands-on" or action learning and dialogue are particularly important;
- members of citizens' groups learn in a variety of situations or settings which contribute significantly to the learning process; these settings include hearings and public meetings, conferences and direct action;
- most groups operate on a form of consensus and maintain an egalitarian spirit;
- small groups are significant for validation, emotional support and social identity and hence provide effective learning environments;
- other contexts provide opportunity for personal and social reflection and hence also are important in shaping learning outcomes.

Synthesizing earlier literature, Alexander also proposes a model of social learning that is consistent with the notion of education through EA. Under this model the prior learning that individuals bring to citizens' groups is classified as attitudes, knowledge and skills. A "disorienting dilemma" interacts with a person's prior learning, activating the person to join a citizens' group. Drawing on their prior learning, members of citizens' group identify their objectives and formulate their strategies. Once this is done, the group takes action. This, in turn engenders experiences. All of this occurs within specific settings, such as the small group context, and uses various modes of learning, such as dialogue and involvement in praxis. The experiences affect prior learning which, in turn, affects group processes and practices. From the constant interplay between action and learning, three broad categories of learning outcomes emerge: empowerment, teamwork and citizenship.

Critical Assessment of Education Techniques

The literature does not reveal a great deal of information on the evaluation of education techniques available for use in EA. For the most part, evaluations of public involvement processes tend to focus on the amount of power given to the public in the decision-making process, not on the education dimension of the involvement process. Although some writers have evaluated the effectiveness of individual education techniques (e.g., Schiboula and Byer, 1991 - knowledge based computer programming; Fortner and Lyon, 1985 - television programming; and, Mcleod, 1987 - local media activities), none have analyzed the techniques within the framework of critical pedagogy.

Although critical EA education is an approach to education, not an educational method, certain education techniques are more suited for use within the critical approach than are others. Using Shor's (1993) descriptors of critical pedagogy and Gibson's (1994) summary of the Freirean process, the following discussion presents a rudimentary framework for classifying the education techniques that are available for use in EA.

Almost all of the education techniques compiled in Table 3.1 could, theoretically, be used within the critical approach but they could also, with as much ease, be employed within the banking approach. Upon further review, however, it is revealed that the techniques can be classified based on their congruence with the fundamental characteristics of critical methodology. It would appear that some of the techniques are well suited to critical EA education, some are poorly suited, while others appear to be neutral.

The techniques that are well suited emphasize interactive learning, are people centered and exhibit many of the descriptors of critical pedagogy. An example is the workshop technique. By definition, workshops are participatory, dialogical, desocializational, research oriented, activist, reliant on group learning and use the teacher as the coordinator. They also tend to be democratic and critical and with proper planning can be situated, multicultural and affective.

The techniques that are poorly suited to critical EA education exhibit few, if any, of the descriptors of critical pedagogy. Generally, they focus on the presentation of "facts"; mere information dissemination with little or no interaction with the affected publics. Typical examples are advertising, direct mail (both e-mail and "snail mail"), posters and central depositories. Other techniques from Table 3.1 that fall into this category include the vast array of publishing techniques (including electronic publishing) and most of the media techniques (excluding talk radio and TV and radio interviews).

In labeling these education techniques as poorly suited to critical EA education, it is not suggested that they be dropped from the EA education process. In the context of a well planned and coordinated critical program, the "lowliest" of the poorly suited techniques can become a valuable tool. For example, central depositories epitomize the banking approach; experts make deposits of authoritative information which are passively withdrawn by members of the public. However, as part of a critical exercise, searching a central depository becomes participatory, desocializational, research oriented, activist, and reliant on praxis; in short a valuable technique for use in critical EA education. In addition, some of the poorly suited techniques serve crucial functions in the EA process. Advertising, direct mail and others are inexpensive techniques used to provide reasonable notice of important events to members of the public. Since reasonable notice is a legal requirement under the principles of natural justice, the value of simple information dissemination techniques is evident.

The education techniques labeled as neutral involve some degree of teacher-learner interaction. This interaction introduces an element of discretion so that a neutral technique can be applied as a banking tool or as a critical tool. Take, for example, panel presentations. The panel format easily fits within the banking approach to education; experts make presentations or deposits of information for the benefit of uninitiated nonexperts. On the other hand, the panel format also easily fits into the critical approach. The key is to incorporate the fundamental characteristics of critical methodology: use resource people from the community or class, situate the dialogue in terms that are relevant to the learners, structure the panel around dialogue and problem posing, respect and value diversity in the class and so on.

The neutral techniques gain value when they are applied in the context or culture of critical pedagogy.

Applying Critical EA Education

Methodology

Informal interviews with officials of Manitoba's EA authority (Manitoba Environment) were conducted for the purpose of selecting an appropriate EA case. Although a number of fairly suitable EA cases were discussed during the interviews, the Pembina Valley Water Supply System emerged as the most appropriate case. First, the case was fairly recent, with the ultimate decision being rendered in June 1994. Second, the case involved a large but manageable number of participants. Third, the strata of participants are quite diverse and included individuals and organizations, cities and towns, lawyers and lay advocates, sophisticated lobby groups and grass-roots community groups, rural and urban representatives, business corporations and non-profit organizations and formal interveners and individuals who were peripherally involved. Fourth, an initial assessment of the case indicated that some degree of public education was attempted by a number of the participants. Finally, the case involved the entire EA process, from preparation and submission of a proposal to the granting and appeal of an Environment License.

Once the case was selected, surveys were conducted to collect primary, normative data. The source of the data was the experiences of the assessment participants. Participants were defined to include a variety of "publics" such as individuals who were peripherally involved, individuals who made the formal record, interveners, the proponent and the EA authority. All participants were surveyed but a non-random sample emerged through a self-selection process. The precise survey methodologies used were structured interviews and questionnaires.

Structured interviews were conducted with a non-random sample of individuals and organizations who participated in the case. The objectives of the interviews were to identify the specific education techniques used by each of the interview subjects during the environmental assessment of the Pembina Valley Water Supply System (Manitoba Environment File No. 3269.00) and to solicit opinion on improving education about EA.

In selecting interview subjects, consideration was given to those key participants who might reasonably have engaged in public education activities. Consideration was also given to ensuring some degree of balance in the points of view presented during the interviews. In the end, interviews were conducted with the proponent (the Pembina Valley Water Supply Cooperative), a consultant retained by the proponent, the provincial EA authority (Manitoba Environment), an interested federal agency (the Prairie Farm Rehabilitation Administration) and two key interveners (Central Plains Inc. and the City of Winnipeg).

Upon completion of the interviews, a questionnaire survey was conducted. The objectives of the survey were to identify the education techniques used in the Pembina Valley Water Supply System case, assess participant knowledge about environmental assessment and the Pembina Valley Water Supply System case, and explore respondent views on EA education.

The surveys were sent to all individuals who participated in the Pembina Valley case. Sample data were obtained from 34 individuals who responded to the survey through a non-random, self-selection process (108 surveys were sent, 8 were returned unopened - effective mailout 100).

The Case

The proposal for the Pembina Valley Water Supply System was subject to both the federal and provincial EA processes. When the proposal was filed in October 1991 the federal process was governed by the Environmental Assessment and Review Process Guidelines Order (EARP) (SOR/84-467). The provincial process was guided by The Environment Act, S.M. 1987-88, c. 26; Chap. E125 and regulations.

The Proponent

The proposal for the Pembina Valley Water Supply System was submitted by the Pembina Valley Water Cooperative Inc., an organization formed in 1991. The Co-op comprises seven rural municipalities and eight towns in the Pembina

Triangle area of southern Manitoba. The members are the Rural Municipalities of Dufferin, Montcalm, Morris, Roland, Rhineland, Stanley and Thompson and the Towns of Altona, Carman, Emerson, Gretna, Morden, Morris, Plum Coulee and Winkler.

The Original Proposal

In the Pembina Valley Water Supply System case, the proponent filed its original proposal on October 18, 1991 (McNaughton, 1993). The Co-op proposed to develop and operate a comprehensive water supply system as a long-run solution to water-related problems in the Pembina Triangle. The project was intended to provide assured supplies of potable water for municipal, industrial and on-farm use (domestic and livestock consumption). Along with the construction of new water treatment plants and pipelines, the proposal included a plan for a water conservation program and a plan for continued use of existing water sources at sustainable levels (Pembina Valley Water Cooperative, 1991).

Figure 3.1 illustrates the Co-op's original proposed project. This involved diverting water from the Assiniboine River (up to 0.57 cubic meters per second by the year 2040) to the Boyne River and eventually to the Stephenfield Reservoir. A new water treatment plant at the reservoir would have been constructed and treated water would have been distributed by pipelines east to Carman and south to the Morden, Winkler and Plum Coulee areas.

A new water treatment plant would also have been constructed in Morris and the existing plant at Letellier would have been expanded. Water would have been diverted from the Red River to meet the demands of these two plants. Up to 0.083 cubic meters per second by the year 2040 would have been withdrawn over and above the 0.057 cubic meters per second currently being withdrawn. The new treatment

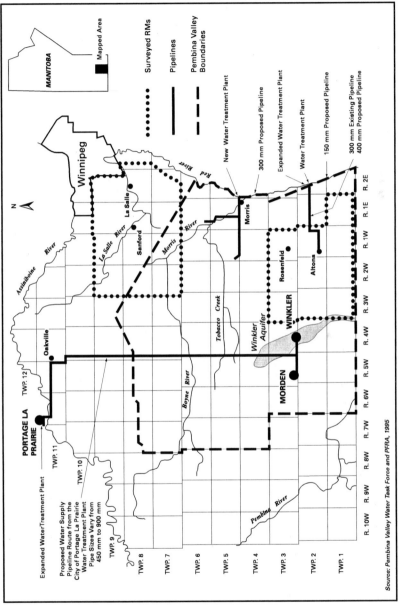

Figure 3.1: Proposed Pembina Valley Regional Water Scheme

Source: Pembina Valley Water Task Force and PFRA, 1995

plant at Morris would have served the Towns of Lowe Farm and Rosenort and the expanded Lettelier plant would have serviced the Towns of Altona, Gretna, St. Jean and Emerson. Existing treatment plants at St. Jean and Emerson would have been closed down. Regional pipelines would have been constructed to service the larger communities and smaller pipeline networks would have been built to meet rural and on-farm needs (M.M. Dillon Ltd., 1992). Chapter eight considers further the economic and social impacts of this case.

Reaction to the Original Proposal

Upon receipt of the proposal, Manitoba Environment filed a public notice of the proposal, filed the proposal in various public registries and provided an opportunity for public comment. Advertisements were placed in newspapers in Winnipeg, Brandon, Portage la Prairie, Treherne, Morris, Morden, Altona, Manitou, Carman, La Liberte and St. Claude (McNaughton and Webb, 1993).

There was significant public reaction to the proposal. Over 400 letters were received by the Minister of the Environment, Manitoba Environment, the Clean Environment Commission (CEC) and the Premier's office. The letters were from private citizens, municipalities and non-government organizations. Some were in favour of the proposal while others raised concerns and objections. Major objections were raised about potential adverse impacts on water rights exercised downstream from the proposed diversions. Objections were also raised about the accuracy of some aspects of the proposal, the scope of the environmental concerns covered in the proposal, and the lack of attention paid to water conservation (McNaughton, 1993).

There was also a substantial response to the proposal from agencies on Manitoba Environment's Technical Advisory Committee. Concerns were raised about a vast array of issues including population projections, water use trends, climate change, risk of damage to the pipeline network, sustainable development, wildlife and plant habitat, fish habitat, increased irrigation, pollution from farm chemicals, water conservation, recreation issues, mitigation, road crossings, heritage resources, the hydrological models employed and storage of diesel fuel supplies at the diversion sites (McNaughton and Webb, 1993).

The Environmental Impact Statement (EIS)

At this stage of the process, the Minister of the Environment, upon the recommendation of Manitoba Environment, required the proponent to provide additional information and to prepare an environmental impact statement. To assist in this regard Manitoba Environment issued guidelines for the preparation of the environmental impact statement. The guidelines were developed in consultation with the Technical Advisory Committee and after consulting with the public at three scoping workshops held in Russell, Portage la Prairie and Winkler in May 1992 (McNaughton, 1993).

The environmental impact statement was submitted on December 15, 1992. Manitoba Environment placed the document in the public registries and advertised its availability through local media outlets. The environmental impact statement divided potential impacts into three main categories: the impacts of engineered facilities; the impacts of water resource management operations; and, socioeconomic impacts. It identified the potential for some adverse residual impacts, made a number of recommendations regarding research and monitoring, and concluded that the project was acceptable, with insignificant long-term adverse impacts (M.M. Dillon Ltd. 1992).

The Modified Proposal

On February 4, 1993, before the period for public review of

the environmental impact statement had expired, the proponent modified its original proposal by submitting an addendum to the EIS (McNaughton and Webb, 1993).

Under the modified proposal, the Assiniboine-Boyne diversion and the Stephenfield treatment plant were abandoned. In their stead it was proposed to expand the City of Portage la Prairie's existing withdrawal and treatment facilities. A water supply pipeline network was still proposed but under the modified proposal the potential service area was expanded to include the Rural Municipalities of Portage la Prairie, Grey, Cartier and St. François Xavier (M.M. Dillon Ltd., 1993).

Reaction to the EIS and Addendum

Even with the modified proposal, significant public concern remained. Most of the comments received by Manitoba Environment in response to the EIS and addendum were critical. The technical advisory committee was less critical but also identified a number of inadequacies in the EIS documents. At this point Manitoba Environment requested supplemental information from the proponent to clarify technical details, provide further information and address items in the EIS guidelines that were not addressed in the EIS (McNaughton and Webb, 1993).

Public Hearings

The Commission held some 40 hours of public hearings in the Pembina Valley Water Supply System case in the spring of 1993. Hearings were held in Portage la Prairie, Russell and Altona. On June 29, 1993 the Commission adjourned the hearings and requested the provision of additional information from the Manitoba Department of Natural Resources, the provincial Sustainable Development Coordination Unit and the proponent (Manitoba Clean Environment Commission, 1994).

Following the adjournment of the hearings, the proponent amended its proposal yet again. This amendment deleted the portion of the project related to diversion of water from the Assiniboine River. The project now focused solely on withdrawals from the Red River and the Stephenfield Reservoir (Manitoba Clean Environment Commission, 1994).

In March 1994 the Commission reconvened the hearings, this time in Winnipeg and Carman. On the instruction of the Minister of the Environment, the reconvened hearings focused on the proponent's amended, modified proposal. Through both rounds of hearings the Commission heard presentations and received written submissions from the major participants namely, the proponent, the provincial EA authority and interested government agencies providing technical assistance, i.e., Manitoba Natural Resources and the Sustainable Development Coordination Unit. It also received 41 submissions from diverse individuals and organizations including, cities, towns, rural municipalities, environmentalists, social activists, chambers of commerce, small farmers and large farming corporations (Manitoba Clean Environment Commission, 1994). In the end, the Commission recommended that a conditional licence be granted for the amended, modified proposal.

The Federal Process

In a typical review under EARP (when it was still in force), the first step was a preliminary assessment by the "lead" federal initiating department. In the Pembina Valley Water Supply System case there were a number of initiating federal departments but the lead department was the Prairie Farm Rehabilitation Administration (PFRA). The final decision on the preliminary assessment was never actually registered with FEARO since PFRA was never formally approached for funding assistance.

Education Techniques Used in the Case

Table 3.2 presents a listing of the education techniques used in the Pembina Valley Water Supply System case. It compiles the techniques that were revealed by the case file review, the interviews and the questionnaire survey and classifies them according to format. It also identifies the agencies that sponsored the education activities and the roles the agencies played in the case (i.e., proponent, EA authority, adjudicator, intervener, etc.).

Table 3.2
Education Techniques Used During the Environmental Assessment
of the Pembina Valley Water Supply System

Proponent - Pembina Valley Water Co-op (Pembina Valley Water Task Force)

√ *audio/visual/electronic:*	slide presentations
√ *traditional publishing:*	brochures, newspaper inserts, reports, newsletters, information kits
√ *direct/individualized:*	direct mail, phone line, technical assistance
√ *media:*	advertising, news releases, news conferences, talk radio, call-in television, interviews, public service announcements
√ *presentations/events:*	panels, open houses, exhibits, meetings, town hall meetings
√ *formal education:*	integration into existing curricula

Provincial EA Authority - Manitoba Environment

√ *audio/visual/electronic:*	slide presentations
√ *traditional publishing:*	notices, reports, information kits, translation, central depositories
√ *direct/individualized:*	direct mail
√ *media:*	advertising
√ *presentations/events:*	workshops, open houses, meetings, town hall meetings

Interveners - Manitobans Against the Assiniboine Diversion, City of Winnipeg, Central Plains Inc., Assiniboine River Campaign, Coalition to Save the Assiniboine River

√ *audio/visual/electronic:*	slide presentations
√ *traditional publishing:*	brochures, notices, feature articles, position papers, reports, newsletters, information kits, posters
√ *direct/individualized:*	direct mail
√ *media:*	advertising, news releases, news conferences, talk radio, interviews
√ *presentations/events:*	workshops, open houses, meetings, town hall meetings, exhibits

Adjudicator - Manitoba Clean Environment Commission

√ *traditional publishing:*	notices, final report, final decisions, transcripts, central depositories
√ *direct/individualized:*	direct mail
√ *media:*	coverage of hearings

Lead Federal Initiating Department - Prairie Farm Rehabilitation Administration

√ *direct/individualized:*	technical assistance
√ *presentations/events:*	workshops, open houses, meetings, town hall meetings, exhibits

Techniques Identified by Participants During the Questionnaire Survey (Sponsoring Agency Not Identified)

√ *audio/visual/electronic:*	films
√ *traditional publishing:*	booklets, manuals
√ *presentations/events:*	simulations, conferences, dialogues

While a variety of techniques was used in the Pembina Valley case, few were well suited to critical EA education. In fact, only three such techniques were identified: simulations, dialogues and workshops. The majority of the techniques used was either poorly suited to critical EA education or was neutral. There was heavy emphasis on traditional publishing and provision of notice (e.g., direct mail and advertising). Among the neutral techniques used, emphasis was on open houses, town hall meetings, exhibits/displays and meetings. Media techniques involving some degree of teacher-learner interaction, such as talk-radio and call in television, were also used.

The party that attempted the most public education during the assessment was the proponent, the Pembina Valley Water Cooperative. It is interesting to note that all of the techniques used by the Co-op fall into the poorly suited or neutral categories. This is not surprising given that the Co-op would have had little interest in engaging in critical education leading to conscientization. Its main interest would have been in conducting forms of public relations to promote or "sell" its project to its constituents and to political power brokers.

The techniques used by the provincial agents, i.e., Manitoba Environment and the CEC, tend towards the poorly suited or neutral variety, although Manitoba Environment did use the workshop format early in the EA process when it developed the EIS guidelines. For the most part, provincial authorities focused on traditional publishing and information dissemination for the purpose of providing notice.

The techniques used by interveners also tend towards the neutral and poorly suited variety (e.g., traditional publishing, notice provision, slide presentations, videotape, meetings and town hall meetings). However, what few well suited techniques were used in this case, were used by interveners. The data indicate that intervener groups not only used the workshop format, they also used simulations and dialogues. It is true that simulations and dialogues were identified during the questionnaire survey and therefore, the sponsoring agency was not identified. However, it is safe to assume that these techniques were used by interveners since these techniques were not referenced in the official case files, nor in the interviews with the proponent and the EA authority.

Appraising Participant Knowledge

The questionnaire survey explored various aspects of participant knowledge about environmental assessment and the Pembina Valley Water Supply System case.

Readership Rates of "Dominant Documents"

Three questions were about whether respondents had read the documents offering the dominant discourses (the draft EIS guidelines, the EIS and the CEC decision and report). The results of the survey are that:

- eight respondents (24%) read each of the documents;
- 14 of the respondents (41%) did not read any of the reports;
- 19 respondents, or 56% of the sample, read the EIS;
- 12 individuals, or 35%, read the draft EIS guidelines; and,
- 11 respondents, or 32%, read the CEC decision and report.

Knowledge of Process-Related Information

Nine questions provided a measure of knowledge of process-related matters (e.g., jurisdiction, the players in the process, the outcome of the case). On average, the respondents answered less than 40% of these questions correctly. An examination of numerical measures of central tendency of the percentage correct reveals a mean ($\bar{x}$) = 37 and a median = 39.

It is interesting to compare the means of the percentage correct for sample subsets consisting of data from respondents who read each of the dominant documents ($\bar{x}$ = 61) versus data from respondents who read none of the documents ($\bar{x}$ = 17). The differences are striking and suggest a correlation between readership of dominant documents and knowledge of process-related information. In fact, using the Spearman rank correlation coefficient reveals an (r_s) value of .777, indicating a strong correlation between these two variables.

Critical Consciousness

Four survey questions provided a measure of critical consciousness. Four indicators of critical consciousness were used to score each respondent on a five-tier ordinal scale (zero to four):

- Did the respondent challenge the official position on the purpose of the project asserted by the proponent and the provincial government? Alternatively, did the respondent demonstrate an understanding of interdependency in resource systems and resource communities?
- Did the respondent express an informed, critical opinion on the efficiency, efficacy or fairness of the EA process?
- Did the respondent emphasize the value of working with other concerned citizens during the EA process?
- Did the respondent agree that education conducted during the Pembina Valley EA could have been improved?

The survey results for the second indicator were particularly interesting, and provide a glimpse of respondent opin-

Table 3.3
Critical Respondent Comments Regarding the Efficiency, Efficacy
or Fairness of the EA Process

Definite feeling that the process was not the objective. Because of political considerations the environmental impacts in the Portage area were minimized. The proponent was not objective and was self-serving. There appears to have been a hidden agenda on the part of the provincial government. PFRA also seemed to be a proponent. The CEC is just another provincial government department.

The EA should have been done by an independent source. Not by the government or influenced by the parties involved.

In the PVWC case - the CEC was not an impartial body and independent (government appointed people).

Too much was political rather than common sense concern.

It's just a lot of paper work and expense to look good. In the end the government does whatever it wants anyway.

I got the impression they were going ahead with their plans without any advice from anyone else, good or bad.

Ideally, the CEC should be an impartial body - but in reality the chairperson (and the others) I believe were political appointees and as a result made the recommendations desired by the body appointing them (the Minister of Environment or the government?).

It should have been explained clearly that the Manitoba government supported the project, and was not objective.

I know that the CEC does not always hold fair hearings.

We have learned that the whole process is a "farce" - if the government wants the proposal to go ahead, there is no thought of sustainability.

When the government is the proponent (along with PVWC) and uses a large amount of taxpayers' money assisting with the project - the whole process is a "farce".

It is all a case of politics. Tell you whatever the government wants to hear. In the case of the Pembina Valley Water Supply System, the EA process was a complete farce.

ion of the efficacy of the EA process in Manitoba, as shown in Table 3.3.

The respondents were then ranked and the Spearman rank measure of association was used to determine correlations between critical consciousness and two other variables namely, readership of "dominant documents" and knowledge of process-related information. Since a large proportion of ties were present, Siegel's (1956) corrected formula for r_s was used.

A Spearman rank correlation coefficient (r_s) of .404 was determined for the association between critical consciousness and knowledge of process-related information. This indicates a weak association between these variables. A Spearman rank correlation coefficient (r_s) of .527 was found for the variables critical consciousness and readership of "dominant documents". This indicates a moderately strong association between these two variables.

Levels of Participation

Two of the survey questions dealt with participation in the public hearings and were meant to identify whether the respondent participated and, if so, in what manner.

For the purpose of analysis, the modes of participation were ranked on a three-tier ordinal scale based on the level of participation and complexity of each mode. SUBMISSION OF A LETTER and ATTENDANCE were placed in the lowest rank. SIGNING A PETITION, which was identified in a response to the open-ended part of question 3b, was also placed in the lowest rank. ORAL PRESENTATION and SUBMISSION OF A WRITTEN BRIEF were placed in the middle rank. FORMAL INTERVENTION was in the highest rank. Using scores on the ordinal scale, the respondents were then ranked and the Spearman rank correlation coefficient was used to determine correlations between level of participation and other variables such as critical consciousness and knowledge of process-related information. However, before examining the Spearman rank correlation coefficients, contingency coefficient (C) analysis was done.

A 2 x 8 contingency table was built on two variables, namely, knowledge of process-related information and whether the respondent participated in the public hearings. Knowledge was measured by the number of process-related questions answered correctly. There were nine such questions but the most anyone answered correctly was seven. Based on the table, χ_2 was calculated as 14.23 and $C = .543$, revealing a moderately strong association between the variables.

Given the strong association, the correlation between participation and critical consciousness was examined. A 2 x 5 contingency table was constructed, χ_2 was calculated as 6.24 and C was determined as .394, which indicates a weak association.

With the discovery of positive correlations between participation, knowledge and critical consciousness using the contingency coefficient, the Spearman rank correlation coefficient was used to determine two correlations: one between level of participation and critical consciousness and the other between level of participation and knowledge of process-related information.

Based on the data for level of participation and critical consciousness the r_s was computed as being .157, revealing a weak correlation between the two variables. Based on the ranks on knowledge of process-related information and level of participation, the r_s value was determined as being .568, revealing a moderately strong correlation.

Views on EA Education

One of the survey questions asked whether there were any education techniques used in the case that were particularly effective. Seven respondents (21% of the sample) answered YES. Five of the seven identified the particular event or activity. Two of the comments referred to the public hearing process. Although the public hearing process is not an educational technique within the analytic framework used earlier in this chapter, the hearing process is a key element in the notion of education through EA. The fact that respondents identified participation in public hearings as an event that particularly affected their understanding reinforces the whole participatory approach underlying critical EA education.

Another comment refers to published studies and reports. This suggests that information dissemination, particularly publication of technical studies or reports, has a valid role to play in EA education. This is consistent with the point made earlier that information dissemination is important but becomes even more so when it is supplemented with a coordinated critical education program.

Another dimension of respondent views explored in the survey concerns public demand or need for EA education. Asked whether EA education is necessary for the public's involvement in environmental assessment to be effective, a strong majority of respondents (24 or 71%) answered YES while only 3 respondents or 9% answered NO. This empirical evidence supports the literature reviewed earlier which asserts that public demand for environmental education exists and is a component of the rationale for critical EA education.

Comments to this question such as: "Person needs to be educated on the matter before [he/she] can make sound decisions"; "Create awareness of process and implications for future"; and, "Lack of knowledge about the process discourages participation", also express a clearly perceived need for EA.

Conclusions

The literature indicates that education is a crucial aspect of the public involvement process. The notion explored in this research is that education is a necessity; a precondition to advanced levels of public involvement. The type of education introduced in this research is critical EA education, the foundation of which is critical pedagogy. It was argued that critical EA education is consistent with fundamental democratic principles and, by facilitating the development of counter-hegemonic discourse, has potentially far-reaching benefits for the advancement of sustainability.

Critical EA education encompasses both "education about EA" and "education through EA" and should result in citizen empowerment and social action. In this way, the notion of critical EA education is congruent with environmental adult transformation, environmental adult learning and social learning theory.

Nonparametric statistical analysis of variables at work in the Pembina Valley case provides empirical evidence for the concepts of critical EA education. Data reveal a strong correlation between readership of dominant documents and knowledge of process-related information (r_s = .777). There were also moderately strong correlations between knowledge of process-related information and whether the respondent participated in the public hearings (C = .543) and between knowledge and level of participation (r_s = .568).

Weak correlations were found between whether the respondent participated in the public hearings and critical consciousness (C = .394), and between level of participation and critical consciousness (r_s = .157). Critical consciousness was then related back to readership of dominant documents (r_s = .527) and knowledge of process-related information (r_s = .404).

The research illuminated that the majority of education techniques applied in the case was not well suited to critical EA education. In spite of this, there was support for the theoretical assertions underlying critical EA education, as evidenced by process-related knowledge among case participants, higher levels of public participation, and a degree of critical consciousness. These findings do not stand counter to the notion of, and need for, "critical EA education" since the case study was not a test of well-suited critical EA techniques. What remains, then, is to determine the effect on these key variables of a well-designed curriculum of EA education.

Critical EA education also requires further conceptual development to more fully integrate it with environmental adult transformation and social learning theory. As well, although some of the elements of "education about EA" are evident, research is required to more fully define both substantive and procedural elements. And while the general notion of "education through EA" is presented, additional research is required to fully explore the dynamics of the concept. The identification of indicators of critical consciousness also requires clarification, given that only a weak correlation is evident between level of participation and critical consciousness (r_s =.157).

Further research into the area of critical EA education may be difficult, however, since most cases utilize few well suited techniques, as was the situation in the Pembina Valley case. Moreover, in recent years governments have tended to emphasize information dissemination and communication practices among stakeholders, rather than encouraging critical debate about a proposed project or about larger environmental management issues. Recently, governments have also expressed a strong interest in streamlining EA process, often through limiting public involvement. These reasons may make it difficult to test what may seem to be a more complex public involvement process.

Despite this, the research results show good reason to further test the application of critical education in environmental assessment as part of the continuing effort to make the EA process more efficient, effective and fair. Critical EA education may also prove to be valuable in the advancement of sustainability, particularly if EA becomes more fully integrated in broader land-use planning approaches, as is being called for in many quarters. Finally, in an interesting twist of irony, policy makers may find the efficiency advantages they seek for EA by promoting informed and critical evaluation of pro-development discourse.

End Notes
[1]The chapter is based on an article that has appeared in *The Canadian Geographer* (1997).

References

Alderson, G. (1992) "Focus on current purposes of public legal education and information in Canada," in *National Public Legal Education and Information (PLEI) Policy Consultation Package*, Ottawa, ON: The National PLEI Policy Working Group, 42 pp.

Alexander, D. (1994) *Planning as Learning: The Education of Citizen Activists*, PhD Thesis, Waterloo, ON: University of Waterloo, School of Urban and Regional Planning.

Aronowitz, S. (1993) "Paulo Freire's radical democratic humanism," in McLaren, P. and Leonard, P. (eds.), *Paulo Freire, A Critical Encounter*, New York, NY: Routledge, 8-24.

Apps, J.W. (1991) *Mastering the Teaching of Adults*, Malabar, FL: Krieger.

Axelrod, R. and Hamilton, W.D. (1981) "The evolution of cooperation," *Science* 2(11): 1390-1396.

Berkes, F. (1989) *Common Property Resources: Ecology and Community-Based Sustainable Development*, London, UK: Belhaven.

_____ (1993) "Application of ecological economics to development: the institutional dimension," in *Ecological Economics: Proceedings of a Workshop*, Ottawa, ON: IREE/CIDA, 61-75.

Bush, M.A. (1990) *Public Participation in Resource Development After Project Approval*, Ottawa, ON: Canadian Environmental Assessment Research Council.

Costanza, R. (1987) "Social traps and environmental policy," *Bioscience*, 37: 407-412.

Cranton, P. (1994) *Understanding and Promoting Transformative Learning: A Guide for Educators of Adults*, San Francisco, CA: Jossey-Bass Publishers.

Diduck, A. (1995) *Critical Education for Environmental Assessment*, Masters Thesis, Winnipeg, MN: Natural Resources Institute, University of Manitoba.

Finger, M. (1989) "Environmental adult education from the perspective of the adult learner," *Convergence: An International Journal of Adult Education*, 22(4): 25-32.

Fortner, R.W. and Lyon, A.E. (1985) "Effects of a Cousteau television special on viewer knowledge and attitudes," *Journal of Environmental Education*, 16(3): 12-20.

Freire, P. (1970) *Pedagogy of the Oppressed*, New York, NY: Seabury Press.

_____ (1985) *The Politics of Education*, South Hadley, MA: Bergin and Garvey.

_____ (1993) "Forward," in McLaren, P. and Leonard, P. (eds.), *Paulo Freire: A Critical Encounter*, New York, NY: Routledge, ix-xii.

Gadgil, M., Berkes, F. and Folke, C. (1993) "Indigenous knowledge for biodiversity conservation," *Ambio*, 22(2-3): 151-156.

Gibson, A. (1994) "Freirean versus enterprise education: the difference is in the business," *Convergence: An International Journal of Adult Education*, 28: 46-56.

Goodland, R., Ledec, G. and Webb, M. (1989) "Meeting environmental concerns caused by common-property mismanagement in economic development projects," in Berkes, F. (ed.), *Common Property Resources: Ecology and Community-Based Sustainable Development*, London, UK: Belhaven, 148-164.

Grima, A.P. (1985) "Participatory rites: integrating public involvement in environmental impact assessment," in Whitney, J.B.R. and Maclaren, V.W. (eds.), *Environmental Impact Assessment: The Canadian Experience*, Toronto, ON: University of Toronto, 33-52.

Grima, A.P. and Berkes, F. (1989) "Natural resources: access, right-to-use and management," in Berkes, F. (ed.), *Common Property Resources: Ecology and Community-Based Sustainable Development*, London, UK: Belhaven, 33-54.

Holling, C.S. and Bocking, S. (1990) "Surprise and opportunity: in evolution, in ecosystems, in society," in Mungall, C. and McLaren, D.J. (ed.), *Planet Under Stress: The Challenge of Global Change*, Toronto, ON: Oxford University Press, 285-300.

hooks, b. (1993) "bell hooks speaking about Paulo Freire - the man, his work," in McLaren, P. and Leonard, P. (eds.), *Paulo Freire: A Critical Encounter*, New York, NY: Routledge, 146-154.

Ibikunle-Johnson, V. (1989) "Managing the community's environment: grassroots participation in environmental education," *Convergence: An International Journal of Adult Education*, 22(4): 13-23.

Imel, S. (1993) *Guidelines for Working with Adult Learners*, ERIC Digest No. 154, in URL: gopher: //ericir.syr.edu/100/clearinghouse/16houses/CACVE /CEDigests/Digest154, Columbus, OH: ERIC Clearinghouse on Adult, Career, and Vocational Education.

Kirkwood, G. and Kirkwood, C. (1989) *Living Adult Education: Freire in Scotland*, Milton Keynes: Open University Press.

Kockelmans, J.J. (1979) "Why interdisciplinarity?" in Kockelmans, J.J. (ed.), *Interdisciplinarity and Higher Education*, London, UK: The Pennsylvania State University Press, 123-160.

Knowles, M.S. (1980) *The Modern Practice of Adult Education*, Chicago, IL: Association Press / Follett.

_____ (1984) "Introduction: the art and science of helping adults learn," in Knowles, M.S. (ed.), *Andragogy in Action: Applying Modern Principles of Adult Learning*, San Francisco, CA: Jossey-Bass, 1-22.

Lankshear, C. (1993) "Functional literacy from a Freirean point of view," in McLaren, P. and Leonard, P. (eds.), *Paulo Freire: A Critical Encounter*, New York, NY: Routledge, 90-118.

Manitoba Clean Environment Commission (1994) *Report on Public Hearings, Pembina Valley Water Cooperative Inc.*, Pembina Valley Regional Water Supply Proposal, Steinbach, MN: Manitoba Clean Environment Commission.

McLaren, P. and Leonard, P. (eds.) (1993a) *Paulo Freire: A Critical Encounter*, New York, NY: Routledge.

Mcleod, J. (1987) "Communication and energy conservation," *Journal of Environmental Education*, 18(3): 29-37.

McNaughton, D. (1993) *Clean Environment Commission Hearing Exhibit 2*, Pembina Valley Regional Water Supply, Opening Submission, Winnipeg, MN: Manitoba Environment.

McNaughton, D. and Webb, B. (1993) *Clean Environment Commission Hearing Exhibit 16*, Pembina Valley Regional Water Supply, Proposal Summary, Winnipeg, MN: Manitoba Environment.

Meredith, T. (1992) "Environmental impact assessment, cultural diversity, and sustainable rural development," *Environmental Impact Assessment Review*, 12: 125-138.

Mezirow, J. (ed.) (1990) *Fostering Critical Reflection in Adulthood: A Guide to Transformative and Emancipatory Learning*, San Francisco, CA: Jossey-Bass Publishers.

_____ (1991) *Transformative Dimensions of Adult Learning*, San Francisco, CA: Jossey-Bass Publishers.

M.M. Dillon Ltd. (1992) *Pembina Valley Water Cooperative Inc., Environmental Impact Statement for the Pembina Valley Regional Potable Water Supply Proposal*, Altona, MN: Pembina Valley Water Cooperative Inc.

_____ (1993) *Pembina Valley Water Cooperative Inc., Environmental Impact Statement for the Pembina Valley Regional Potable Water Supply Proposal, Addendum*, Altona, MN: Pembina Valley Water Cooperative Inc.

Peck, J.R. and Feldman, M.W. (1986) "The evolution of helping behaviour in large randomally mixed populations," *American Naturalist*, 127: 209-221.

Pembina Valley Water Cooperative Inc. (1991) *Pembina Valley Water Supply Proposal, Environmental Impact Statement*, Altona, MN: Pembina Valley Water Cooperative Inc.

Pratt, D.D. (1988) "Andragogy as a relational construct," *Adult Education Quarterly*, 38(3): 160-172.

Praxis (1988) *Public Involvement: Planning and Implementing Public Involvement Programs*, Calgary, AB: Praxis.

Regnier, R. and Penna, P. (1996) "The limits of empowerment in anti-nuclear advocacy: a case study of adult education for technological literacy," *The Canadian Journal of Adult Education*, 10(2): 35-57.

Richardson, M., Sherman, J. and Gismondi, M. (1993) *Winning Back the Words, Confronting Experts in an Environmental Public Hearing*, Toronto, ON: Garamond Press.

Schibuola, S. and Byer, P.H. (1991) "Use of knowledge-based systems for the review of environmental impact assessments," *Environmental Impact Assessment Review*, 11:

11-27.

Shor, I. (1993) "Education is politics: Paulo Freire's critical pedagogy," in McLaren, P. and Leonard, P. (eds.), *Paulo Freire: A Critical Encounter*, New York, NY: Routledge, 25-35.

Siegel, S. (1956) *Nonparametric Statistics For the Behavioral Sciences*, New York, NY: McGraw-Hill.

Sinclair, A.J. and Diduck, A. (1995) "Public education: an undervalued component of the environmental assessment public involvement process," *Environmental Impact Assessment Review*, 15: 219-240.

Smith, G. (1993) *Impact Assessment and Sustainable Resource Management*, New York, NY: John Wiley and Son.

Storey, K., Durst, D., Ross, K., Shrimpton, M. (1991) *ISER Offshore Oil Project: Monitoring for Management*, Institute of Social and Economic Research, St. John's, NF: Memorial University of Newfoundland.

Sullivan, W.C., Kuo, F.E. and Prabhu, M. (1996) "Assessing the impact of environmental impact statements on citizens," *Environmental Impact Assessment Review*, 16: 171-182.

Thompson, E. (1989) *Committee Report*, An unpublished paper presented to The Manitoba Law Foundation by the Ad Hoc Committee on Public Legal Education, Winnipeg, Manitoba.

Usang, E.N. (1992) "Strategies for green literacy," *Convergence: An International Journal of Adult Education*, 25(2): 46-53.

Webler, T., Kastenholz, H. and Renn, O. (1995) "Public participation in impact assessment: a social learning perspective," *Environmental Impact Assessment Review*, 15: 443-463.

West, C. (1993) "Preface," in McLaren, P. and Leonard, P. (eds.), *Paulo Freire: A Critical Encounter*, New York, NY: Routledge, xii-xiv.

Chapter 4

Information Limitations in Participatory Impact Assessment

Thomas C. Meredith
McGill University

In sustainable development, everyone is a user and provider of information considered in the broad sense. That includes data, information, appropriately packaged experience and knowledge. The need for information arises at all levels, from that of senior decision makers at the national and international levels to the grass-roots and individual levels. The following two program areas need to be implemented to ensure that decisions are based increasingly on sound information:
(a) Bridging the data gap;
(b) Improving information availability (Agenda 21, 40, UNCED, 1992).

The principle — if not the phrase — of "sustainable development" is widely accepted as the appropriate response to what may be the definitive crisis of our period of history, that is, reconciling humanity's increasing power to change the biophysical environment with its increasing vulnerability to the consequences of that change. The crisis is as complex as it is urgent. Jacobs and Sadler (1990: 171) have argued that environmental impact assessment "is a *necessary* but not sufficient process for achieving sustainable development" (emphasis added). Public involvement is a prerequisite for effective impact assessment (for example, see Iacofano, 1990; Renn et al., 1995) but this begs the question of the nature and quality of information that "the public" incorporates in its participation. Holling's

(1978: 131) seminal work noted that "communication is the bridge between environmental analysis and decision making". "Informing the public" in impact assessment is often thought of as an essentially top down process (e.g., Jain et al., 1993), but as is noted in Agenda 21 (quoted above), this notion of information flow is questionable, particularly in the context of adaptive, participatory and/or anticipatory (as opposed to reactive) impact assessment (Meredith, 1992 and 1995).

Maser (1996: 106) discusses the process of learning as a step in resolving environmental conflict. There are many factors that contribute to the empowerment of a "public" through learning. But even given both a willingness and an ability to learn, gaining access to information — including information beyond what project proponents or regulators choose to provide — can be a critical limitation to full and fair participation in environmental decision making and impact assessment. This chapter explores barriers that obstruct access to information. Seven categories that have been encountered in the author's experience are discussed.

The importance and impact of information flow on change and development are well recognized if not fully understood (Menou, 1993). The underlying assumption of this chapter is that a more acute awareness of societal inter-linkages with environmental systems is a prerequisite for defining and conducting effective impact assessment. The chapter therefore begins with a discussion of the growth in self-awareness of humans as agents of environmental change. It then looks at the processes by which individuals are motivated to arrest or reverse processes that are environmentally damaging, non-sustainable, and/or ultimately self-destructive. This process defines the "demand" for data and information against which limits to "supply" can be assessed. The chapter argues that, despite the accepted desirability of a "general" solution to the environmental crisis, in the foreseeable future decisive action will be needed at the community level to protect local environments. Impact assessment has a vital role to play in community-level reconciliation of anthropogenic stress and ecosystem capability, but central to its effectiveness is accurate information about the causes, character and probable consequences of environmental change.

Anthropogenic Environmental Change and Community-Level Responses

There is a strong tradition within geography, anthropology and sociology of the study of human-environment relationships (Butzer, 1990). Central to this study has been the question of the unity or duality of human-nature systems (Kates et al., 1990). Cultural ecology and various other ecosystem approaches in social science identify the interactive nature of this relationship (Rappaport, 1990) and there is an emerging sense that human activity can only be meaningfully assessed as part of an ecosystem. Bennett (1990) suggests the name "socio-natural system" for this but the term "socioecosystem" has been used elsewhere (Meredith, 1991a, 1995) and is used here.

There is also a strong tradition — going back at least to 1864 when Marsh published *The Earth as Modified by Human Action* — of attempting to define the nature of the human impact on the environment (Simmons, 1989). What has changed in recent decades is awareness of the magnitude of the human impact, the threat it poses for human well-being and environmental integrity, and the need for action. The background and evolution of this change are treated in Turner et al. (1990a). The scale and rate of acceleration of the human impact are described. They note that global scale change can result from systemic changes (like greenhouse gas accumulations) or from the aggregate of local actions (deforestation). The "proximate" causes of change (forest clearance) need to be distinguished from "ultimate" causes (market demand for wood, population demand for land) (Turner et al., 1990b). The technological, economic and demographic pressures that are the "ultimate" causes of environmental change will continue to mount (WCED, 1987). Canadian policy dimensions are treated in Boardman (1992), Mitchell (1991) and Fleming (1997).

Ironically, despite the obvious importance of human agency in environmental change, it was possible to write in 1992:

> . . . any effort to understand global environmental change that does not include . . . the human dimension cannot succeed. Awareness of that simple truth is now spreading throughout the scientific community.
> Stern et al., 1992:v

This truth will affect the way impact assessment is conducted: understanding the role of human actors as both stakeholders and ecological entities is critical, as is understanding questions of scale in assessing the role of human action.

The Scale of Human Involvement: Community-Level Adaptation to Environmental Change

> . . . our understandable wish to preserve the planet must somehow be reduced to our scale of competence - that is, to the wish to preserve all of its humble households and neighbourhoods.
> Wendell Berry, quoted in Boychuck, 1991:24

Global sustainability is an abstract concept. It is, ultimately, the aggregate of individual human experiences in local environments. Environmental crises — whether resulting from local or remote causes — are experienced at specific sites, by specific groups, at specific times. Underlying the logic of the phrase "think globally, act locally" is the knowledge of the importance of individual concern and domestic environmental stewardship. Even in the face of global change, sustainability will be won or lost differentially, site by site. Local crises arise in proportion not only to the degree of absolute stress experienced, but also to the degree to which ameliorative or compensatory action can be taken.

Impact assessment is a formal process for exploring the implications of proposed actions. It works reasonably well in the constrained circumstances in which it is conventionally applied — a named proponent, a specific project and site, and a legally defined scope and format. However, a more general, inclusive and iterative form of impact assessment would meet the objectives of adaptive environmental management (Holling, 1978) and a community-based, proactive, engagement of impact assessment procedures could both increase the effectiveness of impact assessment and make a major contribution to ecosystem sustainability (Meredith, 1992). This requires three conditions: a *willingness* to use impact assessment more generally (rather than simply where it is legally mandated); an *ability* to define the root causes of locally significant environmental change; and a degree of *belief* that local action can influence the root causes or compensate for their effects.

People are more likely to be motivated by factors that affect immediate, perceived human well-being (Maslow, 1954) than factors which affect long-term ecosystem viability (Figure 4.1) (Meredith et al., 1994). The ability of human systems to compensate for local environmental stress can arise from the ability to import carrying capacity (food, energy, natural resource) and export or defer negative impacts (shipping hazardous wastes to other places, leaving environmental costs of nuclear storage to another generation)(Wackernagel and Rees, 1996). These factors mute local awareness of environmental impacts. Sustainability

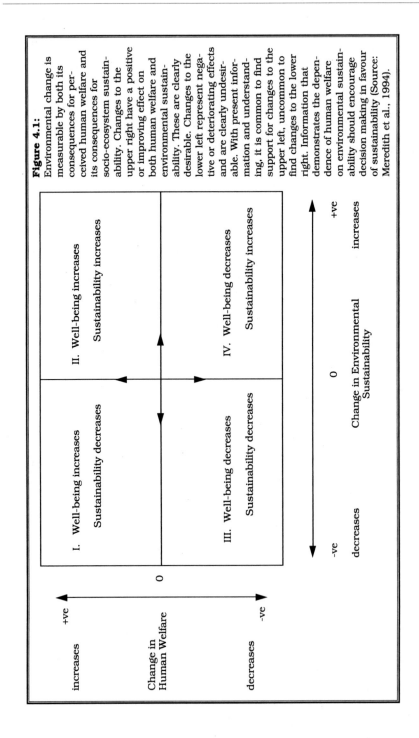

Figure 4.1:
Environmental change is measurable by both its consequences for perceived human welfare and its consequences for socio-ecosystem sustainability. Changes to the upper right have a positive or improving effect on both human welfare and environmental sustainability. These are clearly desirable. Changes to the lower left represent negative or deteriorating effects and are clearly undesirable. With present information and understanding, it is common to find support for changes to the upper left, uncommon to find changes to the lower right. Information that demonstrates the dependence of human welfare on environmental sustainability should encourage decision making in favour of sustainability (Source: Meredith et al., 1994).

requires an impact assessment procedure — formal or informal — that demonstrates human well-being and ecosystem sustainability to be coextensive and mutually supportive.

Burton et al. (1993) study human response to extreme events in nature. Because environmental change can increase the natural extremes, and thereby, increase environmental hazards, much of the theoretical work on natural hazards can be borrowed to study response to environmental change. Burton et al. produce a model which suggests how choices are made by individuals. There is much in the literature to support the selection of the individual as the fundamental unit of evaluation (Moran, 1990; Rappaport, 1990). The phases in the reaction process involve individuals becoming aware of change, interpreting that change as significant (conceptualizing a "problem" (Kasperson et al., 1991), identifying available responses and balancing the costs and benefits of those responses. The sequence is perception, interpretation, and response, and although this occurs ultimately at the level of the individual, information-gathering and action are frequently collective activities. "Local groups . . . are the conjunction between local ecological processes and regional social, economic and political processes" (Rappaport, 1990: 61) and also with distinct elements of the environment (Figure 4.2). This conceptualization demonstrates clearly why local, informed participation in environmental decision making is critical.

Environmental Information: Making the Invisible Visible

While various stakeholders have different tools and specific interests and objectives, each is engaged in understanding and responding adaptively to problems of environmental change. Nonetheless, there should ultimately be a common interest in a sustainable environment (Figure 4.3) based on a common recognition that all interests are served by avoiding environmental collapse. But this requires a common

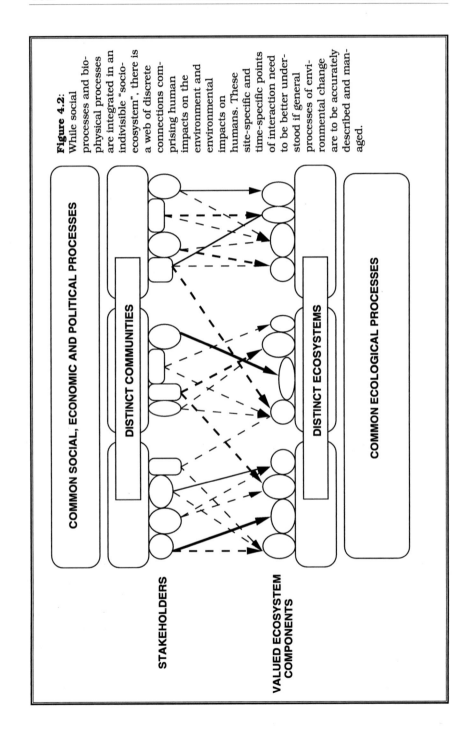

Figure 4.2:
While social processes and bio-physical processes are integrated in an indivisible "socio-ecosystem", there is a web of discrete connections comprising human impacts on the environment and environmental impacts on humans. These site-specific and time-specific points of interaction need to be better understood if general processes of environmental change are to be accurately described and managed.

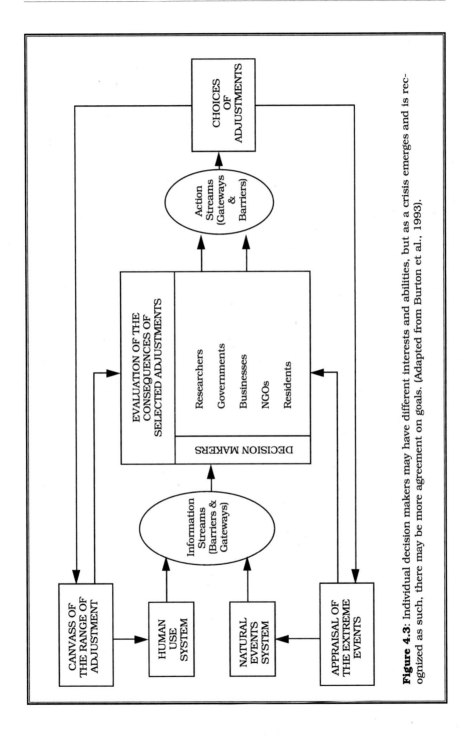

Figure 4.3: Individual decision makers may have different interests and abilities, but as a crisis emerges and is recognized as such, there may be more agreement on goals. (Adapted from Burton et al., 1993).

(and accurate) "perception" of change that is affecting the environment. The result of variations in spatial and temporal scale of potentially important environmental events (Meredith, 1991b, 1995) is that some salient information will not be evident to resource users. The incorporation by individuals of this information into their interpretation of environmental circumstance requires "making the invisible visible" (Burton, 1991). This involves basic science to collect data about change, but also systems to organize and communicate it as useful information. Much of this is not immediately accessible to individuals in communities.

Complex data can be synthesized in indicators or indices. Indicators of environmental quality are of interest to national governments and both Canada and the US have supported research on the topic (Ott, 1978; Turnstall, 1979; CEQ Annual Report, 1992; Inhaber, 1974; VHB Consulting, 1989; Indicators Task Force, 1991; OECD, 1991). Sheehy (1989) and Rapport (1990) reviewed environmental indicators. Several authors have proposed indicators of ecosystem recovery (Kelly and Harwell, 1990), risk (Bascietto et al., 1990), ecosystem health (Schaeffer, 1988, Rapport, 1989), and sustainability (Liverman et al., 1988). But the technology of raw data acquisition and management, the scientific uncertainty of models used to interpret data, and the complexity of many integrating indices, make access to salient data problematic.

Community-level impact assessment, or environmental decision making involves accessing data and information, interpreting it and communicating it. Communities experiencing significant, undesirable, biophysical change offer a microcosm in which to study human response to environmental change. The emergence of crises and the human responses to them are iterative, that is, the transition toward crisis can be accelerated, slowed or reversed on the basis of the human reaction. Reactions can be cultural (values, ethics and awareness), socio-political (control, access), institutional (relation of stakeholders), economic (resource values and market pressures, tax, trade and subsidy issues), technological (harvesting or conservation efficiencies), or biophysical (natural properties of soil, water, biota), but they must be based on an accurate perception and interpretation of the evidence. The interpretation includes assessment of impacts, which must be based on accurate information about real or anticipated environmental change. Barriers to salient information make appropriate assessment impossible (Figure 4.4).

The analysis presented below addresses seven categories of barriers. It is based on projects in which local community members were motivated by concern over the negative impacts of perceived local environmental change and sought information to quantify or interpret the change. These were not, for the most part, formal impact assessment processes but rather more general attempts to assume local responsibility for protecting environmental assets in the face of on-going change. The cases are selected to most clearly illustrate the barrier and are drawn from case experience in rural Canada as well as in East Africa and Mexico.

Seven Barriers to Information Flow

Lack of awareness of information sources

The most obvious barrier to using information or data is simply lack of awareness of the existence of the information or about even the class of information. A Nova Scotia conservation group interested in demonstrating the temporal acceleration in the loss of salt marshes was unaware of archived air photos as a source of information. Once potential users are aware of the source of information there may still be barriers with respect to knowledge of indexes or catalogues of data (determining who has taken air photos and at what dates) and, of course, specific elements in a source of information may not be directly accessible through established indices. In another study of coastal land use, one of

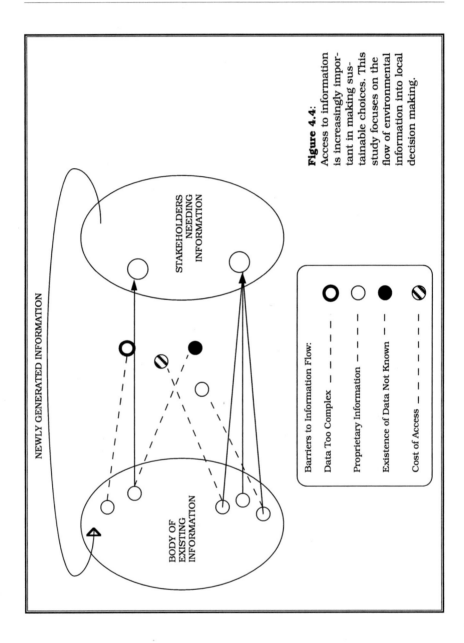

Figure 4.4:
Access to information is increasingly important in making sustainable choices. This study focuses on the flow of environmental information into local decision making.

the most useful air photo sets was an unofficial set taken privately. It was not catalogued in any way but was accessible through networked contacts. Data and information that are not catalogued can be effectively lost (Convis, 1993).

Almost by definition, crossing the "threshold of awareness" will create a demand for new information types that will be outside the prior needs of the individuals involved. There is no way of, and probably no point to, making all types of potentially relevant information sources available to all potential users. Nonetheless, the inherent characteristic of the process of crossing the "threshold of awareness" suggests that the demand for new information will be an almost universal problem, and that some mechanism should be in place to ease the transition. In other words, the means of addressing this barrier is not to make more information available but rather to make it easier to determine what information is available. This may be best achieved through a support network or an environmental information resource centre.

Legal barriers to data access

Data about Arctic oil reserves are won at great expense. It makes no sense for the same expensive data to be collected separately by different potential users (oil companies, government regulators, citizen groups). And yet in practice, especially when research results have strategic significance (corporate, community or national), there is no obvious basis for open access to information. Formal impact assessment can require full disclosure but, as noted, formal impact assessment represents only a small subset of cases (and even in these cases the virtual impossibility of duplicating studies to verify results means a vulnerability to incomplete disclosure). This is one dimension of the "data gap" cited in Agenda 21 and, functionally, it is closely linked to the issue of the cost of data access (see below). It represents a common situation in many resource sectors. For example, forestry inventories that logging companies produce may be required for economic planning but may have considerable significance in environmental conflicts. Survey data and opinion polls, likewise, create data sets that may not be openly accessible despite their potential importance.

It is unlikely that this barrier will be eliminated except, perhaps, in cases of acute conflict for which formal negotiation or even legal mediation is envisioned. It is perhaps arguable that as issues of sustainable development become clearer the mutual benefits of data sharing will become more evident and proprietary information will be less isolated. In the meantime, simple knowledge of data gaps allows the differential to be factored into planning (i.e., knowing what you do not know is better than not knowing that there is information you do not possess: there may be proxy data that will allow some approximation, public information from other comparable sites, or ways of deducing something about the detail of withheld information).

Financial barriers to data access

A community group in Québec was aware of the potential value of satellite imagery for quantifying land cover change in a forested region. Their ambition was halted when they learned of the costs of satellite data (and they noted that this seemed curious given the role of tax dollars in the data collection). Financial limits to data access are inevitable, whether the limit is encountered at a very low level where, for example, it may be impossible to hire a project worker to conduct basic background library searches, or whether it is at a high level of, for example, not being able to purchase proprietary information or to hire experts (legal, technical or scientific). The financial and legal barriers to data and information overlap considerably: if funds are unlimited most information can be accessed or duplicated despite legal barriers. An important subcategory of financially limited data is data collected by governments or with government support and then sold on some sort of cost recovery basis. Satellite imagery is the most relevant example. The actual real costs of collecting images are high because of the complex technology involved, and at present the commercial costs of images are high relative, at least, to the budget of many non-government organizations. The argument can be made that marginal costs of using satellite data are negligible once the infrastructure to collect the data is in place. Given that public funds support much of the data collection, there is some question as to how those data can best serve the public interest. It is not clear that denying access to local conservation organizations ensures their best use. However, this is not a situation that is likely to change immediately and so, in the meantime, knowledge of useful, free or low-cost, remotely-sensed data sources is valuable. AVHRR (airborne, very high resolution radar) data, despite its low resolution, provides frequent coverage and is available at no cost. Videography, that is, VHS video, is very cheap and technically within the grasp of many local groups, although there is little chance of archived material being available. This, however, may imply technical limits, which are discussed further below.

In considering financial barriers it is necessary to recognize that perfect information is rarely if ever available and that more time and money could almost always be used to enhance insight or understanding. It is cripplingly counterproductive to delay decisions or action until perfect information is attained (the excuse that US President Reagan used for inaction on cross-border acid precipitation and that tobacco companies plead against nicotine regulation). But, if imperfect information is inevitable, so too perhaps, is cost-related inequity among stakeholders in the degree of imperfection. It is necessary to be aware of such differentials but it is worth noting that cost is not the only determinant of the quality of information accessed and that community groups can often compensate for deficience in one area by using local knowledge that may come at no cost and yet be exclusive, irreplaceable and pivotal. This is considered further below.

Technical limits on data management

While assisting in developing information resources for a forest community in British Columbia, a trained technician with good experience in Geographic Information System (GIS) methods was able to access electronic spatial data from four different sources. Only one of the four proved to be in a conventional format and straightforward to load and use. The other three each came with particular problems — none of which was insurmountable but all of which required considerable time, equipment and software, and expertise, and all of which would have placed the data beyond the reach of most potential users (in one case it was simply a minor corruption of a diskette).

The "information revolution" is most often associated with the electronic "highway." The rate of change in electronic data acquisition, storage, transmission, analysis and presentation is such that only trained specialists stay at the cutting edge of progress. The resources are powerful and, clearly, of great value in environmental assessment and decision making and yet, equally clearly, it is not possible for all potential users of high-technology information to acquire and maintain the requisite technical skills to use them. This technical barrier, like the cost barrier, is inevitable. The question is not whether it exists but rather where it exists and what its implications are. GIS was very expensive and esoteric only a decade ago. Now, as more students are introduced to it in university and as it becomes cheaper, more powerful and more user-friendly, it is increasingly within the means of community groups. Depending on the issues at stake, it may be very worthwhile for community groups to make the investment in GIS competency. It is increasingly probable in multi-stakeholder environmental issues that at least some of the participants will have access to GIS and electronic data resources. It is likely that these resources will endow some information advantage whether that be in terms of scope or quality of data or in terms of the ability to synthesize information and communicate a position. Groups or individuals who are prevented by technical barriers from using electronic information processing will, all else being equal, be at a disadvantage.

Lack of paradigms for data interpretation

A spokesperson for a Montreal-based environmental group was being interviewed on a popular morning radio show in the city. He was arguing in favour of a municipal forest-protection scheme that had been proposed several years earlier but was being dropped because of the high costs of acquiring the designated sites (which were still in private hands). In pleading for protection of the forests he suggested that the forests were the last source of oxygen for the urban area. He was implying that if they were lost, the city would suffocate. This creates credibility problems that makes the otherwise sound and supportable objectives of the community group seem suspect.

Science advances by adding new data to existing conceptual models (theories or hypotheses) and then testing for consistency. It may be that any knowledge system does precisely the same. In any case, by definition, each site-specific environmental process is unique; the future, as it arrives, is not fully knowable; and the larger context of human-induced environmental change is uncharted. Science is systematically trying to collate new data into rational models and the lay public is having to establish new paradigms of understanding — in essence, a new cosmology — that incorporates the new evidence and data that become available. This is one of the major human challenges. We do not know how to reconcile the evidence of human-induced environmental change with what appear to be tenacious constraints on our economic systems. But at its simplest, there are elements of local environmental change that may appear disparate and unconnected, or connected in some incomprehensible way, but which are, in fact, consistent with existing theories or models. These models may be known by scientific specialists, by local resource users, in traditional ecological knowledge or in folk wisdom, but they may not be immediately accessible to those involved in community action.

The relationship, for example, between forest ecology and stream hydrology or watershed nutrient budgets is vital to understanding the impacts of mountain deforestation. The evidence of impacts may be visible — for example, reduced sport fish catch — but the causal links — spawning-bed siltation — may not be evident. A process needs to be established whereby existing evidence is explored for consistency with existing theories and, where possible, data need to be turned into information by linking evidence that is consistent with sound environmental models. While there are many good reasons for creating regional forest parks, prevention of literal suffocation is not one of them, and damage can be done by linking data spuriously and reducing credibility. But more than that, systematically reviewing data and models, looking for consistencies, is a way to give meaning to otherwise unconnected and therefore valueless evidence. As connections are established, a story line emerges that can direct action. Without the models, the evidence loses power.

Lack of means of managing non-conventional data and information

The outcome of negotiations is often predetermined by the definition of the context, the terms of reference and the pivotal issues. Sometimes, at least from a distance or in retrospect, the issues that become pivotal appear to be the wrong ones. For example, in hydro dam discussions, should the dominant issue be projected power demand in urban centers or concerns about traditional subsistence practices? In James Bay, Quebec, the Cree and Inuit are affected by loss and fragmentation of harvesting areas by the creation of reservoirs. In the case of the Turkwell Gorge dam project in Kenya, Turkana are affected by the diversion of water away from the lake they have depended on for fish. In both cases, the negative impacts were seen as justified by urban populations who also, in fact, define the decision-making process. The ability to set the agenda of a negotiation process may be the single most important part of the negotiation, and so naturally each stakeholder group will try to set the agenda according to what it sees as its own strongest arguments. Once a dialogue has begun, it may be difficult to change the terms of reference or to even recognize that they should be changed.

Community groups have access to many forms of data and information that are qualities of the socioecosystem itself and are therefore not available from any source other than from the community. Traditional ecological knowledge, local spirituality, aesthetic and amenity values are relevant examples. These values may be downplayed by stakeholders who have other value sets and priorities, especially if the values cannot be shown in concrete, quantified, commensurable terms. This is a question of competing strategies and, in that regard, is similar to other elements of conflict resolution. But these values can also be overlooked simply by default. It takes a considerable degree of sophistication and familiarity with resource allocation decisions to intervene with an argument that, for example, the value of nomadic practices should be considered at least as legitimate as the need for hydroelectric power. Craik and Zube (1976) and Eyles (1990) observe that perception of environmental quality is subjective. Beanlands and Duinker refer to "valued ecosystem components" (1983) to describe the part of the environment valued by users. It is change within valued components that will be perceived by local people as being significant.

There is a paucity of experience in and methods for con-
solidating and presenting non-conventional data and information. Where measurements of non-market goods are con-
templated, a number of monetization methods have been
developed (Adamowicz, 1991). Some of these rely on direct
survey approaches, while others depend on indirect inferen-
tial methods (Pearce and Turner, 1990, Turner, 1993). But
concepts that are used to evaluate non-market worth, such
as contingent evaluation, hedonic prices, replacement cost,
willingness-to-pay or willingness-to-accept (Bromley, 1988;
Dixon and Hufschmidt, 1986; Hufschmidt et al., 1983), are
burdened by problems related to their assumptions, their
applicability, and their inability to recognize the ultimate
subjectivity of many environmental values.

If environmental negotiations are couched in the established frameworks of the legal profession or the scientific
community, local community groups may be accepting, *a
priori*, a handicap. If a framework of what might be called
socioecosystem analysis predominates — that is, a framework that recognizes a non-duality between nature and the
human community inhabiting a landscape — then a community group may be able to assert an advantage. Billy Two
Rivers, a Mohawk Chief involved in impact studies related to
a hydro proposal for the St. Lawrence River at the Lachine
Rapids, refused to discuss economic, engineering or even
scientific aspects of the case because of what he viewed as
the historic unreliability of Euro-American agreements
based on good will and mutual understanding. He successfully shifted the agenda to reflect his peoples' paradigms and
values. Likewise, the Crees changed the basis of the James
Bay negotiation by taking an argument based essentially on
human rights to an international audience. However,
because this is an unconventional approach, the norms of
data collection, analysis and presentation have not been
established. This is an area requiring urgent attention in

which leadership can only come from partnerships between local communities and impact-assessment professionals.

Barriers in data presentation

During confrontations related to a multi-national resort development in Mexico, the foreign proponents of the project prepared extensive and visually-impressive promotional material supporting their objectives. The local community felt disadvantaged in the exchanges for many reasons but one of the more significant was that they felt unable to articulate their position and provide supporting documentation in a way that would have the same impact at the decision-makers' level (in this case, national civil servants). Formal impact assessment is largely a matter of communication. The soundest argument means nothing if it is not presented; the flimsiest argument can appear compelling if it is coherently and professionally presented. Overcoming each of the previously discussed information limitations presupposes an outlet for the results. The formality of public hearings can be intimidating and can be a deterrent in itself, particularly if questioning or cross-examination is permitted. While there is a reasonable record of sensitive and supportive impact-assessment hearing chairpersons — Thomas Berger (1978) perhaps setting an example in the Mackenzie Pipeline case — there is no record of how much salient evidence has been withheld or devalued because of limitations in the capacity to present information. As Holling (1978: 120) cautioned: "...as much effort must go into communication as goes into analysis." The skills of presentation must be seen as an essential part of community based action.

The problems of presentation are not limited to formal hearings. Many environmental issues are played out in the media and in public opinion and in these cases too, the ability to present a clear and cogent rendition of a stakeholder perspective is critical. Because environmental issues are inherently spatial, maps are useful if not essential. And because environmental change is generally of concern, an ability to convey temporal sequences is essential. Automated cartography, typically linked with GIS, provides the capacity to produce effective maps of spatial variability and sequential change. The GIGO reality (garbage in, garbage out) has to be recognized, but it is an inevitable part of any assessment process and, all else being equal, good presentation makes the best use of whatever information resources are available.

Conclusions

The human impact on the environment will continue to be a function of our numbers, our affluence and our technology. But, perhaps increasingly, it will also be a function of our will and our values. It has been argued that the predominance of economic thinking has led to consistently poor ecological choices (Daly and Cobb, 1994). Some economic models do allow for better valuation of ecological value (Turner, 1993), but they still presume either an ultimately objective means of reaching decisions or an effectively level playing field for stakeholders. But to the extent that information is power, the playing field is far from level. Barriers to critical information not only prejudice the negotiating ability of some stakeholder groups, but it can also impede the necessary process of "making the invisible visible".

As we more fully see and understand the way in which we are changing the habitat that supports us, the more likely it is that our will and values will shape our technology, focus our affluence (and perhaps limit our numbers) so that protection of what we depend on (and cherish?) is possible. Assessing the impact of what we do is vital. More information is not a guarantee of accurate assessment, effective action or judicious choice. But in cases where people have crossed the "threshold of awareness," as perhaps most informed citizens have by now, or where people are near, at, or over the "threshold of action," as is anyone involved in attempting to participate in environmental assessment — formal or informal — it is essential that action be based as much as possible on sound information. We can do little about inherent unpredictability of ecosystems (Kates and Clark, 1996), little about extant scientific uncertainty (Hare, 1995), and, given the political reality of the market-driven reality (Daly and Cobb, 1994), perhaps we can do little about proprietary data. But within these limitations, it must be recognized that environmental sustainability is a *sine qua non*, that impact assessment is essential to achieving that, and that full and fair public participation is essential to that. The barriers to information flow are barriers to full, fair and effective participation. Defining them may help find ways of overcoming or avoiding them.

References

Adamowicz, W.L. (1991) "Valuation of environmental amenities," *Canadian Journal of Agricultural Economics*, 39: 609-618.

Bascietto, J. et al. (1990) "Ecotoxicology and ecological risk assessment," *Environmental Science and Technology*, 24: 10-15.

Beanlands, G.E. and Duinker, P.N. (1983) *An Ecological Framework for Environmental Impact Assessment in Canada*, Institute for Resource and Environmental Studies, Halifax, NS: Dalhousie University.

Bennett, J.W. (1990) "Ecosystems, environmentalism, resource conservation, and anthropological research," in Moran, E.F. (ed.), *The Ecosystem Approach in Anthropology: From Concept to Practice*, Ann Arbor, MI: The University of Michigan Press, 435-456.

Berger, T.R. (1978) *Northern Frontier, Northern Homeland*, Ottawa, ON: Supply and Services Canada.

Boardman, R. (1992) "The multilateral dimension: Canada in the international system," in Boardman, R. (ed.), *Canadian Environmental Policy: Ecosystems, Politics, and Process*, New York, NY: Oxford University Press, 224-245.

Boychuck, R. (1991) "How green was his valley?," *Saturday Night*, 106: 24-28.

Bromley, D.W. (1988) "Resource and environmental economics: knowledge, discipline, and problems," in Hildreth, R.J. et. al. (eds.), *Agriculture and Rural Areas Approaching the Twenty-First Century: Challenges for Agricultural Economics*, Iowa City, IOWA: Iowa State University Press, 208-209.

Burton, I. (1991) "On making the invisible visible," in Meredith, T. et al. (eds.), *Defining and Mapping Critical Environmental Zones for Policy Formulation and Public Awareness*, Montreal, PQ: McGill University, 121-122.

Burton, I., Kates, R.W. and White, G.F. (1993) *The Environment As Hazard*, 2nd ed., New York, NY: Guilford Press.

Butzer, K.W. (1990) "The realm of cultural-human ecology: adaptation and change in historical perspective," in Turner et al., *The Earth as Transformed by Human Action: Global and Regional Changes in the Biosphere Over the Past 300 Years*, New York, NY: Cambridge University Press, 685-702.

Convis, C. (1993) *ESRI Conservation Program Statement*, Redlands, CA: Environmental Systems Research Institute.

Council on Environmental Quality (CEQ) (1992) *Environmental Quality*, Annual Report of the Council on

Environmental Quality, Washington, DC: U.S. Government Printing Office.

Craik, K.H. and Zube, E.H. (1976) *Perceiving Environmental Quality*, New York, NY: Plenum Press.

Daly, H.E. and Cobb, J.B. (1994) *For the Common Good: Redirecting the Economy Toward Community, the Environment and a Sustainable Future*, Boston, MASS: Beacon Press.

Dixon, J.A. and Hufschmidt, M.M. (1986) *Economic Valuation Techniques for the Environment: A Case Study Workbook*, East-West Environment and Policy Institute, London, UK: The John Hopkins University Press.

Eyles, J. (1990) "Objectifying the subjective: the measurement of environmental quality," *Social Indicators Research*, 22: 139-53.

Fleming, T. (ed.) (1997) *The Environment and Canadian Society*, Toronto, ON: ITP Nelson.

Hare, K.F. (1995) "Contemporary climatic change: the problem of uncertainty," in Mitchell, B. (ed.), *Resource and Environmental Management in Canada*, New York, NY: Oxford University Press, 10-28.

Holling, C.S. (1978) *Adaptive Environmental Assessment and Management*, New York, NY: John Wiley.

Hufschmidt, M.M., James, D.E., Meister, A.D., Bower, B.T. and Dixon, J.A. (1983) *Environment, Natural Systems, and Development: An Economic Valuation Guide*, Baltimore, ML: The John Hopkins University Press.

Indicators Task Force (1991) *A Report on Canada's Progress Towards a National Set of Environmental Indicators*, SOE

Report No. 91-1, Ottawa, ON: Ministry of Supply and Services.

Iacofano, D.S. (1990) *Public Involvement as an Organizational Development Process*, New York, NY: Garland Press Inc.

Inhaber, H. (1974) "Environmental quality: outline for a national index for Canada," *Science*, 186: 798-8.

Jacobs, P. and Sadler, B.(1990) *Sustainable Development and Environmental Assessment: Perspectives on Planning for a Common Future*, Hull, PQ: Canadian Environmental Assessment Research Council.

Jain, R.K., Urban, L.V., Stacey, G.S. and Balbach, H.E. (1993) *Environmental Assessment*, New York, NY: McGraw Hill.

Kasperson, R.E., Turner, B.L., Kasperson, J.X., Mitchell, R.C. and Ratick, S.J. (1991) "A preliminary working paper on critical zones in global environmental change," in Meredith et al. (eds.), *Defining and Mapping Critical Environmental Zones For Policy Formulation and Public Awareness*, Montreal, PQ: McGill University, 37-62.

Kates, R.W. and Clark, W.C. (1996) "Expecting the unexpected," *Environment*, 38: 26-28.

Kates, R.W., Turner, B.L. II and Clark, W.C. (1990) "The great transformation," in Turner et al., *The Earth as Transformed by Human Action: Global and Regional Changes in the Biosphere Over the Past 300 Years*, New York, NY: Cambridge University Press, 1-17.

Kelly, J.R. and Harwell, M.A. (1990) "Indicators of ecosystem recovery," *Environmental Management*, 14: 527-545.

Liverman, D.M., Hanson, M.E., Brown, B.J. and Merideth, R.W. (1988) "Global sustainability: toward measurement", *Environmental Management*, 12: 133-143.

Maser, C. (1996) *Resolving Environmental Conflict*, Delray Beach, FL: St. Lucie Press.

Maslow, A. (1954) *Motivation and Personality*, New York, NY: Harper Inc.

Menou, M.J. (1993) *Measuring the Impact of Information on Development*, Ottawa, ON: International Development Research Centre.

Meredith, T.C. (1991a) "Environmental impact assessment and monitoring," in Mitchell, B. (ed.), *Resource Management and Development*, Toronto, ON: Oxford University Press, 224-245.

_____ (1991b) "Canadian global change program, human dimensions of global change, critical zones working group: a framework for discussion on a work plan," in Meredith et al. (eds.), *Defining and Mapping Critical Environmental Zones for Policy Formulation and Public Awareness*, Montreal, PQ: McGill University, 3-10.

_____ (1992) "Environmental impact assessment, cultural diversity and sustainable rural development," *Environmental Impact Assessment Review*, 12: 125-138.

_____ (1995) "Geographic information and community-based environmental decisions," in Alvarez, R. (ed.), *Memorias: Sociedad Latinamericana de Perception Remota*, SELPER-Mexico, A.C., 203- 215.

Meredith, T.C., Moore, C., Gartner, J. and Smith, W. (1994) *Canadian Critical Environmental Zones: Concepts, Goals and Resources*, Canadian Global Change Program,

Publication 94-1, Ottawa, ON: Royal Society of Canada.

Mitchell, B. (1991) "'BEATing' Conflict and Uncertainty in Resource Management and Development," in Mitchell, B. (ed.), *Resource Management and Development*, New York, NY: Oxford University Press, 268-285.

Moran, E.F. (1990) "Ecosystem ecology in biology and anthropology: a critical assessment," in Moran, E.F. (ed.), *The Ecosystem Approach in Anthropology: From Concept to Practice*, Ann Arbor, MI: The University of Michigan Press, 3-40.

OECD (1991) *Environmental Indicators: A Preliminary Set*, Paris, FR: Organization for Economic Co-operation and Development.

Ott, W.R. (1978) *Environmental Indices: Theory and Practice*, Ann Arbor, MI: Ann Arbor Science Publishers.

Pearce, D.W. and Turner, R.K. (1990) *Economics of Natural Resources and the Environment*, Baltimore, ML: The John Hopkins University Press.

Rappaport, R.A. (1990) "Ecosystems, populations and people," in Moran, E.F. (ed.), *The Ecosystem Approach in Anthropology: From Concept to Practice*, Ann Arbor, MI: The University of Michigan Press, 41-72.

Rapport, D.J. (1989) "Symptoms of pathology in the Gulf of Bothnia (Baltic Sea): ecosystem response to human activity," *Biological Journal of the Linnean Society*, 37: 33-49.

_____ (1990) "Criteria for ecological indicators," *Environmental Monitoring and Assessment*, 15: 273-275.

Renn, O., Webler, T. and Wiedemann, P. (eds.) (1995)

Fairness and Competence in Citizen Participation, Boston, MASS: Kluwer Press.

Schaeffer, D.J. (1988) "Ecosystem health: 1. measuring ecosystem health," *Environmental Management,* 12: 445-455.

Sheehy, G. (1989) *Environmental Indicator Research: A Literature Review for State of the Environment Reporting,* Technical Report Series, Report No. 7, SOE Reporting Branch, Ottawa, ON: Environment Canada.

Simmons, I.G. (1989) *Changing the Face of the Earth: Culture, Environment, History,* Oxford, UK: Basil Blackwell.

Smith, W. (1993) "Measuring the immeasurable: indices of development," in Meredith, T. and Smith, W. (eds.), *Environment, Culture and Quality of Life: An Annotated Bibliography,* Centre for Society, Technology and Development, Montreal, PQ: McGill University, 7-20.

Stern, P.C., Young, O.R. and Druckman, D. (eds.) (1992) *Global Environmental Change: Understanding the Human Dimension,* Washington, DC: National Academy Press.

Turner, B.L. II, Clark, W.C., Kates, R.W., Richards, J.F., Mathews, J.T. and Meyer, W.B. (1990a) *The Earth as Transformed by Human Action: Global and Regional Changes in the Biosphere Over the Past 300 Years,* New York, NY: Cambridge University Press.

Turner, B.L. II, Kasperson, R.E., Meyer, W.B., Dow, K.M., Golding, D., Kasperson, J.X., Mitchell, R.C. and Ratick, S.J. (1990b) "Two types of global environmental change: definitional and spatial-scale issues in their human dimensions," *Global Environmental Change,* 1: 14-22.

Turner, K. (ed.) (1993) *Sustainable Environmental Economics and Management*, London, UK: Bellhaven Press.

Turnstall, D.B. (1979) "Developing indicators of environmental quality: the experience of council on environmental quality," *Social Indicators Research*, 6: 301-347.

United Nations Conference on Environment and Development (UNCED) (1992) *Agenda 21*, Conches, SWITZERLAND: United Nations.

VHB Research and Consulting (1989) *Indicators and Indices of the State of the Environment*, Toronto, ON: VHB Research and Consulting.

Wackernagel, M. and Rees, W.E. (1996) *Our Ecologica Footprint: Reducing the Human Impact on the Earth*, Gabriola Island, BC: New Society Publishers.

World Commission on Environment and Development (WCED) (1987) *Our Common Future*, New York, NY: Oxford University Press.

Section 2

**Methodological Approaches to EA
Components and Process**

Chapter 5

Socio-Economic Assessment Auditing: A Hibernia Case Study

Jim Locke and Keith Storey
Memorial University

Since the passage of the U.S. National Environmental Policy Act in 1969, environmental impact assessment (EIA) has diffused world-wide, with many countries having adopted some form of formal EIA procedures. Since its inception, considerable resources have been allocated to conduct EIAs, but until recently, very little has been done by way of follow-up to determine whether EIA has been effective in terms of predicting impacts or whether the strategies to optimize those impacts have met their objectives. Since the mid-1980s, however, the question of the utility and efficiency of EIA has increasingly arisen. Part of this was the recognition of the need for a formal feedback mechanism within the EIA process to identify and evaluate the actual environmental consequences of a project or action. The EIA audit is a process of obtaining relevant information and examining and evaluating EIA procedures and project or action outcomes.

Although the notion of post-project audits has existed in the literature since 1969, and while interest in the subject of environmental auditing has been increasing over the past decade, the use of and experience with environmental audits is still limited. The 1992 Canadian Environmental Assessment Act (CEAA) is a case in point. The Act requires the development of follow-up programs prior to the granting of project approval. A "follow-up program" under the Act is defined as one designed for the verification of the accuracy of the environmental assessment of a project, and the evaluation of the effectiveness of any mitigative measures developed to address the adverse environmental effects of the project (Canada, 1992:4), and as such parallels the notion of "EIA audit". However, the regulations/guidelines governing the Act's follow-up provisions have yet to be finalized and will have to address a number of issues prior to the implementation of these audit/follow-up procedures. Such issues include the method of conducting an audit, the prerequisites for auditing, the party or parties responsible for conducting as well as paying for the audit, and the authority responsible for administering the overall auditing process.

Objectives

The focus of this chapter is on audit methods, particularly as they apply to the follow-up of socio-economic impact predictions and optimization strategies. Most of audit studies to date have had a biophysical bias, with socio-economic issues having been either significantly under-represented or completely omitted from the studies. The reasons for this are not clear. It may be that socio-economic impacts are less tangible and not as easily quantified, thereby making them more difficult to audit. Or, as some researchers have suggested, the lack of socio-economic impact auditing research may testify to the fact that many EIA researchers view socio-economic issues as less significant than those of a biophysical nature.

In any event, whatever the focus, the impacts predicted for developments have proven difficult to audit. It is the lack of and need for EIA audit research, which emphasizes the socio-economic impacts of human actions, that serve as the rationale for this chapter. The results of a socio-economic audit of the Hibernia offshore oil and gas project illustrate a number of the shortcomings of current audit methodology. The type of problems encountered suggest that improving elements of the current approach is unlikely to address fundamental problems. Accordingly, an alternative approach is suggested which, it is believed, will have greater value for the EIA process in its primary role as an aid to decision making.

The Hibernia Project

The Hibernia project had its beginnings in 1979 with the discovery of oil in the Hibernia P-15 well off the southeast coast of Newfoundland. In 1980, the proponent, Mobil Oil Canada, Ltd., applied to develop the field. As a project on federal lands and involving federal funds, the Environmental Assessment Review Process (EARP) was triggered. Under this process an EIA was conducted and the results summarized in an Environmental Impact Statement (EIS) that was submitted for review in 1985 (Mobil, 1985).

Volume IV of the Hibernia EIS addressed the potential socio-economic impacts of the project. A number of predictions were made with respect to issues such as housing, employment, demography, the fishery, and the effects on Newfoundland's "social fabric". Also, some general management strategies were suggested to optimize particular impacts. Those predictions relevant to the offshore platform construction site at Bull Arm were subsequently reviewed and management strategies spelled out in more detail in Environmental Protection Plans (EPPs) developed for this area. The auditing procedure described here is used to evaluate the accuracy of the predictions made in these documents.

EIA: A Lack of Follow-up

Follow-up procedures are a formal requirement under the CEAA, and were also outlined under EARP. However, unlike the CEAA, which appoints the Minister of Environment responsible for the design and implementation of follow-up programs, there was no specific body established under

EARP to either oversee such activities or to ensure that they were performed. The Federal Environmental Assessment and Review Office was the agency responsible for administering the EARP. However, it was not within the mandate of the assessment and review office to conduct or coordinate follow-up procedures. Rather it was the responsibility of the Initiating Minister to administer follow-up procedures for approved projects. The result was that implementation of follow-up was not widespread. In a 1987 review of federal projects that had been subject to the process, McCallum, (1987:733), concluded that:

> there is little evidence of consistent programs or procedures, scientific or administrative, for a comprehensive approach to follow-up. In addition,.... follow-up is not done to the degree that it should be within the federal system.

Little subsequently changed. Most emphasis continued to be placed on the initial stages of EIA, i.e., the pre-approval stage, with very little attention being given to the post-approval and post-project components. From the inception of the EARP in 1973 up to 1992, 56 of the projects subjected to the process had proceeded to the panel-review stage. Environmental assessment panel reports had been submitted to the Minister of Environment for 39 of these, thus marking the completion of the panel review stage. All of these reviewed projects were granted Ministerial approval to proceed. However, whether follow-up investigations were conducted for these 39 projects is not easily determined as no composite data record of such activities was kept (Barnes, pers. comm., 1992).

The apparent lack of, and uncoordinated approach to, follow-up under EARP was related to the fact that there was no specific follow-up procedure outlined, or indeed even formally required; a shortcoming that the CEAA has since attempted to address (see Canada, 1992, section 6.8).

The inadequacy of follow-up procedures within EIA is not limited to Canada. The monitoring of project impacts is not a formal requirement under the EIA procedures of most countries. For example, the results of a comparative review of EIA systems of several countries (Wood, 1995) indicate that of the seven systems analysed, four did not contain specific requirements for monitoring, while the remaining three contained partial requirements. In many cases, discretionary provisions exist, but in practice, these are rarely employed. The United States is a case in point. Under the National Environmental Policy Act, monitoring is discretionary and, to date, follow-up efforts have been generally weak. In fact, Wood suggests that monitoring is widely recognized as the "weak link" in the American EIA system. The Canadian Environmental Assessment Act, on the other hand, fares well in the Wood comparison!

The importance and value of EIA follow-up is at least acknowledged in the CEAA, and the Act formally defines a follow-up program and contains provisions for the development and implementation of such a program. The details of the follow-up program must be outlined and approved by the responsible government authority prior to project approval. Given that regulations for follow-up have still to be established, it is too early to say how effective the legislation will be.

The EIA Audit

The term "audit", borrowed from accounting, conveys the idea of data certification and verification of practice. The notion of post-project audits, also referred to as post-project studies, evaluations or analyses, has existed in the literature since 1969 but from the mid to late 1970s onward, interest in the subject of environmental auditing has been increasing (Rigby, 1985).

Perhaps the most commonly cited strength of environmental auditing is its feedback function. It is argued that information obtained from auditing should be incorporated into decision-making procedures of subsequent projects. According to Spaling et al. (1993:70):

> Feedback would provide information on the effectiveness of institutional processes, and also on the accuracy and reliability of impact prediction... Expost evaluations would provide hindsight information contrasting the intended and actual EIA process, and comparing the predicted and observed impacts. This information would serve as a learning opportunity to improve project design and impact prediction for other proposed actions at different locations in the future.

Buckley (1991:94) emphasises the immediate rather than hindsight benefits in suggesting that the principal advantage of systematic environmental auditing:

> is that it provides a feedback link in environmental planning and management... Environmental impact audit provides a measure of the accuracy of the initial prediction, and potentially, of the "environmental management effort" needed to bring actual impacts into line with expectations where initial estimates proved inaccurate. This also provides a "learning function" in EIA as a whole: future predictions can take into account the outcomes of past predictions.

Wood (1995:199) points out that in addition to assisting impact forecasting for future projects, the results of the audit also would serve a public relations function; they could demonstrate the concerns of government and industry for the environment and also provide reassurance to the public of the effectiveness and success of their impact management strategies.

The absence of such knowledge of past successes and/or failures of the EIA process inhibits the advancement of such procedures. Without feedback, those techniques and procedures which prove to be effective and successful remain largely unknown. As a result, time and resources may be wasted as EIA practitioners and researchers independently "keep reinventing the wheel" (Munro et al., 1986:28).

Conversely, a lack of feedback may result in the propagation of ineffective or unreliable EIA techniques and procedures. Often, practitioners adopt information and methods from assessments of similar projects or similar environments. However, such an approach may be inappropriate as the validity of many of these techniques is seldom evaluated. As a consequence, it is quite possible that predictive techniques are being employed and, subsequently, decisions being made and actions being implemented based upon models and information whose validity and accuracy are unknown (Tomlinson and Atkinson, 1987a:188).

Some authors suggest that the feedback and learning opportunities associated with auditing could also serve to enhance the general approach to EIA. According to Tomlinson and Atkinson (1987a:188), a major weakness of EIA practice has been its use solely to obtain a development permit instead of as an environmental management tool. Consequently the focus has been primarily on the "front-end" or the pre-approval activities of EIA with little consideration being given to the outcomes of these approved projects (McCallum, 1987).

Sadler (1988:129) described this lack of attention to the effectiveness of the mitigative and management measures as "the paradox" of EIA. The absence of follow-up precludes any opportunity to learn from other project experience and, therefore, inhibits the advancement of EIA. As Bisset and Tomlinson (1988:126) concluded:

> there is a need for a feedback mechanism in EIA which involves the transfer of knowledge from the actual environmental effects of a project or action to future EIAs... This can only be achieved through audits.

The limited use of, and thus experience with, environmental audits is reflected in the fact that there has been no standard definition for "environmental audit" (Rigby, 1985; Tomlinson, 1987; Bisset and Tomlinson, 1988; Buckley, 1991). Since first introduced, the concept has evolved and been expanded. As a result, the term has come to be used to define and describe a wider and wider range of procedures and activities. For example, Tomlinson and Atkinson (1987a) proposed seven different types of auditing within the EIA process:

Review of Draft EIS Audit. This involves a review of the draft EIS vis-à-vis its terms of reference.

Decision Point Audit. This type of audit examines the effectiveness of the EIS within the decision-making process.

Implementation Audit. Its purpose is to determine whether the recommendations of the EIS or the Review Panel were implemented.

Performance Audit. This is an examination of the company's internal environmental management of a project and its ability to respond to environmental incidents during project operations.

Project Impact Audit. Such an audit involves the examination of the environmental consequences of a project. Its purpose is to determine whether these consequences were originally forecast.

Predictive Technique Audit. This involves a comparison between the actual and predicted effects of a project in order to verify and improve predictive techniques.

EIA Procedures Audit. EIA procedures provide the framework within which EIAs for particular projects are carried out. An audit of these procedures would examine the performance of EIA procedures at the macro level and could include any or all of the above forms of audit.

Buckley (1991:121) further expanded the definition and applied it not only to the EIA process but to the other aspects of the environmental management process, including: compliance, monitoring programs, equipment performance, physical hazards, financial risks, products and markets, baselines and benchmarks, management programs and structures, planning procedures and legislation.

Thus, over the past decade the label "environmental audit" has been adopted to represent a broader range of activities than was the case when it was first conceived. Initially, it was used to refer only to a follow-up of EIA predictions. However, "environmental audit" now refers to such things as testing a company's pollution controls and monitoring equipment to ensure that it meets operational specifications; assessing the "greenness" or the environmental friendliness of a company's retail products; or, with regard to corporation mergers and acquisitions, identifying any environmental liabilities associated with the takeover target that may be transferred to the new corporation (Buckley, 1991). As a result, EIA auditing, which was once synonymous with environmental auditing, is now only one of many types of procedures which fall under the umbrella of "environmental auditing".

The fact that the scope of the definition has broadened is indicative of the increased thought and research which have been devoted to environmental auditing. Some of this heightened attention has been directed toward the area of EIA auditing. As a result, EIA audit studies have been undertaken in such countries as Canada, Australia, the United States and the United Kingdom, but, as discussed below, this has not proved to be a simple task.

Difficulties in Predicting and Auditing

The majority of EIA audits that have been carried out would fall under either the Project Impact or Predictive Technique categories defined above. Some of these have addressed single projects, such as the post-project evaluation of the CP Rail Rogers Pass Development (Ross and Tench, 1987), while others have adopted a multi-project focus, for example, Buckley's (1991) national study of Australian impact predictions and Culhane's (1987a; 1987b) follow-up of American EISs.

Of the two, the most common type of EIA audit undertaken has been the Predictive Technique Audit. Such studies are concerned with assessing the accuracy of pre-project predictions and forecasts relative to actual project outcomes. A recurring conclusion of these investigations has been that "the accuracy of such predictions leaves much to be desired" (Tomlinson and Atkinson, 1987b:259).

There are perhaps two general reasons for this. The most basic of these is that the relationships between action, cause, effect and impact are often improperly understood with the result that predictions by type, magnitude, spatial and temporal dimensions and significance are often erroneous. For example, those responsible for estimating the amount of time and resources that will be required for a given project are almost invariably too optimistic - demand for labour, the time to complete tasks and the estimate of

overall costs in particular, are more often than not significantly underestimated (see, for example, Gilmore et al.,
1980).

The other general reason for error is associated with the
essentially static, 'snapshot', nature of the EIA process.
Quite often the design characteristics of the project will
change significantly between the time that the EIA is undertaken and the time that the project is completed. Since the
predictive component of EIA is usually a one-time rather
than recurring exercise, the original impact predictions may
be neither accurate nor relevant once the project actually
occurs (see, for example, Munro et al., 1986:15; Clark et al.,
1987:530; McCallum, 1987:737 and Buckley, 1991:96).
Similarly, changes in exogenous factors, particularly changing economic or social circumstances, may often significantly alter the baseline conditions that are likely to be
affected by the project or action in question, once again
affecting the potential accuracy of any predicted outcomes.

Even if these difficulties can be avoided or overcome,
impact prediction auditing is not as straightforward a task
as it might seem. As noted by Bisset (1980:389), "while the
implementation of audits appears, superficially, to be a conceptually simple exercise, experience shows it is fraught
with difficulties".

In reviewing EIA audit case studies, Locke (1996) found
that there were three general, procedural difficulties common to many of these. One was that many of the predictions
outlined in the EIS and other project documentation were
unsuitable for audit. Buckley (1991:96), for example, discovered that many of these documents contained few
testable predictions and those predictions that were testable
generally addressed only minor impacts while major
impacts were discussed qualitatively. EIS predictions have
also been described as being expressed in "vague, imprecise
and woolly language" (Clark et al., 1987:530), while state-

ments regarding impact significance and probability of occurrence have been seen as "confoundingly vague", lacking quantification and ambiguous with respect to the direction or beneficiality of impacts reported (Culhane, 1987a:374).

A second general problem was a temporal one. First, few forecasts contained any reference as to *when* the impacts were likely to occur (Clark et al., 1987:532). Such a time frame is essential to ensure that appropriate monitoring measures are in place in order to identify project-related variations in a particular environmental component. Otherwise, project impacts would go undetected, ultimately leading to erroneous conclusions regarding the environmental consequences of the project and/or the effectiveness of management systems.

The third problem involved monitoring data. The success of, and indeed, the ability to perform an audit, is contingent upon the availability and quality of pre-project and project-operations monitoring data. In most studies, the monitoring data necessary to evaluate the reliability of impact predictions were found to be either non-existent, insufficient or inadequate (see Bisset, 1980:390; Murdock et al., 1982:337; Canter, 1985:258; Munro et al., 1986:13; Sonntag, 1987:451; CEARC, 1988:2-3 and Buckley, 1991:96).

Monitoring programs and data were seen to be deficient in several respects. Sometimes monitoring programs were not related to the forecasts outlined in the EIS and those programs that were related did not always generate data appropriate for audit. For example, predictions may have been made for a particular location or time period but the monitoring data were collected at a different location or expressed for a different period. As well, monitoring data often did not permit statistically valid testing of the predictions as a function of too few samples, inadequate controls or too many missing data points (Clark et al., 1987:533 and Buckley, 1991:96).

It was also found that baseline or pre-project information was often lacking (Canter, 1985:264 and CEARC, 1988:2). In many cases such data did not cover a sufficient time period to allow the identification of natural or 'without project' patterns in the environmental factors being considered (Clark et al., 1987:533).

The availability and accessibility of monitoring data can be another obstacle in the auditing process. Data may be difficult to obtain either because they have not been published or because circulation of the information has been restricted (CEARC, 1988:3 and Buckley, 1991:118).

Both the nature of the impact predictions and the availability of adequate monitoring data have tended to limit the number of auditable predictions. For example, Buckley (1991) determined that of the thousands of forecasts contained in the 800-1,000 EISs and equivalent documents produced in Australia between 1974 and 1982, monitoring data to test these predictions exist for only 3% of these EISs. Similarly Murdock et al. (1982) found that of the 225 EISs they reviewed, only 44 were suitable for evaluation, and in the CEMP study, of 791 predictions identified, 697 were untestable and only 94 could be audited (Clark et al., 1987).

These examples demonstrate the complexities involved in performing an EIA audit. As the authors of the CEMP study noted:

> The main conclusion of the research, in terms of testing predictions, is that it has been very difficult to audit the impacts predicted for developments. Impact predictions are not phrased in a way which allows auditing, and they become obsolete very easily. In addition, existing monitoring programs are

not very useful in providing data to allow predictions to be tested in a scientifically acceptable manner (Clark et al., 1987:537).

Socio-Economic Impact Audits

The above conclusions have been derived primarily from the auditing of biophysical impact predictions. Indeed, such forecasts have been the focus of most audit studies while socio-economic issues are largely under-represented, the main exceptions being studies conducted by Murdock et al. (1982) and Gilmore et al. (1980). Typically, socio-economic impact predictions either comprise only a small proportion of those being audited, as was the case in the follow-up study of Australian EIS predictions (Buckley, 1991) in which only nine of the 181 reviewed were socially related, or socio-economic issues are altogether excluded from the study, as in the CEMP study of the four development projects in the United Kingdom (Clark et al., 1987).

Since most audits have addressed biophysical impact predictions, much of the research related to auditing has had a biophysical bias (see Rigby, 1985; Sadler, 1987; Davies and Sadler, 1990; and Buckley, 1991). Whether the approaches adopted for biophysical auditing research are appropriate for socio-economic impact projections is debatable, as there has been little research undertaken with respect to this. Davies and Sadler (1990), for example, suggest that, because of the different nature of social impact assessment, it may be necessary to reassess existing auditing procedures in order to accommodate socio-economic impacts.

The practice of social [i.e., socio-economic] impact assessment incorporates a number of assumptions and approaches which differ from those of EIA as it is conventionally defined. Therefore, it is useful to consider how the present guidelines must be reorganized to accommodate social practices. Although social impact monitoring has been the focus of recent research, little development has been achieved in the direction of monitoring and auditing social impacts and assessment methodology (Davies and Sadler, 1990:30).

Socio-Economic Audit of the Hibernia Project

To explore this particular problem further, an audit of the socio-economic predictions made in the Hibernia EIS and related documents was undertaken (Locke, 1996) based on current approaches and most closely corresponding to that adopted by Culhane (1987a), Clark et al. (1987) and Buckley (1991).

The procedure followed is conceptually simple. First a definition of what is meant by a forecast, prediction and projection was determined. From a review of the content of the Hibernia EIS (Mobil, 1985) and subsequent Environmental Protection Plans (NODECO 1991; PASSB 1992) socio-economic predictions were then identified. These were then further screened to determine whether they were auditable based on a number of criteria reflecting the specificity of the prediction, whether it was conditional or independent and its present relevance (see below). For the remaining predictions, actual data were compiled and predicted and actual outcomes compared.

Predictions were categorised under the ten theme headings used in the EIS and classified as follows:

G: wording of prediction too general;
C: prediction contingent on other events which have not yet taken place;
NR: prediction no longer relevant (e.g., because of project changes);
NYR: prediction not yet relevant (e.g., specified time

DS: period not yet reached);
         prediction is a descriptive statement of
         quantitative data presented;

R: prediction a repetitive statement of an impact
         already discussed;

S: prediction suitable for audit.

Table 5.1 summarises the results from the review of the Hibernia EIS. In total 143 socio-economic predictions were identified of which 78 (54.5%) were considered suitable for audit. Of these, 49 (63%) related to predictions about commercial or social infrastructure and a further 12 (15%) concerned public services.

The relevance of some of the EIS predictions was affected by the five-year delay between the submission of the EIS and the commencement of the project. During this period, the site chosen for the construction of the offshore platform was changed and this significantly affected the relevance of a number of the predictions made. No new environmental assessment was considered necessary but Environmental Protection Plans (EPPs) were required. These updated a number of the key issues associated with construction and specified the means to deal with them. Screening the EPPs led to the identification of 50 predictions of which 29 were suitable for audit. Of the remainder, 15 were not yet relevant, 5 were too vague or general and 1 was repetitive of a prediction made earlier.

These predictions were then reviewed in the light of the available monitoring data. Of the 86 original predictions, there were 67 which could not be followed up as there has been no monitoring of these issues. Of the 19 predictions for which there has been some monitoring, a further 11 were excluded as the data collected are either insufficient or inadequate to evaluate the accuracy of the predictions made. Thus, of the original 86 'suitable' predictions made in the EIS and EPPs, only eight were found to be auditable. Of

Table 5.1
Summary of Classification and Category for the 143 EIS Impact Predictions

Category/Classification	Industry	Employment	Demography	Fishery	Housing	Public Services	Commercial/Social Infrastructure	Land/Resource Use	Municipal Gov't/Finance	NFLD. Social Fabric	Total
General (G)	3	0	1	0	0	2	3	2	2	4	17
Conditional (C)	0	0	0	3	0	2	2	0	0	0	7
No Longer Relevant (NR)	0	0	1	9	0	4	0	2	0	1	17
Not Yet Relevant (NYR)	0	0	0	1	0	0	5	0	0	0	6
Descriptive Statement (DS)	0	0	0	0	5	0	2	0	0	0	7
Repetitive Statement (R)	0	0	0	0	3	1	6	0	1	0	11
Suitable for Audit (S)	0	4	4	0	4	12	49	5	0	0	78
Total	3	4	6	13	12	21	67	9	3	5	143

In comparing the predictions made in the EIS with those in the EPPs, those in the EIS that were no longer relevant were excluded, and, those that were updated in the EPPs were replaced. The net result was that 21 of the 78 suitable EIS predictions were removed, and 29 from the EPPs added, for a total of 86 'suitable' predictions.

these eight predictions, two were employment-related, one was demographic, three concerned housing, and the remaining two concerned fishery matters.

In comparing these predictions with the actual outcomes, the 'accuracy' of the predictions varies considerably. In the case of the employment and demographic-related predictions, however, these are related to each other and consequently the patterns of similarity and difference between the predicted and actual values are the same. The expected and actual number of jobs at the platform construction site during the first five years of the project are illustrated in Table 5.2. As can be seen, the numbers were over-predicted for years one (1990) and three (1992) of the project, but substantially under-predicted in all others years. The second employment-related prediction describes the peak number of workers expected at the platform construction site. By July 1995 the construction workforce had peaked at 5,779 — 61% higher than the 3,600 originally forecast. Finally, Table 5.3 illustrates the expected versus actual number of workers living in the workcamp. While the overall pattern of differences remains the same, the number in the camp in years four and five were 268% and 203% greater than predicted. In response to the demand for on-site accommodations, an additional 480 rooms were subsequently added to the camp, bringing the total capacity to 3,480. During peak employment in 1995, the camp was fully occupied.

Housing predictions were originally based on employment expectations. In the EIS forecasts are given both for the St. John's area and the Isthmus of Avalon — the area in the vicinity of the construction camp. As Table 5.4 illustrates, the demand for project-related housing units in the St. John's area was over-predicted, while in the Isthmus area it was generally under-predicted (Table 5.5). A related prediction was that the project was not expected to result in a significant increase in either land or house prices in the St. John's area. Analysis of Canada Mortgage and Housing

Table 5.2
Predicted and Actual Number of Hibernia Jobs Created in the Isthmus Impact Area, 1990-1994

Year	1990	1991	1992	1993	1994
Predicted	250	850	1155	1465	2265
Actual	116	972	898	3060	4019

Table 5.3
Cumulative Increments at the Bull Arm Work Camp: Predicted and Actual Values, 1990-1994

Year	1990	1991	1992	1993	1994
Predicted	143	546	751	958	1465
Actual	N/A	673	642	2569	2969

Table 5.4
Cumulative Household Increments St. John's Impact Area: Predicted and Actual Values, 1990-1994

Year	1990	1991	1992	1993	1994
Predicted	41	67	210	234	262
Actual	N/A	N/A	65	98	231

Table 5.5
Cumulative Household Increments Isthmus Impact Area: Predicted and Actual Values, 1990-1994

Year	1990	1991	1992	1993	1994
Predicted	7	35	49	63	96
Actual	N/A	56	80	90	91

Corporation (CMHC) housing market data over the period in question suggests that while Hibernia personnel have helped to absorb some of the higher priced houses on the market, average MLS sales prices in the St. John's area rose only marginally from $88,993 in 1990 to $92,011 in 1994 — an increase of 3.4% (Woodman, 1995, pers. com.). Hibernia activities did not result in any significant increase in demand for housing in the area and consequently the prices of land and housing were not significantly affected.

The remaining auditable predictions concerned potential impacts on the fishery in the vicinity of the platform construction site. In the first case, it was predicted that the movement of project vessels within a designated traffic lane might interfere with normal fishing and vessel operation and cause damages. There were also concerns that project vessels which did not confine themselves to the designated traffic lane might damage gear or fishing vessels. Data from HMDC indicate that minor damage to gear has occurred as predicted. In 1992 two claims for fishing net damage were made and subsequently settled.

The findings from this audit of Hibernia impacts are similar to those of most audits undertaken to date; poor wording of the predictive statements and the paucity of adequate monitoring data preclude an evaluation of the majority of predictions. The audit of the Hibernia project reveals that, of the 193 socio-economic impact predictions made, only eight are suitable for audit. Of these, outcomes from three are consistent with the original predictions, while the remaining five either under- or over-estimate the impacts of the project.

These findings further confirm that in general neither the format of the EISs being produced nor the quality of the monitoring data being collected is well-suited to the auditing approach employed to date, with its emphasis on impact prediction accuracy. However, this raises the question of whether the current approach to EIA — a "demand" approach, which emphasizes predictive precision — is itself adequate or useful. It is argued here that a "capacity" approach to EIA, with a greater emphasis on impact management rather than impact prediction, is more appropriate to accommodate the dynamic nature of both the development projects and the context in which they operate. Such an approach would also serve to better integrate EIA into the broader environmental planning process.

Predictive Accuracy of Hibernia's EIS and EPP and General Project Outcomes

Due to the small number of predictions that were suitable for inclusion in the final audit, it is difficult to formulate any general conclusions regarding the accuracy of the Hibernia-related socio-economic impact predictions. However, to date, there have been no apparent negative socio-economic impacts of the Hibernia project. In fact, most project impacts generally have been positive (e.g., employment and expenditures). The project-related demographic changes have been such that any impacts have been easily absorbed, while local industry and residents have benefitted from the business and employment opportunities associated with the project. In fact, for many areas of Newfoundland, the spin-offs from Hibernia have been the only bright spot in a generally declining economy over the past five years.

With regard to the adverse impacts of the project, these have proved much less significant than had been originally anticipated before and during the Hibernia public review. The mitigative measures designed and implemented thus far have been successful in addressing the potential problems identified in the project's impact assessment and review process. For example, the construction of the work camp at the GBS construction site has been effective in reducing the level of interaction between project employees and surrounding communities. As a result, even though the data are not available to conclusively demonstrate the outcomes, the initial concerns regarding higher house prices, increased crime rates, an over-extension of existing public services and infrastructure and a general "erosion" of Newfoundland's "social fabric" have not materialized (see Storey, 1995).

Many of these conclusions cannot, however, be drawn from the results of the audit. The results from it instead point to a number of shortcomings and inadequacies of the current approach to EIA auditing. The fact that only eight of the 193 socio-economic impact predictions made for the Hibernia project were suitable for final audit suggests the need for an alternative auditing procedure and/or revision to the way in which EIS predictions are presented. Furthermore, the results call into question the value of attempting to use the audit process to determine predictive accuracy. These issues comprise the focus of discussion in the following section.

The Socio-Economic Impact Audit Procedure

The procedure employed in the Hibernia audit was based primarily upon three case studies: the U.S. Audit (Culhane, 1987a); the United Kingdom Audit (Clark et al., 1987); and the Australian Audit (Buckley, 1991). The methods used in these studies were drawn upon to develop the method applied to the Hibernia project. While the main differences from the case studies were that the Hibernia audit addressed socio-economic issues and had a single-project focus — the case studies were all multi-project investigations and dealt predominantly with biophysical impact predictions — the findings from all were similar.

In all cases there were significant procedural difficulties in undertaking the audit. Volume IV of the Hibernia EIS primarily outlines the issues of concern and, similar to Buckley's Australian findings (1991:96), contains relatively few predictions. Furthermore, as is highlighted in several of the audit studies (Canter, 1985:264; Munro et al., 1986:12; Clark et al., 1987:530; Culhane, 1987a:374 and McCallum, 1987:737), the majority of the EIS predictions are non-quantitative and often are expressed in "vague and woolly language".

The time-related difficulties described in the EIA auditing literature (see Clark et al., 1987:530; McCallum, 1987:737 and Buckley, 1991:96) are also a limiting factor in the Hibernia audit. Most of the predictions identified contain no time frame as to when the impacts are likely to occur. Also, the many delays to the Hibernia project schedule complicate the assessment of the predictions. A span of approximately five and a half years separated the completion date of the EIS and the commencement of project development activities at the Bull Arm platform construction site. During this time interval, significant project changes occurred, including the selection of the new site of platform construction. As a result, many of the original predictions are irrelevant, and many need to be modified in the light of new project information and changes in the "new-project" environment.

The paucity of adequate monitoring data was also problematic as almost all studies have found (see for example, Murdock et al.,1982:337 and Buckley, 1991:96). This is a major deficiency with respect to the socio-economic component of the Hibernia project as indicated by the fact that adequate project monitoring data are available for only eight of the 86 predictions identified as being suitable for audit.

Three general reasons for undertaking socio-economic monitoring have been identified: compliance; project impact management; and policy evaluation. In the first instance, the data collected may be used to ensure that the project is operating in accordance with any agreements, regulations and legislation. In the second case, monitoring data may serve to identify undesirable unexpected consequences and allow for the development of responsive management measures. With respect to evaluation, the monitoring data may provide insight regarding the effectiveness of policies being implemented and developed (Storey et al., 1991:5-6).

The inadequacy of the Hibernia socio-economic monitoring seems related to the purpose for which it is being used. The main purpose of the monitoring undertaken for the project seems to be that of compliance, i.e., to ensure that monitoring commitments made within the EIS or the EPP are being fulfilled, and not specifically as a means for management. As a result, in some cases data have been collected or recorded but are of little value by way of managing project impacts. For example, in the quarterly monitoring reports generated by the Hibernia Construction Sites Environmental Management Committee (HCSEMC), it is noted that social services caseloads in the area near the Bull Arm construction site have increased during the course of the project. However, it is then stated that these changes cannot be directly attributed to project activities. Thus, while the social services requirements in the area are being monitored, the monitoring is not designed to highlight project-related change. Consequently, the resultant data cannot provide critical feedback concerning actual project outcomes. Such feedback is the primary function of monitoring and is essential for effective project impact management.

In order to overcome some of these problems, changes would have to be made at the terms-of-reference stage which would in turn affect recommendations for monitoring and auditing made in the EIS. The general wording of such a large proportion of EIS predictions in the Hibernia case, as well as other case studies, indicates that the notion of auditing was not a consideration at the time of their writing. Several authors have described the "ideal" prediction for auditing purposes as one which is written in hypothesis format (Beanlands and Duinker, 1983 and Spaling et al., 1993) indicating the magnitude, areal extent, time-scale, probability and significance of the predicted impact (Clark et al., 1987:528; Culhane, 1987a:362 and Tomlinson and Atkinson, 1987b:260). Such a format would work toward the development of the necessary monitoring programs and increase the proportion of auditable predictions as has been the case with the monitoring of Hibernia-related biophysical impacts.[1]

Another issue is that of interpretation of the audit results. As illustrated in Tables 5.2-5.5, there are differences between the predicted and actual values. In some cases these are quite large in terms of percentage values, and in all cases the predictive values are both less and greater than the actual ones. Do these differences make the original predictions 'inaccurate'? How close should the values be in order for them to be considered 'accurate'? Herein lies a problem with respect to the relevance of 'accuracy' and the need to reconsider the current emphasis on it in the EIA process.

The EIA Process: A Different Emphasis

A primary objective of the EIA audits conducted to date has been to evaluate the accuracy of the predictions within the EIS by comparing these to the actual project outcomes. An implicit assumption of this approach is that the activity in question and the environment within which the activity occurs will remain as originally projected. In reality, projects themselves and the context in which they exist are dynamic, and changes in either can make the original predictions irrelevant. This is particularly likely if any considerable time elapses between initial project definition and project completion.

Such has been the case with the Hibernia project, where 16 years have elapsed since field discovery in 1979 and the present. During this period there have been significant changes to the project, in terms of design, the location of activity and implementation plans. Similarly there have been significant and unexpected social and economic changes, particularly those arising from the 1992 fisheries moratoria. These changes have made many of the original EIS predictions irrelevant and consequently any audit based on them inappropriate.

In order to accommodate any project or environment changes, there needs to be a process which is dynamic and adaptive in nature. Given a set of goals and objectives for a project, the EIS must not be seen as the final product but rather as the "first cut" at impact identification and prediction. The predictions within the EIS would be better treated as perishable products with limited shelf-lives that require regular review and replacement. One way of achieving this is to revise the format of the EIS. Clark et al. (1987:537), for example, propose that the EIS assume a loose-leaf form to allow for continual updating through additions and subtractions over the course of the project.

In addition, there may need to be fundamental changes to the way in which predictions are developed and presented. In most cases, Hibernia included, predictions are made during the early stages of the planning process when there exists a high degree of uncertainty with respect to project parameters. There is nonetheless a strong preoccupation with predictive precision, whereby the primary focus is to quantify the demands of the project on the environmental variables in question. A widely held view among EIA practitioners and EIS writers is that the more quantitative and exact, the better the prediction; in Duinker's (1987) view, quantitative prediction is the only one worth having. The spuriously precise predictions which are often produced may have a serious downside by implying a predictive capability that is rarely justified and raise false expectations regarding our ability to manage the biophysical and socioeconomic consequences of our actions.

An alternative approach, which downplays the need for quantitative precision in making socio-economic predictions, involves a shift from what might be described as a 'demand' to a 'capacity' emphasis. Rather than focusing upon the demands that the project will place upon the various components of the environment - the 'unknowns', it might be more appropriate to emphasise the 'known' existing capacities of these environmental components.

To use Hibernia as an example, there was concern that the project would encourage in-migration which in turn would result in an increased demand for housing. The traditional 'demand' approach emphasizes prediction of the number of migrants, their demographic composition and potential demand for housing. Under a capacity approach, an assessment of the housing supply within the area would start by establishing the current housing supply situation and determining the area's housing threshold, i.e., the maximum housing demand that could be accommodated without exceeding the existing supply. The EIA would then assess the project's housing requirements in the light of this threshold value. Rather than attempting to generate precise project demands in the face of uncertainty, it would be sufficient to estimate the order of magnitude of demand relative to existing supply. Housing demands below the threshold value would be considered as project 'effects' requiring no avoidance or mitigative actions, while demands exceeding the threshold would indicate potentially adverse 'impacts' — such as an increase in rental rates and/or land and house prices — requiring mitigative strategies if the project is allowed to proceed.

A shift from a demand to a capacity perspective would result in the emphasis of the EIA moving from impact prediction to impact management. Decisions will still need to be made on the basis of the available evidence as to whether the project should proceed, but if EIA is to be integrated into the broader planning process then more attention needs be given to the goals and objectives that the project is designed to achieve. The complexities of the environments within which any project exist suggest that it is arrogant to imagine that we can accurately and precisely predict eventual outcomes. There is consequently a need to develop strategies that are flexible in order to accommodate such changes in the project and the environment in which the project operates to allow for quick reassessment and modification of predictions.

Under this revised approach to EIA, the format and the role of the EIS would change. Instead of being viewed as a definitive document containing a list of precisely defined predictions, it would be treated as an initial inventory of possible project consequences at that particular point in time. It would outline the thresholds of the various environmental components under consideration, a predicted range of project impacts on these components, as well as an assessment of these predictions relative to the thresholds. The EIS, then, would still remain the basis for the approvals process but it would not be seen as a final product of the EIA process. Rather it would be treated as an ongoing working document to be referred to, reviewed and revised through the entire life of the project. As a result, the emphasis of EIA and the resultant EIS would change from impact prediction to impact management. This would retain the decision-making assistance function of EIA but would be more attuned to the post-decision requirements of managing potential environmental impacts associated with human activities in a context of uncertainty. More importantly, the adoption of the concept of a dynamic EIS would help establish an ongoing feedback link between assessment results and management decisions, thereby integrating EIA into the broader environmental planning process.

Such a shift in emphasis is of equal relevance to impact assessment audits. Given project and environment dynamics, it may be of little value to compare the numerical values of predicted and actual outcomes. Instead it would seem to be more relevant to consider whether the predictions are sufficiently accurate to allow particular socio-economic project objectives to be achieved. Audits which attempt to determine the accuracy of EIA predictions as though the exercise were a business plan or budget seem to have lost sight of the fundamental purposes of environmental assessment and management. These are first to provide decision makers with the information to make decisions, e.g., to allow the project to proceed, and then to provide information that will allow a determination of whether optimization objectives (avoiding or minimizing adverse impacts, and creating or maximizing positive impacts) are being met.

Undertaking a "relevant" audit implies that, at least in the socio-economic context, we must be much more conscious of the purpose of monitoring and more careful about the choice of variables and the measures used. All too often socio-economic monitoring data have proved useful only for compliance purposes but largely irrelevant for project management purposes, policy development or knowledge building (see Storey et al., 1991). Developments in the theoretical and practical aspects of socio-economic impact assessment have usually lagged behind and often followed developments in biophysical EIA. While socio-economic assessment is frequently significantly different from its biophysical counterpart, it may be that we can learn much from the more scientifically rigorous, impact-hypothesis testing approaches used in many biophysical environmental effects monitoring programs. In adopting such an approach, the development of socio-economic "maximum allowable effects levels" ties in closely with the "capacity" approach discussed above.

Conclusion

Over the past 25 years, significant developments have taken place in EIA procedures and methods at the 'front end' of the process, e.g,. in screening and scoping and the identification, prediction and assessment of impacts. However, as this chapter has attempted to show, much still needs to done at the 'back end' or post-approval stage to determine and evaluate the effectiveness of these 'front end' initiatives. EIA auditing and monitoring programs allow for such evaluation. However, the method adopted in socio-economic impact assessment audits conducted to date — a simple accounting framework which calculates and examines the difference between predicted and actual outcomes — is an inadequate approach, given the dynamic nature of projects and the socio-economic context in which they operate. At the end of the day, it's more important that the results of the assessment process promote effective decision making and contribute to the avoidance of the unexpected, the minimization of adverse effects and the enhancement of beneficial project outcomes than it is for EIS predictions to prove accurate. The EIA auditing approach employed to date, however, does not concern itself with such considerations.

Over the past decade, there has been an increased emphasis placed on post-approval activities. Much attention has been given to monitoring and auditing, with the importance and benefit of such follow-up procedures being widely recognized. Monitoring and auditing are essential components of the EIA process if that process is to have credibility. It will not be sufficient, however, to treat these elements independently of other stages in the EIA process. Greater awareness of the need for follow-up is required to ensure that the 'back end' of the process is considered when the 'front end' is being designed.

Notes:

[1]This is in marked contrast to the biophysical monitoring program established to check on environmental impacts at the Bull Arm construction site. Eight environmental indicators were identified and maximum allowable effects levels (MAEL) established for each. Impact hypotheses (i.e., null hypothesis) for each measured variable state that project activities would not elevate the concentration or degree of the variable to a level that exceeds the MAEL for that variable. The monitoring program was designed to collect data to test the hypotheses, and more particularly to detect environmental change well before any changes exceed the acceptable limits (see LGL, 1993:3-4).

References

Barnes, D. (1992) Personal Communications, Ottawa, ON: Federal Environmental Assessment Review Office.

Beanlands, G.E. and Duinker, P.N. (1983) *An Ecological Framework for Environmental Impact Assessment in Canada*, Halifax, NS: Institute for Resource and Environmental Studies, Dalhousie University and Federal Environmental Assessment Review Office.

Bisset, R. (1980) "Problems and issues in the implementation of EIA audits," *Environmental Impact Assessment Review*, 1: 379-396.

Bisset, R. and Tomlinson, P. (1988) "Monitoring and auditing of impacts," in Wathern, P. (ed.), *Environmental Impact Assessment: Theory and Practice*, London, UK: Unwin Hyman, 117-128.

Buckley, R. (1991) *Perspectives in Environmental Planning*, New York, NY: Springer-Verlag Berlin Heidelberg.

Canada (1992) *Bill C-13 An Act to Establish a Federal Environmental Assessment Process*, Ottawa, Ontario.

CEARC (Canadian Environmental Assessment Research Council) (1988) *Evaluating Environmental Impact Assessment: An Action Prospectus*, Ottawa, ON: Ministry of Supply and Services, Canada.

Canter, L.W. (1985) "Impact prediction auditing," *The Environmental Professional*, 7: 255-264.

Clark, B.D., Bisset, R. and Tomlinson, P.   (1987) "Environmental assessment audits in the U.K.: scope, results and lessons for future practice," in Sadler, B. (ed.), *Audit and Evaluation in Environmental Assessment and Management: Canadian and International Experience*, 2 Vols., Proceedings of the Conference on Follow-up/Audit of EIA Results, Ottawa, ON: Ministry of Supplies and Services, Canada, 519-540.

Culhane, P.J. (1987a) "Decision making by voluminous speculation: the contents and accuracy of U.S. environmental impact statements," in Sadler, B. (ed.), *Audit and Evaluation in Environmental Assessment and Management: Canadian and International Experience*, 2 Vols., Proceedings of the Conference on Follow-up/Audit of EIA Results, Ottawa, ON: Ministry of Supplies and Services, 357-378.

_____ (1987b) "The precision and accuracy of U.S. environmental impact statements," *Environmental Monitoring and Assessment*, 8: 217-238.

Davies, M. and Sadler, B. (1990) *Post-project Analysis and the Improvement of Guidelines for Environmental Monitoring and Audit*, Prepared for the Environmental Assessment Division, Conservation and Protection, Ottawa, ON: Environment Canada.

Duinker, P.N. (1987) "Forecasting environmental impacts: better quantitative and wrong than qualitative and untestable!," in Sadler, B. (ed.), *Audit and Evaluation in Environmental Assessment and Management: Canadian and International Experience*, 2 Vols., Proceedings of the Conference on Follow-up/Audit of EIA Results, Ottawa, ON: Ministry of Supplies and Services, 399-407.

Gilmore, J.S., Hammond, D., Moore, K.D., Johnson, J.F. and Coddington, D.C. (1980) "The impacts of power plant construction: a retrospective analysis," *Environmental Impact Assessment Review*, 1: 417-420.

LGL (1993) *The Hibernia GBS Platform Construction Site Marine Environmental Effects Monitoring Program, Year One*, Report prepared for the Hibernia Management and Development Company Ltd., St. John's, NF: LGL Limited.

Locke, J.C. (1996) "Socio-economic auditing: a critique using the case study of the Hibernia Offshore Oil Development Project," Unpublished MA Thesis, St. John's, NF: Department of Geography, Memorial University of Newfoundland.

McCallum, D.R. (1987) "Environmental follow-up to federal projects: a national review," in Sadler, B. (ed.), *Audit and Evaluation in Environmental Assessment and Management: Canadian and International Experience*, 2 Vols., Proceedings of the Conference on Follow-up/Audit of EIA Results, Ottawa, ON: Ministry of Supplies and Services, 731-749.

Mobil (1985) *The Hibernia Environmental Impact Statement, Volume IV - Socio-Economic Impact Assessment*, St. John's, NF: Mobil Oil Canada, Ltd.

Munro, D.A., Bryant, T.J. and Matte-Baker, A. (1986) *Learning From Experience: A State-of-the-Art Review and Evaluation of Environmental Impact Assessment Audits*, Ottawa, ON: Canadian Environmental Assessment Research Council.

Murdock, S.H., Leistritz, F.L., Hamm , R.R. and Sean-Shong Hwang (1982) "An assessment of socioeconomic assessments: utility, accuracy, and policy considerations," *EIA Review*, 3/4: 332-350.

NODECO (Newfoundland Offshore Development Constructors) (1991) *Hibernia Development Project Platform Construction Sites Environmental Protection Plan*, St. John's, Newfoundland.

PASSB (PCL-Aker, Stord-Steen-Becker) (1992) *Hibernia Development Project Platform Construction Site, Topsides Environmental Protection Plan*, St. John's, Newfoundland.

Rigby, B. (1985) "Post-development audits in environmental impact assessment," in Maclaren, V. and Whitney, J.B. (eds.), *New Directions in Environmental Impact Assessment in Canada*, Toronto, ON: Methuen Publications, 179-220.

Ross, W.A. and Tench, G.D. (1987) *CP Rail Rogers Pass Development: A Postproject Analysis*, An unpublished report, Ottawa, ON: Environment Canada.

Sadler, B. (ed.) (1987) *Audit and Evaluation in Environmental Assessment and Management: Canadian and International Experience*, 2 Vols., Proceedings of the Conference on Follow-up/Audit of EIA Results, Ottawa, ON: Ministry of Supplies and Services.

_____ (1988) "The evaluation of assessment: post-EIS research and process development," in Wathern, P. (ed.), *Environmental Impact Assessment: Theory and Practice*, London, UK: Unwin Hyman, 129-142.

Sonntag, N.C. (1987) "Predicting environmental impacts of hydro-electric developments in Canada," in Sadler, B. (ed.), *Audit and Evaluation in Environmental Assessment and Management: Canadian and International Experience*, 2 Vols., Proceedings of the Conference on Follow-up/Audit of EIA Results, Ottawa, ON: Ministry of Supplies and Services 435-453.

Spaling, H., Smit, B. and Kreutzwiser, R. (1993) "Evaluating environmental impact assessment: approaches, lessons and prospects," *Environments*, 22: 63-74.

Storey, K. (1995) "Managing the impacts of Hibernia: a mid-term report," in Mitchell, B. (ed.), *Resource and Environmental Management in Canada: Addressing Conflict and Uncertainty*, Toronto, ON: Oxford University Press, 310-334.

Storey, K., Durst, D., Klein, R. and Shrimpton, M. (1991) *Monitoring for Management: Towards a Process for Managing the Socio-Economic Impacts of Offshore Oil Development in Newfoundland and Labrador*, ISER Offshore Oil Project, Institute of Social and Economic Research, St. John's, NF: Memorial University of Newfoundland.

Tomlinson, P. (1987) "Editorial," *Environmental Monitoring and Assessment*, 8: 183-185.

Tomlinson, P. and Atkinson, S.F. (1987a) "Environmental audits: proposed terminology," *Environmental Monitoring and Assessment*, 8: 187-198.

_____ (1987b) "Environmental audits: a literature review," *Environmental Monitoring and Assessment*, 8: 239-261.

Wood, C. (1995) "Monitoring and auditing of actions," in *Environmental Impact Assessment: A Comparative Review*, Harlow, UK: Longman Scientific and Technical, 197-211.

Woodman, M. (1995) Senior Market Analyst, Canada Mortgage and Housing Corporation (CMHC).

Chapter 6

Environmental Assessment of Non-Project Activities: Assessing Water Contamination by Agriculture[1]

Harry Spaling
The King's University College
and
Bruce MacDonald
Agriculture and Agri-Food Canada

Environmental impact assessment (EIA) is applied most commonly at the project level. There are at least two explanations for this. First, EIA is generally limited by policy or regulation to consider only individual actions of significant magnitude and duration. Project attributes such as size, intensity and timing, among other criteria, are used to include or exclude a proposed action from the formal requirements of an impact assessment (i.e., screening). Generally, only those actions that exceed a predetermined threshold are assessed. An implication of current EIA policy and legislation is that non-project activities are not assessed for their environmental impacts. This is important because non-project activities may disturb large areas of the landscape and be active for long periods of time. Examples include farmland drainage, timber harvesting and growth of urban settlements.

Second, a methodological explanation is that analytical tools for impact analysis are more highly developed for site-specific assessment than regional- or national-scale assessment. This is because spatial considerations are typically confined to local scales, commonly delineated by project or jurisdictional perimeters. Similarly, the temporal dimension is generally characterized by short time frames, usually determined by the project's life cycle with emphasis on the implementation phase. These limited temporal and spatial boundaries generally restrict impact analysis to consideration of immediate effects and site-specific changes. There is a need to develop methods of environmental assessment for application at broader spatial and temporal scales.

This chapter is focused on assessing activities of a non-project nature. These are actions similar in kind that are repeated over time and expansive over space. They are generally characterized by small, independent decisions by numerous individuals. The environmental impact of any one non-project action may be deemed insignificant, but they may accumulate over time and across space as significant cumulative effects. For example, a single farmer makes annual, seasonal and daily decisions regarding the management of a land unit (e.g., amount and timing of fertilizer and pesticide application). Each decision may contribute to an increment of environmental change that is individually insignificant but, repeated over time and dispersed across space by a myriad of farmers, may accumulate and contribute to significant cumulative environmental change (Spaling, 1995).

A method to analyze and assess the cumulative impact of non-project activities is developed in this chapter. Agriculture is selected as the non-project activity. The environmental component of concern is water quality. The method is based on an indicator of risk of water contamination known as IROWC.[2] It uses a partial budget approach representing the change in contaminant levels which result from agricultural activities. IROWC is demonstrated using available data for plant nutrient nitrogen and the triazine group of herbicides at the ecodistrict level in Southern Ontario for 1981-1991.[3]

General Concepts

IROWC is based on three concepts: the notion of risk, priority contaminants, and hierarchical systems.

Risk of Water Contamination

Agriculture is one human activity with potential to contaminate surface and ground water supplies from a non-point source. The potential of agricultural activities to contaminate water can be measured, analyzed and reported as risk (Miller et al., 1992). Risk is characterized by two general attributes (Covello and Merkhofer, 1993):

1. a possibility of an adverse or undesirable outcome, and

2. uncertainty about the occurrence, timing or magnitude of the undesirable outcome.

Both conditions are necessary for risk to occur. In this case, the undesirable outcome is water contamination by agriculture, and uncertainty is related to the probability of coincident occurrence of those factors that affect contamination. These factors are the properties of a contaminant or agent of risk (e.g., solubility, mobility, persistence), environmental attributes (e.g., soil texture, slope, precipitation) and land use and farm management (e.g., crop type, intensity of farm inputs).

The risk of contamination generally differs between surface water and ground water because of dissimilar processes. The risk of surface water contamination is influenced by solution (i.e., runoff, tile flow, base flow) and sediment transport, whereas risk of ground water contamination is affected by leaching below the root zone (i.e., beyond tile depth) and deep percolation.

Thus, the level of risk of water contamination by agriculture may be analyzed and assessed for surface or ground water, or both, given a set of agricultural practices, environmental conditions and contaminant properties.

Priority Contaminants

In general, contaminants originate from farm inputs that are not completely utilized in the production of food or fibre, or are released by decomposition of residual materials (from crops and livestock manures). These inputs differ in their purpose (e.g., addition of plant nutrients, control of pests), and in their physical, chemical and biological properties. This means that the risk of contamination varies for different contaminants. Two contaminants of scientific and public concern are residues from pesticides and nitrogen fertilizer.

There is evidence to suggest that the risk of pesticides as a water contaminant has decreased because pesticides have evolved from general biocides with limited selectivity and high persistence to highly selective and concentrated forms with relatively rapid breakdown (Environment Canada, 1991). Management practices have also changed from routine use to application only when pest infestation exceeds a threshold level. Applying IROWC to pesticides may demonstrate the reduced risk of advanced and properly managed pesticides.

Nitrogen is an essential plant nutrient applied in organic (e.g., manure) and inorganic (e.g., fertilizer) forms. Nitrogen uptake by crops reduces the amount available for contamination, but the risk of water contamination still may be high because crop requirements and the amount and timing of nutrient application are rarely synchronized. For example, availability of fertilizer nitrogen usually exceeds crop needs at early stages of plant growth (e.g., spring) and again during post-harvest as crop residues break down and release nutrients back into the environment. The risk of contamination is also increased because nitrogen is ubiquitous, has anionic forms, and undergoes various chemical and biological transformations in the environment. For these reasons, IROWC is used to assess the risk of water contamination from nitrogen.

Hierarchical Systems

Hierarchy theory organizes complex ecological problems into manageable units of space and time while retaining a holistic approach to problem solving (Allen and Starr, 1982; Dumanski et al., 1993; Kay, 1993). This theory may be used to structure the problem of defining the risk of water contamination into a series of nested levels. Each level within a nested hierarchy is delineated by spatial and temporal boundaries. Different ecological factors and processes may predominate and constrain each level. Scale defines the entities, structures and processes that are operational at each level.

A system of hierarchical levels for IROWC is shown in Table 6.1. A nested hierarchy is developed for the major contaminants at risk (i.e., nutrients, pesticides), and for each of the main factors affecting risk of water contamination (i.e., climate, soils, land use, management). Each level of the hierarchy is defined by spatial and temporal scales.

The factors that affect water contamination are likely to differ in their relative importance, or degree of interaction, at each level. Those factors most likely to be differentiated and associated at each level are shown in Table 6.2. The type and number of factors incorporated into IROWC increases as spatial and temporal resolution also increases within the hierarchy. Thus, the sensitivity and reliability of IROWC increases with downward movement through the hierarchical levels.

Table 6.1

Hierarchical Levels for the Indicator of Risk of Water Contamination (IROWC)

Hierarchical Level	General agent of risk	Specific agent of risk	Management	Land Use	Climate	Soils, Topography, Drainage	Processes
Level 7 National Environment Strategy for Agriculture	Broad agro-environmental indicators						
Level 6 National Scale: 1:7,500,000 to 1:5,000,000 Time: 10 to 5 years	**Plant Nutrients (N and P)** **Pesticides**	-Fertilizer -animal wastes		**agricultural intensity - proportion of farmland in crop**	temperate (normals data)		
Level 5 Regional provincial or ecozone (Mixed Woods Plain) 1:5,000,000 to 1:1,000,000 Time: 5 to 1 year	Plant Nutrients (N and P) Pesticides	**-fertilizer -animal wastes -urban sources Classes of herbicides Classes of pesticides**	general levels of intensity and contiguity; general management and conservation practices	**general practices - cash crop-ping, summerfal-low livestock; general class of crop e.g. grain corn, spring wheat**	**Meso or small order Macro (e.g. monthly or seasonal rainfall and moisture deficits)**		
Level 4 Major drainage basin or ecological region (Lake Erie low-lands) 1:1,000,000 to 1:250,000 Time: annual to seasonal	Plant Nutrients (N and P) Herbicides Insecticides Nematocides	-fertilizer -animal wastes by livestock enterprise -urban and rural by specific centres Groups of similar compounds e.g. phe-noxy	**mix of manage-ment practices (e.g. con-ventional and no-till), general times of field opera-tions**	**mix of farming systems with defined crops and rotations**	**Meso (e.g. monthly or daily climate including spatial and temporal variability across the area)**	Great groups, associations thereof; Broad groups of texture and parent material **Topography and drainage**	-Surface water by runoff; -Surface water by sediment; -ground water

The items in bold represent constraints which have been added at the various hierarchical levels. The complete set of constraints at any level include those in bold and all the bold constraints from the higher levels. In some cases, the constraints represent increased specificity of a particular kind of constraint; in other cases they are additional kinds of constraints.

Table 6.1 (continued)
Hierarchical Levels for the Indicator of Risk of Water Contamination (IROWC)

Hierarchical Level	General agent of risk	Specific agent of risk	Management	Land Use	Climate	Soils, Topography, Drainage	Processes
Level 3 Watersheds (Lower Thames River watershed) 1:250,000 to 1:50,000 Time: seasonal to monthly	Plant nutrients (N and P) Herbicides Insecticides Biological pathogens	-**fertilizer general amounts of specific carriers** -**specific kinds of operations** -**specific pesticides** -**livestock source** -**wildlife source (e.g. gulls)** -**human source**	specific mix of tillage operations, input sources and methods of application	-specific mix of farming systems, crop types and rotations	Meso to small order micro (e.g. daily data on climate events)	**Subgroups or associations thereof. Limited ranges of texture class and parent materials**	Surface water, by water course for solution and sediment -ground water related to specific aquifers -general information on the **extent of subsurface tile drains**
Level 2 Farm/Field scale (farm unit, ecosite) 1:50,000 to 1:5000 Time: monthly to daily	Plant Nutrients (N and P) Pesticides Biological pathogens	-**source, form, and amounts for fertilizer amendments and/or animal wastes Specific compounds, rates etc.** source for human and livestock -localized area for wild	specifics of timing, equipment, conservation tillage, buffer strips, etc.	specifics of farming operation, crop type and variety by land management parcel	Micro - **specifics of events daily or smaller time steps as required**	Families of related soils to soil series (specific textures of surface and parent material, known mixture of soil profiles)	-Surface runoff, tile flow, base flow -wind erosion vs water erosion -ground water levels to specific depths and connected to known aquifers -water retained in the soil and used by plants
Level 1 Plot scale (experimental plot, ecoelement) 1:5000 to 1:1000 Time: daily to hourly	as above	as above	as above with specific experimental treatment(s)	as above with specific experimental treatment(s)	small order micro	Soil series or homogeneous soil (to the extent possible)	-**runoff, sediment & tile flow by field** -**ground water** -**flow paths** -**soil reaction, -specific processeses e.g. rill vs sheet erosion**

Table 6.2

Hierarchical Levels and Spatial and Temporal Resolution for IROWC

Hierarchical Level	Spatial Extent	Spatial Analysis	Temporal Extent	IROWC Sensitivity/Resolution
Level 7	Canada	Canada	decades to centuries	comprehensive analysis
Level 6	Canada	Province	decades to centuries	population, livestock numbers, kinds of crops, extents and quantities of inputs
Level 5	Ecozone	Ecodistrict	5 years to decades	relative risks from nutrients and pesticides
Level 4	Ecoregion	SLC polygon	5 to 10 years	relative risks by specific nutrient and class of pesticide associated with specific crops and soil textures
Level 3	Ecodistricts or Subwatersheds	SLC polygon or detailed soil map	1 to 5 years	relative risks by specific nutrient and class of pesticide associated with specific crops, soil types and pathways (surface or groundwater)
Level 2	SLC Polygon or farm	detailed soil map polygon or field	season to 5 years	estimated actual risks associated with specific crop, soil and land management conditions with estimates for surface and subsurface pathways
Level 1	Field or detailed soil map polygon	plot area or pedon (soil profile)	season to 5 years	measured/modeled/actual risks associated with specific crop, soil and land management conditions partitioned to surface and subsurface pathways

SLC = Soil Landscape of Canada

Methodological Considerations

Hydrology

Excess water plays a fundamental role in ascertaining the level of risk of contamination. It determines the quantity of water available for dilution of contaminants, and their movement to water resources (surface or ground).

A water balance approach can be used to determine the quantity of excess water which is available to transport any residual amount of a contaminant. Ideally, the water balance of an area is represented by the difference between precipitation (P) and actual evapotranspiration (AE). However, data for AE are frequently lacking. It is possible to determine a crude water balance at any location based on annual or seasonal values of P and potential evapotranspiration (PE). When P exceeds PE, surplus moisture is assumed to exist and water accumulates in the soil until field capacity is reached. Any further excess is available as surface water (i.e., runoff, subsurface tile flow) or ground water recharge. When P<PE, a water deficit occurs, and there is no surplus moisture available.

A water balance approach can contribute to the proposed methodology in three ways. First, data on excess water can be distributed over time throughout the year. Seasonal or monthly values of water surplus or deficit can be calculated, and analyzed against the temporal distribution of excess nitrogen or pesticide residue. Second, the variation between years can be assessed. Third, the water balance approach partitions output flow into surface (e.g., runoff, seepage) and ground water (e.g., infiltration, deep percolation) components. Data on the proportion of flow through each pathway are needed to analyze and assess the risk of contamination according to destination.

Agriculture is directly dependent on the hydrological cycle (e.g., soil moisture for crops and drinking water for livestock), but agriculture also alters the cycle, particularly the transfer mechanisms and pathways of flow. For example, tillage practices affect infiltration rates; crop type and planting pattern influence runoff; and, land drainage impacts percolation and lateral flow. These impacts become increasingly important at lower spatial and temporal scales. Thus, calculation of excess water at these scales needs to account for the effects of land management on the water balance of an agricultural area.

While the pathways of the hydrologic cycle are reasonably well understood, reliable quantitative estimates of the magnitude of flows in specific components are rare.

Nutrients

Nitrogen cycles in intensive, arable agriculture are generally characterized by the addition of nitrogen via fertilizer, animal manures or decomposing crop residues, and the removal of nitrogen in the harvested crop and cover crops. Other inputs include atmospheric deposition and nitrogen fixation, while losses occur through leaching, denitrification and immobilization.

Nitrogen in the form of fertilizer and manures often constitutes a large fraction of the total nitrogen input in intensive, arable agriculture. Generally, crops respond positively to increased fertilizer and manure inputs, but this response also increases nitrogen removed in the harvested material. Losses via leaching are also usually higher with increasing nitrogen input. As fertilizer nitrogen is increased, the efficiency of nitrogen use is decreased (i.e., percentage of total fertilizer nitrogen taken up by the plant declines). Nitrogen use efficiencies for crops have been broadly estimated at 50-60% (e.g., Briggs and Courtney, 1989; Juergens-Gschwind, 1989). This means that a considerable quantity of nitrogen not taken up by plants is potentially available for leaching or other dissipation pathways of the nitrogen cycle. The amount can be inferred from the current crop production recommendations, the amounts harvested in crop yields, and survey information about the amounts produced or sold.

Pesticides

An ideal approach to analyzing the risk of pesticide contamination first determines the quantity of a pesticide, and its chemical derivatives in the soil, and then ascertains the susceptibility of these chemicals to various transport and transformation processes (Mackay, 1992). Following application, a pesticide is partitioned into various phases (e.g., vapour in soil air, asorbed by organic matter, solution in soil water). Of particular concern is the amount partitioned in mobile soil water, which represents the quantity potentially available for leaching or surface runoff. The proportion directed toward leaching can be relatively high for herbicides such as atrazine. The risk of surface transport (in solution or attached to eroding soil particles) is especially high if rainfall closely follows pesticide application.

Quantitative models of chemical fate in soil have been used to estimate the amount of a pesticide partitioned in soil water (e.g., PRZM, LEACHM) (Ecologistics Limited, 1993; de Jong et al., 1994). These models are generally site-specific and applicable only at lower hierarchical levels (levels 1-3). Their data demands are extensive. At higher levels (e.g., levels 3-5), understanding of and data on partitioning, transformation and transport are lacking, but information is available on pesticide inputs (e.g., recommended application rates by crop, surveys of pesticide use).

Proposed Budget Model for IROWC

IROWC is based on a partial budget (i.e., input-output) model. This is part of a broader methodological approach that integrates the budget model with other tools (e.g., GIS) and approaches (e.g., spatial analysis of risk). The essential function of the model is to calculate the flow-weighted mean concentration of each potential contaminant for comparison with an appropriate standard (e.g., drinking water).

The Potential Contaminant Concentration (PCC) consists of two parts: i) determination of the Potential Contaminant Present (PCP) in mg/ha, and ii) calculation of Excess Water (EW) in L/ha, representing the available quantity of surplus water. Thus:

$$PCC_c = \frac{PCP \ (mg/ha)}{EW \ (L/ha)} \tag{1}$$

c = contaminant type (e.g., nitrogen, triazine)
PCP = f(crop type, input rates, soil, management, etc.)
EW = f(precipitation, evaporation, crop moisture use (yield)).

At each level of the hierarchy, the differentiating characteristics and associated factors are incorporated into the determination of the amount or potential contaminant present (PCP). For example:

$PCP_5 =$ f(crop type, crop area, nitrogen in fertilizer and manure, nitrogen in harvested crop, herbicide class (e.g., triazine)).

The calculated value is a **relative** indication where the non-crop or unmanaged state is 0 and risk increases in proportion to nitrogen content of the harvested crops or level of pesticide use.

$PCP_2 =$ f(all information and constraints from higher levels plus crop rotations, soil texture, subsurface drainage, conservation practices, specific pesticide, etc.).

The calculated value is the **quantity** in mg/ha for the specific contaminant.

Where 5 and 2 correspond to levels of the hierarchy (Table 6.2).

IROWC is characterized as the ratio of the average PCC to the concentration allowable to maintain a desired standard (e.g., drinking water). Thus:

$$IROWCc = \frac{PCC_c \text{ mg/L}}{\text{Maximum Allowable concentration (mg/L)}_c} \qquad (2)$$

Ideally, this calculation would be carried out for each (precipitation) event which constitutes a risk for water contamination. In practice, this will only be possible at the most detailed level of assessment. The hierarchical levels at which the indicator is required (Table 6.2) determine the kinds of data available and the detail and precision which can be achieved.

In hierarchical fashion, we can start at the highest level and determine the constraints, and then consider lower levels within these. For example, it is feasible to characterize IROWC at the ecoregion or ecodistrict level (levels 5-4). The proportion of the ecoregion or ecodistrict occupied by various crops can be determined. At these levels, only a relative indicator based on annual average conditions can be estimated. It is sensitive to changes in crop type, crop area, livestock density and climate. It is not feasible to incorporate "friendly" practices (e.g., minimum tillage, crop rotation) because it is not possible to associate them with specific crops (Table 6.1).

At lower levels (levels 1-3), the indicator will more nearly reflect **actual** conditions. It will require many more types of data in much greater detail to incorporate spatial variability in soil, topography and drainage; the degree of adoption of "friendly" practices, and more specific details of climate. Temporal sensitivity is also better at lower levels allowing for calculations of risk on a monthly or event basis.

With the calculation of IROWC on the basis of soil units (e.g., soil landscape polygon for level 3, detailed soil maps for level 2, and on-site soil characterization for level 1), it should also be possible to partition the risk of contamination into surface or subsurface water and possibly, tile drainage water. In addition, with movement from highest to lowest levels, the probability of coincident occurrence (the certainty that the specific crop is grown on a known soil type using particular tillage practices, etc.) increases, thereby enhancing the level of confidence for the estimate.

Application of IROWC

Ideally, IROWC would be implemented at all hierarchical levels. In reality, it is only possible to determine all parameters required at the lower levels. At the higher levels only a relative IROWC rating is possible based on the principles outlined; namely, an estimate of the amount of potential contaminant(s) available, the amount of excess water and the amount which could be accommodated within the standards of concern. Furthermore, it is only at the lower levels that the calculations can be verified by field observations. There is benefit in building confidence in, and validating, the procedure by verifying the lower levels through direct observation and using these results for comparing and verifying the higher levels.

This application of IROWC should be considered a preliminary demonstration due to data constraints and the preliminary nature of the methodology. Only a relative indicator based on annual average conditions is estimated. Notwithstanding the preliminary nature of this demonstration, the application indicates the kinds of information that are required, the type of resolution that can be achieved, and the levels of effort and detail that are needed to calculate actual indicators of risk of water contamination.

For this demonstration, IROWC is applied at the ecodistrict level (level 5-4) for the Southern Ontario region. At this level or higher, spatial units are so large that the land use and management practices cannot be associated with specific soils, topography and drainage systems. Consequently, it is not possible to partition the IROWC between surface and ground water. Variations in specific land management practices, or variation throughout the year or between years, can be incorporated but are not illustrated in this demonstration.

The nutrient nitrogen, and the herbicides atrazine and simazine, are the contaminants for which IROWC is calculated. The moisture conditions were estimated from climatic normals data for 1951-80. These data were extracted from the Land Potential Data Base (Kirkwood et al., 1983) and associated with ecodistrict and soil landscape of Canada (SLC) polygons by taking the largest area of overlap. A geographical information system (GIS) was used for spatial analyses.

Calculations

The relative annual excess water (REW) or deficit was calculated from the annual precipitation (P) and the potential evaporation (PE), using 1951-80 climatic normals data, as:

$$REW = Annual (P - PE) \tag{3}$$

It is recognized that this approach to calculating annual excess water is not without problems. Actual evapotranspiration (AE) is only a fraction of PE for most conditions of crop and soil (e.g., prairies). This means that the above approach may underestimate annual excess water. However, the approach is maintained because it is difficult to obtain data for AE at broad scales for a mix of crops. A related problem is basing spatial screening on a single criterion (i.e., REW). For example, it is possible to have both a small REW and a large potential contaminant concentration (PCC). The criterion of EW is maintained over concentration because the fundamental matter of concern is water transport of the contaminant. This does not imply that the steady accumulation of a contaminant under dry conditions and over the long term (e.g., geologic nitrate) is not important, but rather that its potential for transport to surface or ground water is significantly reduced.

Ideally, PCC should incorporate variation in nutrient uptake efficiency and time of uptake for each crop, as well as the temporal variability of excess water. Thus:

$$PCC = \frac{f(\text{crop type, nutrient uptake efficiency, time of uptake})}{\text{excess water } f(\text{time period}) \times \text{crop area}} \quad (4)$$

Data constraints and the comprehensiveness of the analysis resulted in a simplified version of this equation for the purposes of this demonstration. This analysis used mean annual values for P and PE (1951-1980 climatic normals) to estimate REW, and a mean nutrient uptake efficiency of 60% for all crops over the entire growing season (see below).

Based on the above rationale, the following series of equations were used to estimate IROWC at the ecodistrict levels for Southern Ontario:

$$RPCC_N = \frac{\sum_{ED} \text{Crop Area}_{by\ crop} \times \text{Nitrogen Harvested}_{by\ crop}{}^4}{REW \times \text{total crop area}} \quad (5)$$

$$RPCC_M = \frac{\sum_{ED} \text{Nitrogen in Manure} \times 0.1}{REW \times \text{total crop area}} \quad (6)$$

$$RPCC_H =$$
$$\frac{\sum_{ED} \text{Crop Area}_{by\ crop} \times \text{Average rate for herbicides}_{by\ crop}}{REW \times \text{total crop area}} \quad (7)$$

$RPCC_{Ha} =$

$$\frac{RPCC_H \times (P\text{-}PE)_{May} + (P\text{-}PE)_{June} \times 0.5 + (P\text{-}PE)_{July} \times 0.25}{(\text{Annual Precipitation} - PE \text{ from } 1951\text{-}80 \text{ climatic normals})} \quad (8)$$

where,

RPCC = relative potential contaminant concentration for nitrogen in the harvested crop (N), long-term nitrogen from manure (M), herbicide (H), herbicide concentration adjusted for the susceptible time (month) for transport (Ha) for each ecodistrict (ED)

Three additional considerations were included in these equations:

1. Data on nitrogen use efficiency plotted against proportion of optimum yield (Sander et al., 1994) show an efficiency of 40-60% for corn. Data from Europe (Juergens-Gschwind, 1989) also suggest a nitrogen use efficiency of 60% and further indicate the other sink terms for the additional nitrogen (e.g., denitrification, soil biomass, transport off-site by water). This implies that the quantity available for other pathways is approximately equivalent to the Nitrogen Harvested (equation 6). This efficiency is assumed for all crops.

2. Nitrogen values for manure vary over time. Generally, 50% of the total manure nitrogen (75% for poultry) applied in the spring is available in the year of application. In the second year approximately 10% of the remaining nitrogen becomes available, 5% in the third year. For this calculation, the nitrogen during the year of application is included in the estimate based on harvested crop. For subsequent years a factor of 10% is used to account for the long-term value and also for the nitrogen lost from manure applied (equation 7).

3. For herbicides, equation 8 is adjusted by the proportion
    of the excess moisture in May, June and July as these
    are the times the herbicide will be most susceptible to
    transport. These monthly figures are further weighed
    (1.0, 0.5 and 0.25 respectively) to account for declining
    susceptibility to movement off-site. After this time it is
    assumed to have been degraded by natural processes.
    Atrazine and simazine are aggregated as triazines, and
    specific properties of individual herbicides (e.g., solubil-
    ity, half-life, partitioning coefficient) are not considered
    at levels 4-5.

Finally, IROWC provides a measure of the relative
amount by which the current water quality standards are
exceeded (equation 2). The current drinking water standard
for nitrogen is 10 mg/L and the standard for atrazine is
0.005 mg/L, and for simazine is 0.01 mg/L. The latter standard is used to calculate IROWC for herbicides.

Spatial Analyses

Spatial analyses of the above parameters were conducted
using GIS. Figure 6.1 shows the change between 1981 and
1991 in relative potential contaminant concentration for
nitrogen, based only on levels harvested in the crop, for
ecodistricts in Southern Ontario. Results are reported in
units of mg/L with the range going from a decrease of 5 or
less to an increase of 5 or more. In general, the results are
quite encouraging for much of the province showing no
change or a slight decline in potential contamination of
water by nitrogen from crop sources. The greatest increase
is indicated in the ecodistrict which occupies north
Middlesex and the western portion of Huron Counties (west
of Toronto). In addition, there is some indication of an
increase in Eastern and Southern Ontario, as well as the
northern fringe.

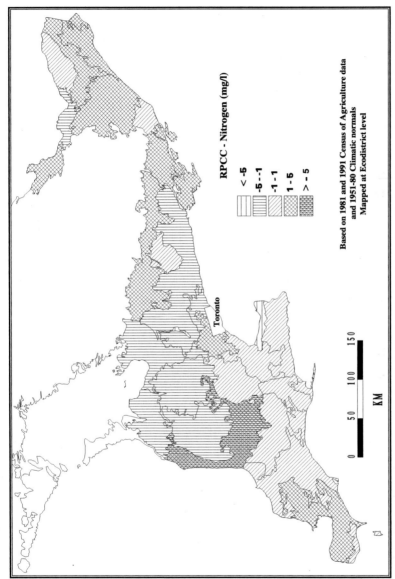

Figure 6.1: IROWC - Change in Relative Potential Contaminant Concentration (RPCC) in Southern Ontario — Nitrogen (crop) 1981 - 91

The ratio of the relative potential contaminant concentration (RPCC) to the maximum concentration allowed by current drinking water quality standards provides an indication of risk (equation 2). The provincial standard for nitrogen is 10 mg/L. The risk of contamination from nitrogen relative to the acceptable water quality standard for 1991 is shown in Figure 6.2. Nitrogen sources include both crop production and residual amounts from previous manure applications. Risk of water contamination from these sources is the highest in ecodistricts of Southwestern Ontario.

Similar to nitrogen, the relative risk of contamination may also be calculated for potential herbicide (triazine) concentration and its associated drinking water standard. The Ontario standard is 0.01 mg/L for simazine, which is used here for all triazine herbicides. The relative risk ratio for triazine and water quality standard for 1993 is displayed in Figure 6.3. Like nitrogen, the highest relative risk is also in Southwestern Ontario with moderate risk in adjacent ecodistricts. Risk generally declines in eastern and northern ecodistricts. In these regions, triazine use (as atrazine) is significantly less because climatic conditions are not as suitable for corn.

The spatial distribution of risk of water contamination by nitrogen and herbicides generally reflects the geographic pattern of agriculture in Ontario. Ecodistricts with relatively high risk are typically characterized by intensive production of row and specialty crops, and livestock. These crops are usually associated with higher rates of application of nitrogen fertilizer and herbicide. Intensive livestock farming generates large quantities of manure for disposal, resulting in relatively high rates of land application. Overall, ecodistricts with relatively high nitrogen input and herbicide use are associated with increased relative risk of water contamination.

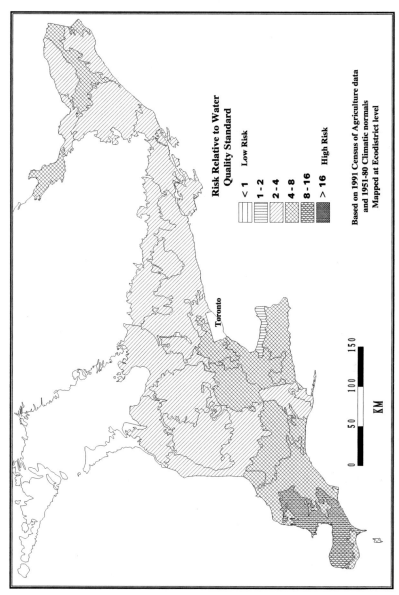

Figure 6.2: IROWC - Relative Risk of Contamination in Southern Ontario Nitrogen (crop and residual manure) 1991

Risk Relative to Water Quality Standard

< 1   Low Risk
1 - 2
2 - 4
4 - 8
8 - 16
> 16   High Risk

Based on 1991 Census of Agriculture data and 1951-80 Climatic normals
Mapped at Ecodistrict level

Toronto

0   50   100   150

KM

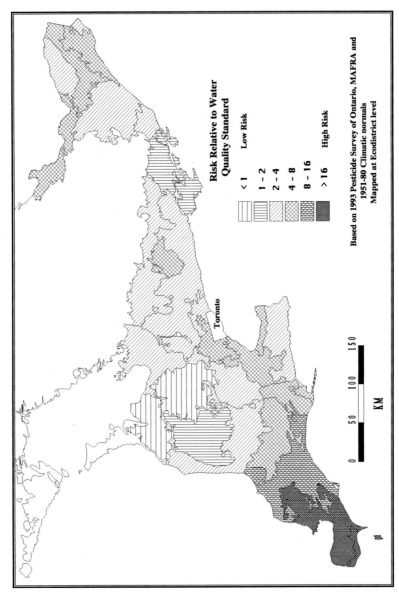

Figure 6.3: IROWC - Relative Risk of Contamination in Southern Ontario Triazine 1993

Conclusion

Non-project activities are generally exempted from policies and legislation governing EIA. Consequently, environmental effects of these activities remain largely unassessed and unknown. There is a need to develop tools that can be used to analyze and assess the environmental changes attributable to non-project activities. Information generated by these tools may contribute to more effective environmental assessment of all human activities, projects and non-projects alike.

Agriculture is one non-project activity that is likely to continue to impact valued environmental components such as water quality. This chapter has proposed an indicator of risk of water contamination (IROWC) to assess the probability of water contamination from agriculture. Conceptually, the methodology is based on:

1. a hierarchical framework that organizes and classifies the various components of IROWC into a series of nested hierarchies defined by temporal and spatial attributes.

2. a risk-based approach, in which risk is a function of i) contaminant properties, ii) environmental attributes (e.g., soil, climate), and iii) management and land use.

3. integration into IROWC of the risk factors and the probability of their coincident occurrence or reliability.

4. a unit of expression that measures change in risk over time and across space, relative to some acceptable level of water quality (e.g., drinking water standard).

Demonstration of IROWC at the ecodistrict level in Southern Ontario showed temporal and spatial variation in the risk of water contamination from nitrogen and atrazine.

IROWC successfully integrated key factors that affect the risk of water contamination from agriculture (e.g., soil and landscape properties, amount and distribution of precipitation, intensity of inputs, crop type). It is data demanding and subject to the limited resolution and availability of data sets (e.g., climate, soils). For this reason, IROWC requires further testing, particularly at lower hierarchical levels where other related research is underway and where some data constraints may be overcome.

IROWC has operational utility because it allows for spatial comparison and temporal analysis of the factors affecting risk of water contamination. Changes in land management and production practices are readily incorporated into the methodology. Data requirements are extensive, but it uses existing or obtainable information. A map of the risk of water contamination is easily communicated to policy and decision makers.

Water quality is an important policy issue for agriculture. This issue is best addressed at the regional scale. Incremental changes to water quality at the field or farm scale generally accumulate at broader temporal and spatial scales. The cumulative response of water quality to various agricultural activities can be investigated at the level of the ecodistrict. Results can be used to formulate agri-environmental policies at the ecodistrict level.

Targeting specific geographic areas is an important factor in implementing policy. Information provided by IROWC may facilitate the targeting of remedial policies and programs to those ecodistricts characterized by a higher relative risk of contamination from agriculture. IROWC may also be used to evaluate the effectiveness of policies and programs for reducing the risk of water contamination from agricultural activities for any ecodistrict over time.

For example, data that compare the risk of water contamination from conventional and conservation tillage can be used to identify best management practices for protecting water quality and reducing pollution. This information could be incorporated into a policy initiative such as a national soil and water conservation program, or a more regional initiative aimed at environmental farm plans. Over time, as best management practices are implemented, changes in the risk of water contamination associated with tillage can be measured and reported by IROWC. In this way, IROWC can contribute to targeting and evaluating remedial policies for water quality.

The indicator of risk of water contamination developed and applied here can be used to identify ecodistricts where agri-environmental policy to protect and restore water quality are most needed. This contribution should be helpful for achieving a more environmentally sustainable agriculture.

Notes:
[1]This chapter is based on two earlier reports by MacDonald and Spaling (1995a, 1995b).
[2]IROWC is one of several indicators currently under development by Agriculture and Agri-Food Canada to monitor environmental impacts of agricultural activities (see McRae et al., 1995).
[3]An ecodistrict is a spatial unit of the ecological land classification system in Canada with a typical scale of 1:3,000,000 - 1:1,000,000 (Ecological Stratification Working Group, 1996).
[4]The calculation determines the average quantity of nitrogen harvested per hectare of cropped land in an ecodistrict based on the following levels of nitrogen in the harvested crop: corn, grain and silage - 175 kg/ha; soybeans and white beans - 150 kg/ha; barley - 45 kg/ha; spring wheat - 55 kg/ha; winter wheat - 85 kg/ha; fall and spring rye and oats - 35 kg/ha; alfalfa and other tame hay - 200 kg/ha.

Acknowledgements

We acknowledge the technical input of the Water Contamination Risk Team of the Agri-environmental Indicator Project of Agriculture and Agri-Food Canada, the GIS analysis and map preparation by Fenghui Wang, and the helpful comments of Hank Bestman and anonymous reviewers.

References

Allen, T.F.H. and Starr, T.B. (1982) *Hierarchy: Perspectives for Ecological Complexity*, Chicago, IL: University of Chicago Press.

Briggs, D. and Courtney, F. (1989) *Agriculture and Environment: The Physical Geography of Temperate Agriculture Systems*, Harlow, UK: Longman Scientific and Technical.

Covello, V. and Merkhofer, M. (1993) *Risk Assessment Methods: Approaches for Assessing Heath and Environmental Risks*, New York, NY: Plenum Press.

de Jong, R., Reynolds, W.D., Vieira, S.R. and Clements, R.S. (1994) *Predicting Pesticide Migration through Soils of the Great Lakes Basin*, Centre for Land and Biological Resources Research, CLBRR Contribution No. 94-70, Ottawa, ON: Agriculture and Agri-Food Canada.

Dumanski, J., Pettapiece, W., Acton, D. and Claude, P. (1993) "Application of agro-ecological concepts and hierarchy theory in the design of databases for spatial and temporal characterization of land and soil," *Goderma*, 60: 343-358.

Ecological Stratification Working Group (1996) *A National Ecological Framework for Canada*, Centre for Land and

Biological Resources Research Branch, Agriculture and Agri-Food Canada and State of the Environment Directorate, Ottawa, ON: Environment Canada, Minister of Supply and Services.

Ecologistics Limited (1993) *Assessing the State of the Agricultural Resources - Wilmot Township and the Town of Whitchurch-Stouffville*, Draft report prepared for Agriculture and Agri-Food Canada (Guelph), Waterloo, ON: Ecologistics Limited.

Environment Canada (1991) *The State of Canada's Environment*, Ottawa, ON: Environment Canada.

Juergens-Gschwind, S. (1989) "Ground water nitrates in other developed countries (Europe) - relationships to land use patterns", in Follett, R.F. (ed.), *Nitrogen Management and Ground Water Protection*, Amsterdam: Elsevier, 75-138.

Kay, J. (1993) "On the nature of ecological integrity: some closing comments," in Woodley, S., Kay, J. and Francis, G. (eds.), *Ecological Integrity and the Management of Ecosystems*, St. Lucie Press, 201-212.

Kirkwood, V., Dumanski, J., Bootsma, A., Stewart, R.B. and Muma, R. (1983) *The Land Potential Database for Canada (revised 1989)*, LRRC Technical Bulletin 1983-4E, Ottawa, ON: Research Branch, Agriculture Canada.

MacDonald, B. and Spaling, H. (1995a) *Indicator of Risk of Water Contamination: Concepts and Principles*, Prepared for the Water Contamination Risk Team of the Agri-environmental Indicator Project, Guelph, ON: Agriculture and Agri-Food Canada, Ontario Land Resource Unit.

_____ (1995b) *Indicator of Risk of Water Contamination: Methodological Development*, Prepared for the Water

Contamination Risk Team of the Agri-environmental Indicator Project, Guelph, ON: Agriculture and Agri-Food Canada, Ontario Land Resource Unit.

Mackay, D. (1992) "A perspective on the fate of chemicals in soils", in Miller, M. et al. (eds.), *Agriculture and Water Quality*, Proceedings of an Interdisciplinary Symposium, Guelph, ON: Centre for Soil and Water Conservation, University of Guelph, 1-11.

McRae, T., Hillary, N., MacGregor, R.J. and Smith, C.A.S. (1995) *Design and Development of Environmental Indicators With Reference to Canadian Agriculture*, Paper presented to the North American Workshop on Monitoring for Ecological Assessment of Terrestrial and Aquatic Ecosystems, Mexico City, September 1995, Ottawa, ON: Agriculture and Agri-Food Canada.

Miller, M.H., FitzGibbon, J.E., Fox, G.C., Gillham, R.W. and Whiteley, H.R. (eds.) (1992) *Agriculture and Water Quality*, Proceedings of an Interdisciplinary Symposium, Guelph, ON: University of Guelph.

Sander, D.H., Walters, D.T. and Frank, K.D. (1994) "Nitrogen testing for optimum management", *Journal of Soil and Water Conservation: Nutrient Management Special Supplement*, 49: 46-52.

Spaling, H. (1995) "Analyzing cumulative environmental effects of agricultural land drainage in Southern Ontario, Canada", *Agriculture, Ecosystems & Environment*, 53: 279-292.

Chapter 7

Strategic Environmental Assessment and Regional Planning: Practical Experience from the National Capital Commission

E. Nicholas Novakowski and Barry Wellar
University of Ottawa

This chapter reports on the application of strategic environmental assessment (SEA) to the National Capital Commission's *Plan for Canada's Capital*, a strategic regional land-use plan concerning the federal presence (e.g., land holdings and real assets) in the National Capital Region (NCR). To date, four activity stages of SEA — needs justification, scoping, additional policy alternatives and prediction — have been made operational at the National Capital Commission (NCC) and are the focus of attention here. It is intended that this overview of the NCC experience may provide assistance to other agencies and interested parties in their efforts to apply SEA principles and practices to planning processes and products.

The National Capital Region

The National Capital Region approximates the geographical boundaries of the Ottawa-Hull Census Metropolitan Area or CMA. With a metropolitan population exceeding one million in 1996, the Ottawa-Hull CMA is the fourth largest CMA in Canada and the only one to cross provincial boundaries (Statistics Canada, 1997). The NCR is also a complex jurisdiction for land-use planning since 28 local governments, three regional governments, and several federal agencies are involved in decisions about what goes where.

The National Capital Commission

The National Capital Commission is a federal Crown Corporation. The *National Capital Act* empowers the NCC "to acquire and dispose of properties; construct and maintain parks, parkways, bridges and other structures; cooperate with local municipalities, public and private agencies in joint projects; administer, preserve and maintain historic places; and carry out planning related to proper development of public lands in the National Capital Region" (NCC, 1991:32). The NCC retains land-use approval power for all initiatives on federal lands in the NCR.

Background to the Plan for Canada's Capital

The *Plan for Canada's Capital* is a strategic regional prescription for the federal presence in the NCR in two major respects. First, it presents the federal perspective on the types and amounts of real assets — land, parkways, parks, buildings, bridges, statuary — that the Government of Canada should own or provide in the Capital. And, second, it provides the federal vision concerning the prescribed uses and functions to be associated with federal assets.

Background to Strategic Environmental Assessment

Emphasis in this paper is on the *application* of strategic environmental assessment (SEA) within the NCC during the plan formulation stages of the new *Plan for Canada's Capital*. As a result, a detailed discussion of the genesis and elaboration of SEA concepts, methods and procedures is not included. In the interests of completeness, however, it is appropriate and instructive to present several fundamental considerations which underlie this case study treatment of SEA. Readers wishing to pursue the fundamentals in depth are invited to examine the selected references.

First, strategic environmental assessment is a combination of three complex domains: assessment, which is one of many types of inquiry; environment, which is one of many research domains; and, strategy or the strategic, which is one of several domains wherein or whereby governments or other agents can choose to act or not to act with respect to plans, policies, programmes, and/or projects. Second, numerous disciplines, agencies, researchers and practitioners have contributed, both formally and informally, to the concepts, methods and procedures which are candidates for inclusion in strategic environmental assessment applications.

And, third, the concepts, methods and procedures associated with SEA are by no means new. Rather, they tend to be variations on themes whose origins and elaborations can be traced back through the past half-century. The following contributions to the SEA-related literature are selected for reference because of both their methodological orientation and their regard for the fundamentals noted above: Steger and Lakshmanan, 1968; Schofer et al., 1974; Wellar and Lavallée, 1976; U.S. Department of Housing and Urban Development, 1981; Wellar, 1981, 1982, 1984, 1987; Whitney and Maclaren, 1985; Wood and Djeddour, 1991; Therivel et al., 1993; Glasson, 1995; Partidário, 1996 and Sadler, 1996.

What is Strategic Environmental Assessment?

Early treatments of strategic environmental assessment in the North American experience include Schofer et al. (1974) and the U.S. Department of Housing and Urban Development or USDHUD (1981). The areawide methodology of the USDHUD is, in many respects, analogous to project-level environmental assessment (EA). Articles specifically referring to SEA date back to at least 1983 (e.g., Ratick and Lakshmanan, 1983).

Due to provisions in the *California Environmental Quality Act*, California is considered a particularly important proponent of SEA practice in the North American context (Bass, 1990; Bass, 1991). In addition to the United States, a number of countries have formalized SEA processes, including Japan, the Netherlands and New Zealand (Therivel et al., 1993). In Canada, a number of federal agencies (e.g., Parks Canada, the NCC) have formulated their own protocols for policy assessment, *ergo* strategic environmental assessment. Partidário (1996) itemizes some of the many names that forms of this process have been called in their various contexts: policy environmental assessment or policy EA; policy impact assessment; EA of policy, plan and program (PPP); integration of EA into policy making, planning and program development; and, integration of environmental issues into decision-making processes.

Moving beyond labels to generics, Therivel et al. (1993: 20) define strategic environmental assessment as:

> the formalized, systematic, and comprehensive process of evaluating the environmental impacts of a policy, plan or programme and its alternatives, including the preparation of a written report on the findings of that evaluation, and using the findings in publicly accountable decision-making.

As defined, there are two primary dimensions concerning the application of SEA. First, SEA pertains to the environmental assessment of plans, policies or programmes (Gilpin, 1995). Consequently, the policy framework in which individual projects are developed will already be assessed, thereby concentrating the attention of all subsequent site-level EAs (if required) on the specifics of the project. This reveals the basis for differentiation between EA and SEA. In brief, EA is concerned with project-level activities and SEA is concerned with strategic-level activities (e.g., the earlier stages of decision making where strategies are being generated). Similarly, SEA is or should be integrated with the planning process, and is consequently applied before and during the design stages (Rickson et al., 1989; Perks et al., 1995).

As for the second dimension, SEA can be used as an instrument to make sustainability operational. Plans lacking an environmental orientation (e.g., an organizing concept such as healthy communities, bioregionalism, the ecosystem approach or sustainability) can be enlarged in scope and environmental sensitivity through the application of SEA (Therivel et al., 1993; Partidário, 1993; Glasson, 1995).

Beyond the project-level versus strategic-level distinction, an ongoing issue involves a determination of whether SEA methods are different from those of project-level EA as discussed in some detail by Lawrence in Chapter 9. Wood and Djeddour (1991: 11) assert that:

> the vast majority of tasks involved in SEA are identical to those in project-level EIA. It follows that many of the methods employed are directly transferable, though many will differ in degree of detail and level of specificity.

Just as projects can be defined for EA purposes by activity envelopes (site preparation, construction, operations, etc.), municipal or regional plans can be defined for SEA purposes by policy interests (greenspace, transportation, aesthetics, etc.) and then further refined into their policy-driven activities — which then become both the sources of environmental effects and the units of study. As indicated, the factors that distinguish strategic-level from project-level activities tend to involve the greater diffusion of associated environmental impacts over both space and time.

Alternative Rational Planning Models and Their Relationship To SEA: A Brief Review

There are, in fact, numerous rational planning models (RPMs). With respect to subject matter, they can be attached to the following domains, among others: environmental, economic, social, developmental, structural-functional, institutional, organizational, regional and geo-political. Each of these RPM domains is supported by a large to very large body of literature. And, each appears eligible or susceptible to the kind of strategic assessment discourse that is presented here for the environmental domain. In a number of ways, strategic environmental assessment can be considered a so-called *transdiscipline*-like evaluation, statistics or logic — modes of data treatment that can be applied across a multitude of research interests.

The context point is that while many domains are candidates for an RPM-related discussion, the focus of this paper is on environmental considerations or inputs-outputs. Further, RPM features can vary within, between and among subject matter considerations. By way of brief elaboration, RPMs can vary temporally (e.g., near-term to long-term); spatially (e.g., small-scale to large-scale, or local to global); they can be process- and/or product-oriented; they can be directed by theoretical and/or practical considerations; they can be directed by political or apolitical interests; and, they can be based on various ways of knowing, including intuition, common sense, and the procedures of scientific inquiry (Wellar, 1995).

While the SEA (rational planning) model at the NCC is most readily distinguished by its environmental subject matter, it is also marked by a second distinguishing characteristic. That is, whatever features are selected for the SEA (model), they are selected for reasons that are methodologically sound from a scientific perspective.

The SEA Framework

The framework adopted for the SEA of the *Plan for Canada's Capital* is adapted from Whitney and Maclaren (1985) and has regard for reviews of their work (see Spalding et al., 1991; Smith, 1993; Novakowski, 1993). This framework was chosen because: (1) it represents an ideal research design; (2) considerable commentary and familiarity with the framework is found in the Canadian environmental assessment experience; and, (3) it is specifically formulated for cross-applicability to policies, programmes and projects. Consequently, subsequent site-level EAs can be consistent with the SEA in terms of methodology.

Ten activity stages are used to organize the SEA: needs justification, scoping, additional policy alternatives, prediction, significance assessment, evaluation, public participation, plan implementation, mitigation and monitoring (Figure 7.1). Although the positioning of the additional policy alternatives stage (as an input to the prediction stage) within the process is modified in the adopted approach, the consistency and methodological considerations of the Whitney and Maclaren framework are maintained. Each activity stage has its own potential envelope of EA methods and techniques, as well as decision criteria.

Content Considerations for the SEA of the Plan

Needs Justification

There are two dimensions to needs justification. On the one hand, there may be some interest in whether the initiative (plan revision in this case) is actually needed or justified. On the other hand, justifying the need for applying SEA also requires attention (Wood and Djeddour, 1991; Therivel et al., 1993). With respect to the need to revise the *Plan for Canada's Capital*, regional municipalities within the National Capital Region are in the process of revising their plans, and the NCC recognizes the opportunity to harmo-

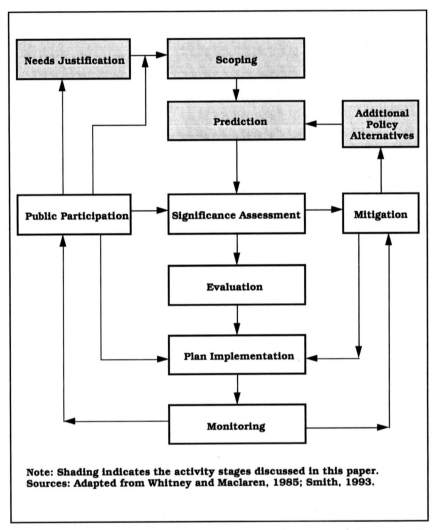

Figure 7.1: Framework for the Strategic Environmental Assessment

nize efforts with the work being done at other jurisdictional levels. As well, considerable changes are occurring to planning law on the Ontario side (Wood, 1995) and greater sensitivity to those changes is warranted. Finally, federal interventions like Program Review (the elimination of 45,000 federal jobs, one third of which are to be lost in the NCR) and institutional restructuring also alter the planning landscape of the Capital (Seasons, 1995).

As to justifying the need for SEA in a particular case, this is an important consideration because it establishes the original rationale and agenda for the entire exercise. The utility of integrating or applying SEA to land use planning is well-documented (Armour, 1989, 1991; Wood and Djeddour, 1991; FEARO, 1992; Therivel et al., 1993; Novakowski, 1993). The salient point made is that the *needs justification* addresses what SEA will accomplish in a particular context.

At the NCC, the decision to undertake and fund the SEA of land-use plans follows from an internal policy mandate. SEA is recognized as a best practices measure that will increase the environmental sensitivity of planning efforts supporting the *Plan for Canada's Capital*, and will offer many specific advantages, including the following:

- The SEA will have an important and proactive role in shaping plan content and planning-related activities. Overall, this is to be accomplished with a four-stream SEA process that: (1) brings environmental considerations directly into the planning process at planning meetings and during environmental review of plan drafts. Specific policy directions with an environmental orientation (and which have not been employed in the plan) must be suggested by the planner undertaking the SEA at every opportunity, whether by formal procedures or otherwise; (2) generates interim draft SEA reports that accompany each plan draft being distributed to committee; (3) produces a final SEA Report (which spec-

ifies the important environmental impacts, how to mitigate them, and the monitoring measures needed to
track them over time), thereby facilitating further participation of affected parties; and (4) provides the archi-
tecture for site-specific EAs that may be undertaken at
a later date under the aegis of the new Plan;

- The SEA is to incorporate Environmental Planning
  Objectives (EPOs). EPOs are specific environmental
  maxima and minima that express the central environmental values to be served by the Plan. They provide
  guidance for decisions about plan-driven activities;

- The identification and consideration of cumulative
  impacts are made explicit, a factor that cannot be adequately dealt with at the project level;

- The SEA involves a strong policy appraisal component
  designed to address the internal and external consistency of plan policies; and,

- The SEA is to contribute to state-of-the-art SEA through
  its efficiency, effectiveness, comprehensiveness and tai-
  lor-made approach within a context of fiscal restraint.

As shown, the SEA is undertaken to bring specific benefits
to the planning process and to planning products (Kingsley,
1993). The *needs justification* stage permits an opportunity
to set out the major organizing concepts for application of
the approach.

Scoping

Scoping is the process of identifying priorities — it attempts
to focus an environmental assessment on a manageable
number of important issues (Duffy, 1986). In other words,
the scoping stage of SEA is critical because it targets the priority issues, objectives, problems, etc. Consequently, the

associated challenge is to specify the means — that is, the how — for identifying, ranking and acting upon needed initiatives. Within the public sector, for example, such general criteria as the following have been used in the prioritizing process for many decades (Wellar and Lavallée, 1976; Wellar 1982, 1987):

- the interests of a government agency are involved;
- the interests of an agency partner are involved;
- the public or other interest is served; or,
- a need-to-know exists.

In the SEA for the Plan, six dimensions were selected for scoping:

- the definition of the environment;
- identification of boundaries;
- identification of key affected parties;
- generation of environmental planning principles and objectives;
- identification of key environmental issues for the NCR; and,
- identification of key indicators.

Due to space constraints, it is not possible to present a detailed account of the procedures behind selecting and prioritizing all the scoping dimensions. This is, however, an important methodological matter, and even an illustrative discussion could be instructive. As a result, the *hows* underlying two of the dimensions — generation of environmental planning objectives and identification of key environmental issues — are made as explicit as conditions permit.

The Scoping of Environmental Planning Objectives

Environmental planning objectives (EPOs) are analogous to other planning objectives in that they are components of (desirable) future goals. And, similarly, the substantive reasons for emphasizing specific objectives rather than general goals include the following: planning based on specific objectives can provide a focus that helps to prevent the agency involved from drifting; the approach promotes a results-oriented agenda; and, very importantly, it focuses organization-wide attention on doing the right things and doing things right.

Caring for the Earth (IUCN et al., 1991) was especially valuable as a guide for identifying appropriate EPOs. In addition, a body of evidence and recommendations from more than twenty other sources in the international literature was synthesized for input into the scoping process surrounding the adoption of the EPOs. Some of the references considered include the following: WCED, 1987; Button and Pearce, 1989; Rees, 1989; Richardson, 1989; Government of Canada, 1990; Fowler, 1991; RCFTW, 1991; Rees and Roseland, 1991; Maclaren, 1992; RCFTW, 1992; Roseland, 1992; Buchholz, 1993; Gurstein and Curry, 1993; Harker et al., 1993; Badami et al., 1994; Tomalty et al., 1994 and Beatley, 1995.

Selection of the EPOs (Table 7.1) was undertaken according to the following criteria.

1. The EPOs are pertinent to one or more planning principle used in the Plan itself and can be used as organizing concepts for environmental considerations. Cross-applicability to more than one planning principle aids in prioritizing the EPOs under conditions of conflict between and among issues, objectives, interests, etc.;

2. The EPO must not only be possible, but attainable. For

Table 7.1
Environmental Planning Principles and Environmental Planning Objectives (EPOs)

	Planning Principles	EPOs	Potential Examples of Appropriate NCC Strategies
1	RESPECT THE COMMUNITY OF LIFE IN THE NCR	MAXIMIZE EQUITY • economic • employment • gender • social • generational	• distribute NIMBYs fairly throughout the NCR • maintain 75/25 federal employment location by province. use of NCC assets for public transit • safety for women/men through urban design • equal accessibility to public space, facilitate conversion of surplus buildings to low-income housing • sustainable forestry and agricultural practices on NCC land
2	IMPROVE THE QUALITY OF LIFE IN THE NCR	OPTIMIZE (MAXIMIZE-MINIMIZE) QUALITY OF LIFE FACTORS • maximize public space for human needs • maximize protection of cultural heritage/heritage landscapes • minimize environmental impacts of development (including cumulative)	• maintain land base for educational, recreational, cultural and natural programming • densification of downtown, maintain Greenbelt integrity, monitor approval process • apply SEA to policies and plans, EA to projects, monitor mitigation
3	CONSERVE THE NCR'S DIVERSITY AND VITALITY	OPTIMIZE (MAXIMIZE-MINIMIZE) DIVERSITY (biophysical, social & economic) • maximize ecosystem, species and genetic diversity • maximize networks and corridors MAXIMIZE ECOSYSTEM HEALTH • minimize threats to water quality • minimize threats to air quality	• enlarge planning toolkit to protect conservation areas (mitigation banking, easements, covenants etc.) • harmonize practices with other governments, protect shoreline corridors • appropriately site snow dump sites, naturalize shorelines, stormwater management strategies • integrate systems of alternative transportation modes, concentrate federal employment in Core
4	RESPECT THE NCR'S CARRYING CAPACITY	MINIMIZE ECOLOGICAL FOOTPRINT MAXIMIZE OPERATIONAL EFFECTIVENESS	• stress densification, mixed uses, facilitate conversion of surplus buildings to social uses • keep PCBs on-site until technology advances, implement the 3Rs, use of compost sites
5	EDUCATE AND CONSENSUS-BUILD THROUGH PUBLIC PARTICIPATION	MAXIMIZE COMMUNICATION ABOUT THE IMPORTANCE OF ECOLOGICAL HEALTH	• use volunteers for conservation exercises, press releases, Ideas Fairs, programming • use recycling stations during NCC-sponsored festivals on federal land - Canada Day, Tulip Festival
6	EMPOWER COMMUNITIES	OPTIMIZE PUBLIC PARTICIPATION	• profile NCC planning principles (mixed uses, densification, environmental stewardship)
7	PROVIDE A REGIONAL FRAMEWORK FOR INTEGRATING DEVELOPMENT AND CONSERVATION	MAXIMIZE KNOWLEDGE BASE	• implement plan monitoring, information sharing with local governments and universities etc.

Source: Adapted from IUCN et al., 1991.

example, an EPO that states an air quality target of zero pollution would not be realistic for the National Capital Region (where car purchases continue to escalate as the baby boom ages); and,

3. The *Plan* must be capable of influencing the EPO, either directly or indirectly. Clearly, from an operational point of view, it would be pointless to include an EPO that is outside the NCC's mandate and *Plan*.

Scoping of Environmental Issues

An inventory of priority environmental issues (Table 7.2) was generated by interviewing a range of experts/officials (policy, plan and research) within the NCC. Their list of issues was then externally supplemented with a consultant's report on priority issues (Haug and Associates, 1992), and a public participation exercise called the *Ideas Fair* (RMOC, 1994). From the extensive list of environmental issues identified by these sources, the scoped list was distilled by applying criteria proposed by Duffy (1986) and Klein (1992):

- The issue must pertain to the *Plan for Canada's Capital* and the environmental dimensions that the *Plan* can affect — *the jurisdiction criterion*.

- Only issues that pertain to the NCR as a whole are considered — *the scale criterion*. Site-specific issues are dealt with at the sector plan, area plan or development plan levels.

- Only issues that were validated by NCC experts and identified by either the consultants or members of the public at the *Ideas Fair* were retained — *the level of concern criterion*.

Table 7.2
Scoped Environmental Concerns

Scoped Environmental Concerns	Attributes of the Concerns
Agricultural Land	Conservation on High Quality Soils
Approaches to the Capital	Appearance
Archaeological Sites	Preservation
Built Form	Appearance
Contaminated Soils	Rehabilitation
Greenspace-rural	Conservation
Greenspace-systems	Conservation
Greenspace-urban	Preservation of High Quality Space
Heritage Sites	Preservation
Parkways	Appearance
Shorelines	Conservation
	Stormwater Management
Valued Ecosystem Components	Preservation
Wetlands	Preservation
Woodlands-rural	Conservation
Woodlands-urban	Preservation of Mature Woodlands

Prediction

Once the significant issues and concerns related to the plan initiative have been identified in the scoping, prediction becomes the focus. Prediction involves ascertaining probable future states after the imposition of plan-driven or -regulated activities. With respect to the SEA, however, this activity has a clear and defined purpose: whether and how specific policies may generate environmental impacts. During this exercise, individual policies are subjected to a series of SEA questions and the answers (predictions) may be based on empirical studies, literature reviews, expert judgment via panels, etc.

The question sequence is defined and documented using a matrix (Figure 7.2) for each policy envelope (e.g., policies pertaining to *federal accommodations*, policies pertaining to *natural heritage areas*) within the land use plan.

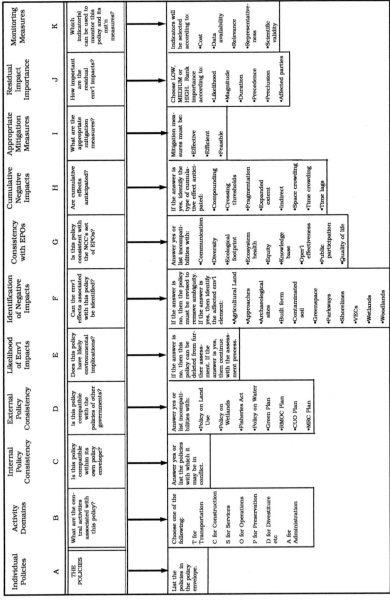

Figure 7.2: The 'How To' Matrix for Strategic Environmental Assessment at the NCC
Source: Adapted from DOE, 1991.

The individual policies comprising the envelope are treated as row entries. If there are 20 policies envelopes, then there are 20 matrices, each with one or more individual policy. If it is a compound policy, then the policy is divided into its component parts. Each individual policy is correlated to its likely and associated activities, which are then subjected to the question sequence of the matrix.

Text accompanying each matrix has the following sub-sections:

- *General Commentary* — involving an overview of the matrix contents and areas of concern;

- *Additional Policy Alternatives* — where environmental policy alternatives that may have been overlooked or downplayed are suggested or stressed. This step represents a first possible layer of mitigation; and,

- *Minor Adjustments* — where the policy can be reworded, re-oriented or optimized by a minor alteration. This represents a second possible layer of mitigation.

Matrix Construction

Here, the *whats* and *hows* of employing the SEA framework are outlined, using the *Plan for Canada's Capital* as a case study.

A. Column A (Individual Policies) of the question matrix (Figure 7.2) lists the individual policies within the policy envelope.

B. Column B (Activity Domains) identifies the central activities associated with the individual policy. The following activity codes are used:

- T for **Transportation** (activities that may change traffic and circulation patterns including bridge construction, new roads through the Greenbelt, new parking facilities, bike corridor creation);

- C for **Construction** (building of major new institutions, attractions and recreational facilities);

- S for **Services** (the provision of visitor kiosks, directories, amenities by the NCC or commercial operators on federal land);

- O for NCC **Operations** (land management practices);

- P for **Preservation** or conservation of land for park and other purposes;

- A for **Administration** (designation and other planning process activities, research, intergovernmental cooperation, etc.); and,

- D for **Divestiture** or disposal (sale, offloading or downloading of NCC land).

As practitioners will notice when applying the activity code strategy, many activities will have a consistent range of specific and cumulative impacts.

C. Column C (Internal Policy Consistency) involves policy appraisal and ascertains whether existing and impending NCC policies are consistent with each other within the envelope.

D. Column D (External Policy Consistency) establishes whether NCC policies are compatible with those of other relevant organizations, viz., federal partners and provincial or regional governments.

E. Column E (Likelihood of Environmental Impacts) identifies whether environmental impacts are considered likely for a particular policy. If they are likely, then negative or positive identifiers are inserted into the cell. If the identifier is negative, then the remaining columns of the matrix must be addressed. If no negative environmental impacts are anticipated, then the assessment process for the policy can be stopped.

F. Column F (Identification of Negative Environmental Impacts) reflects the scoped environmental components that the policy may have an impact upon. If the policy involves an activity that is best considered by using a site-specific EA, then it is excluded from further assessment. For example, a policy may refer to the construction of a specific monument or building. However, unless the details of a particular site are known, prediction of the environmental impacts of constructing and maintaining the initiative is a hollow exercise. In such cases, a recommendation for site-specific EA is inserted into the appropriate matrix cell.

G. Column G (Consistency with EPOs) questions whether policies are consistent with the environmental planning objectives identified in the scoping exercise. If consistency is not demonstrated, then this must be discussed in the accompanying text and mitigated by deleting the policy, formulating companion policies, or rewording the policy.

H. Column H (Cumulative Negative Effects) addresses cumulative effects, and identifies the specific characteristics of impacts that are deemed likely to be cumulative over space and time. The strength of SEA can depend on how well it deals with the cumulative effects issue. Using an analytical framework from Spaling (1994), this column addresses eight comprehensive attributes of cumulative effects:

1. *time crowding* — frequent and repetitive effects on a single environmental component;

2. *space crowding* — a high density of activity on a single environmental component;

3. *compounding* — synergistic effects arising from multiple negative environmental effects converging on a single environmental component (e.g., an urban lake or pond being affected by many sources or types of contamination);

4. *time lags* — long delays are involved before effects become tangible and measurable;

5. *expanded spatial extent* — effects that occur at some distance from the source or sources;

6. *crossing thresholds* — a disruption to a system threshold that fundamentally changes system behaviour. For example, with respect to the hydrological cycle, snow dumps (resulting from intensive snow removal activities) located adjacent to water courses can cause chloride pulses capable of killing all aquatic biota immediately downstream;

7. *indirect* — effects that occur due to a change in a component of a different system; and,

8. *fragmentation* — larger systems being separated into disconnected spatial units resulting in the loss of viability of some function or component of the larger system (e.g., when a mature woodland is bisected by a roadway).

The nature, degree and extent of any cumulative effect or impact must be discussed in the accompanying matrix text.

I. Column I (Appropriate Mitigation Measures) addresses the ways and means of ameliorating negative environmental impacts and can be elaborated upon in the written commentary that accompanies each matrix. Strategies for enhancing environmental benefits should also be discussed.

J. Impacts that persist after mitigation (residual impacts) and their importance are the subject matter of Column J (Residual Impact Importance).

K. Column K (Monitoring Measures) involves the selection of indicators which track the environmental variables of concern identified in the residual impacts column and are cross-referenced to scoped environmental priorities.

As shown, the prediction stage systematically incorporates other elements of the SEA framework: additional policy alternatives, significance assessment, mitigation and monitoring (see Figure 7.2).

Additional Policy Alternatives

At the strategic level, it is during the prediction stage that policy weaknesses (voids, oversights, flawed assumptions, contradictions, ambiguities, etc.) are likely to be most identifiable and apparent. This occurs because policy expectations (or lack thereof) are extended into time and/or space, and involve the language of *could* and *should* rather than known facts and evidence (Smith and Wellar, 1992). In that circumstance, policy weaknesses are highly susceptible to exposure, especially when the foundation(s) underlying the predictions lack robustness. The salient point behind treating policy alternatives as an input to the prediction stage is based on direct, personal, policy process experience, and is supported by the literature (Verheem, 1992; Lee and Walsh, 1992). The challenge, and one which can only be acknowledged in this paper, is to document the discussion of the alternatives and consequently provide an indication of the options that were considered and assessed.

Next Steps

The NCC will be engaged in the outstanding activity stages (e.g., public participation, evaluation) over the course of 1997/1998. As those activities are completed, it would be appropriate to prepare similar status reports on them. As well, it would be useful to re-evaluate the extent and degree of any progress made regarding the application of SEA to the *Plan* activities discussed in this report and in a previous paper (Novakowski and Wellar, 1995).

Concluding Remarks

Methods and techniques for comprehensively identifying and quantifying the regional impacts of a land-use plan are better established in principle than in practice, in part because of the heavy data, expense and time burden of real-world applications. The *how* dimension of the approach discussed here outlines NCC efforts to achieve effective and efficient SEA procedures in the face of onerous time and resource constraints. Drawing on NCC experience to date, important concerns and questions that need to be raised within the critical needs justification, scoping, prediction and additional policy alternatives activity stages of SEA are presented.

A final observation concerning SEA effectiveness concerns vigilance. The playing field involving environmental and economic considerations is not level, even with the application of SEA. As SEA results start to be integrated into the planning process, they may meet resistance at two levels: within the planning process of the organization itself; and, from decision makers both internal and external to the organization. Land-use planning is, after all, politicized in all pluralistic democracies and this means that there are choices to be made.

The burden of the environmental planner, therefore, is to demonstrate methodological competency (description of process to substantiate replicability, minimization of arbitrariness, etc.) and perseverance in terms of getting environmental arguments heard. Once the wheels inside the black box of the underlying political machinery have been set in motion, the conscientious environmental planner must feel confident that every opportunity for consensus building, statement of environmental priorities, sharing of environmental knowledge and public dissemination of information has been explored. The SEA of the *Plan for Canada's Capital* is still unfolding; however, it appears to be an instructive approach that may lend itself to many other strategic-level exercises.

References

Armour, A. (1989) "Integrating impact assessment in the planning process: from rhetoric to reality," *Impact Assessment Bulletin*, 9: 3-14.

_____ (1991) "Impact assessment and the planning process: a status report," *Impact Assessment Bulletin*, 9: 27-34.

Badami, M. et al. (1994) *Sustainability and Planning, A Draft Discussion Paper for the Canadian Institute of Planners*, Ottawa, ON: Canadian Institute of Planners.

Bass, R. (1990) "California's experience with environmental impact reports," *Project Appraisal*, 5: 220-224.

_____ (1991) "Policy, plan and program EIA in California," *EIA Newsletter*, 5: 4-5.

Beatley, T. (1995) "Planning and sustainability: the elements of a new (improved?) paradigm," *Journal of the Planning Literature*, 9: 383-394.

Buchholz, R. (1993) *Principles of Environmental Management: The Greening of Business*, New Orleans, LA: Loyola University.

Button, K. and Pearce, D. (1989) "Improving the urban environment: how to adjust national and local government policy for sustainable urban growth," *Progress in Planning*, 32: 135-184.

DOE (Department of the Environment) (1991) *Policy Appraisal and the Environment*, London, ON: HMSO.

Duffy, P.J.B. (ed.) (1986) *Initial Assessment Guide*, Ottawa, ON: FEARO.

FEARO (Federal Environmental Assessment Review Office) (1992) *Developing Environmentally Responsible Policies and Programs: A Sourcebook on Environmental Assessment*, Ottawa, ON: FEARO.

Fowler, E. (1991) "Land use in the ecologically sensible city," *Alternatives*, 18: 26-35.

Gilpin, A. (1995) *Environmental Impact Assessment: Cutting Edge for the Twenty-First Century*, Cambridge, UK: Cambridge University Press.

Glasson, J. (1995) "Regional planning and the environment: time for a SEA change," *Urban Studies*, 32: 713-731.

Government of Canada (1990) *Canada's Green Plan*, Cat. No. En21-94/1990E, Ottawa, ON: Ministry of Supply and Services.

Gurstein, P. and Curry, J. (1993) "Implementing concepts of sustainable community planning," *Plan Canada*, March: 7-15.

Harker, D. et al. (1993) *Landscape Restoration Handbook*, Ann Arbor, MI: Lewis Publishers.

Haug and Associates (1992) *Environmental Management in the NCR: Challenges and Opportunties, Perceptions of Selected Ontario Municipal/NCC/Provincial Officials and Lobby Groups*, Final Report, Arnprior, ON: Haug and Associates.

IUCN (International Union for the Conservation of Nature) et al. (1991) *Caring for the Earth: A Strategy for Sustainable Living*, Gland, Switzerland: The World Conservation Union, United Nations Environment Programme and World Wide Fund for Nature.

Kingsley, L. (1993) *Environmental Assessment of the Plan for Canada's Capital: Some Initial Considerations*, Unpublished Report for the National Capital Commission, Ottawa.

Klein, H. (1992) *Environmental Assessment and Land Use Planning: The Greenbelt Environmental Assessment*, Unpublished Report for the National Capital Commission, Ottawa.

Lee, N. and Walsh, F. (1992) "Strategic environmental assessment: an overview," *Project Appraisal*, 7: 126-136.

Maclaren, V. (1992) *Sustainable Urban Development in Canada: From Concept to Practice*, Volume 1: Summary Report, Toronto, ON: ICURR Publications.

NCC (National Capital Commission) (1991) *A Capital in the Making: Reflections of the Past, Visions of the Future*, Ottawa, ON: National Capital Commission, Planning Branch.

Novakowski, E.N. (1993) *Impact Assessment and Urban Planning: An Investigation of their Integration in the Larger Municipalities of Ontario*, Unpublished M.A. Thesis, Ottawa, ON: University of Ottawa.

Novakowski, E.N. and Wellar, B. (1995) "The environmental assesment of the plan for Canada's capital: an inside look," *New City Magazine*, 16: 60-62.

Partidário, M. (1993) "Anticipation in environmental assessment: recent trends at the policy and planning levels," *Impact Assessment Bulletin*, 11: 27-44.

_____ (1996) "Strategic environmental assessment: key issues emerging from recent practice," *Environmental Impact Assessment Review*, 16: 31-55.

Perks, W., Thompson, D. and Bilkhu, J. (1995) *EIA + MP: Situation and Prospects*, Canada: ICURR.

Ratick, S. and Lakshmanan, T.R. (1983) "An overview of the strategic environmental assessment system," in Lakshmanan, T.R. and Ratick, S. (eds.), *System and Models for Energy and Environmental Analysis*, Aldershot, UK: Gower, 127-152.

RCFTW (Royal Commission on the Future of the Toronto Waterfront) (1991) *Planning for Sustainability: Towards Integrating Environmental Protection into Land-Use Planning*, Cat. No. Z1-1988/1-41-12-E, Ottawa, ON: Ministry of Supply and Services.

_____ (1992) *Regeneration: Toronto's Waterfront and the Sustainable City*, Cat. No. Z1-1988/1-1992E, Ottawa, ON: Ministry of Supply and Services.

Rees, W. (ed.) (1989) *Planning for Sustainable Development: A Resource Book*, Vancouver, BC: UBC Centre for

Human Settlements.

Rees, W. and Roseland, M. (1991) "Sustainable communities: planning for the 21st century," *Plan Canada*, 31: 15-26.

Richardson, N. (1989) *Land Use Planning and Sustainable Development in Canada*, Cat. No. En 92-911989E, Ottawa, ON: Ministry of Supply and Services.

Rickson, R., Burdge, R. and Armour, A. (1989) "Future prospects for integrating impact assessment into the planning process," *Impact Assessment Bulletin*, 8: 347-357.

RMOC (Regional Municipality of Ottawa-Carleton) (1994) *Ideas Fair Catalogue*, Ottawa, ON: Planning and Property Department, RMOC.

Roseland, M. (1992) *Toward Sustainable Communities*, Ottawa, ON: National Round Table on the Environment and the Economy.

Sadler, B. (1996) *Environmental Assessment in a Changing World: Evaluating Practice to Improve Performance*, Final Report, Ottawa, ON: Ministry of Supply and Services.

Schofer, J. and Stuart, D. (1974) "Evaluating regional plans and community impacts," *Journal of the Urban Planning and Development Division*, Proceedings of the American Society of Civil Engineers, 100/UP1: 93-109.

Seasons, M. (1995) "The federal budget's impact on planners," *Plan Canada*, July: 3-4.

Smith, L. G. (1993) *Impact Assessment and Sustainable Resource Management*, New York, NY: Longman Scientific and Technical.

Smith, R. and Wellar, B. (1992) "A progress report on public policy objectives achieved through IS/GIS/LIS," in Wellar, B. and Parr, D. (eds.), *IS/GIS/LIS and Policies, Plans & Programs: 30 Years in Perspective*, 1992 Annual Conference Proceedings, *Urban and Regional Information Systems Association*, V: 117-144.

Spalding, H., Smit, B. and Kreutzwiser, R. (1991) "Evaluating environmental assessment: approaches, lessons and prospects," *Environments*, 22: 63- 74.

Spaling, H. (1994) "Cumulative effects assessment: concepts and principles," *Impact Assessment*, 12: 231-251.

Statistics Canada (1997) *A National Overview: Population and Dwelling Counts*, Cat. No. 93-357-XPB, Ottawa, ON: Minister of Industry.

Steger, W. and Lakshmanan, T.R. (1968) "Plan evaluation methodologies: some aspects of decision requirements and analytical response," in Jackson, E.W. (ed.), *Urban Development Models*, Proceedings of a Higher Research Board Conference, June 26-30, Hanover, NH: 33-71.

Therivel, R., Wilson, E., Thompson, S., Heaney, D. and Pritchard, D. (1993) *Strategic Environmental Assessment*, London, UK: Earthscan Publications, Ltd.

Tomalty, R., Gibson, R., Alexander, D. and Fisher, J. (1994) *Ecosystem Planning for Canadian Urban Regions*, Toronto, ON: ICURR Publications.

U.S. Department of Housing and Urban Development (1981) *Areawide Environmental Assessment*, Washington, DC: Office of Policy Development and Research (HUD).

Verheem, R. (1992) "Environmental assessment at the strategic level in the Netherlands," *Project Appraisal*, 7:

150-156.

WCED (World Commission on Environment and Development) (1987) *Our Common Future*, New York, NY: Oxford University Press.

Wellar, B. (1981) "Impact assessment and conflict management: confirming analytical approaches to development planning," in *International Symposium on Conflict Management*, Kyoto, Japan: Department of Transportation Engineering, Kyoto University, 80-103.

_____ (1982) "Urban impact assessment in public policy processes: the Canadian record, 1968-1982," *The Canadian Journal of Regional Science*, 1: 39-65.

_____ (1984) "Information for decision-making by rural public authorities," in Maher, M. (ed.), *Local Leadership and Rural Development: Implications for Research and Extension*, Washington, D.C.: USDA and OECD, 31-39.

_____ (1987) "Urban impact assessment and MSUA: two guiding lights that flickered and ....," in Oberlander, H.P. and Fallick, A.L. (eds.), *The Ministry of State for Urban Affairs: A Courageous Experiment in Public Administration*, Vancouver, BC: Centre for Human Settlements, University of British Columbia, 65-91.

_____ (1995) "Evaluating information systems performance using informational activity criteria," in *Information Technology Linking the Americas...Your Network to an Explanded World*, Annual Conference Proceedings, Washington, DC: Urban and Regional Information Systems Association, 97-111.

Wellar, B. and Lavallée, L. (1976) "A methodology for selecting R & D studies in a policy-oriented organization," in Anochie, O. (ed.), *Papers from the 1975 Annual URISA*

Conference, Chicago, IL: Urban and Regional Informaton Systems Association, 1: 391-405.

Whitney, J.B.R. and Maclaren, V.W. (1985) "A framework for the assessment of EIA methodologies," in Whitney, J.B.R. and Maclaren, V.W. (eds.), *EIA: The Canadian Experience*, Toronto, ON: Institute for Environmental Studies, University of Toronto, 1-31.

Wood, C. and Djeddour, M. (1991) "Strategic environmental assessment: EA of policies, plans and programmes," *Impact Assessment Bulletin*, 10: 3-22.

Wood, D. (1995) *The Planning Act: A Sourcebook*, Scarborough, ON: Carswell, Thomson Professional Publishing.

Chapter 8

Regional Economic and Social Impact Assessment of Infrastructure Development and Water Service Provisions

C. Emdad Haque
Brandon University

Various forms of impact assessment, such as Regional Economic Impact Assessment (REIA), Technical Assessment (TA) and Social Impact Assessment (SIA), have emerged since the introduction of assessment procedures under the National Environmental Policy Act (NEPA) in the United States in 1969 (Bisset, 1983; Caldwell, 1988; Vig and Kraft, 1990; Smith, 1993). Despite the great diversity among impact assessments, some variants may complement one another. This study assesses impacts of improved water service systems in rural and rural-urban fringe areas of the province of Manitoba, Canada. It is asserted that REIA is a necessary but inadequate basis for comprehensive and effective policy decision and planning purposes. The possibilities of adding an SIA to an existing REIA are explored through an empirical study of water improvement projects in Manitoba. The case of piped water service projects, which were implemented in rural municipalities (RMs) over the past three decades, is used to exemplify a community-based SIA.

In this chapter, the relationship between REIA and SIA is first reviewed, an overview of the REIA for the proposed Pembina Valley Water Supply project is then presented, the limitations of REIA are determined, and an SIA of water supply improvements in two municipalities of Manitoba is offered, before conclusions are drawn.

Regional Economic and Social Impact Assessments

Regional Economic Impact Assessment (REIA) identifies, predicts, and evaluates economic impacts of development projects at the regional level. It offers measures of likely changes in a region's principal economic variables caused by the flow-on effects of a proposed or already executed project (Flynn et al., 1983; McDonald, 1990). The scope of REIA is restricted to determining changes in (i) regional production of goods and services or total output, (ii) regional salaries and wages or income, and (iii) employment. The regional account contributes to the national economic development (NED) account which measures the net value to the nation of the increased output of goods and services, and the net value of output resulting from external economies (McDonald, 1990; Hamilton et al., 1991). Overall, REIA deals with macro-level economic effects of deliberate measures for growth and development.

In contrast to this emphasis on economic growth, SIA appraises social well-being and its scope is therefore broad. For D'Amore (1978: 336-7):

> Social Impact Assessment is an attempt to predict the future of policy decisions (including the initiation of specific projects) upon people, their physical and psychological health, well-being and welfare, their traditions, lifestyles, institutions, and interpersonal relationships.

A comprehensive review of literature on SIA offers five characteristic features: (i) it systematically identifies, analyzes, and evaluates social impacts; (ii) it develops alternatives to the proposed course of actions and determines the full range of consequences; (iii) it increases the knowledge of both the project proponent and the impacted community;

(iv) it raises consciousness and the level of understanding of the community and puts residents in a better position to understand the broader implication of the proposed action; and finally (v) it includes within it a process to mitigate or alleviate the social impacts likely to occur, if that action is desired by the impacted community (see Burdge and Robertson, 1990: 83). Carley and Bustelo (1984) drew attention to the significance of the political and institutional dimensions in impact assessment.

SIA requires a greater emphasis on broad public participation in the planning process (Finsterbusch and Wolf, 1977; Finsterbusch, 1980; Finsterbusch et al., 1983; Leistritz and Murdock, 1981; Tester and Mykes, 1981). For SIA, the recognition of pluralism in political decision making and the need for public participation in impact assessment is thus critical (Doern and Phidd, 1983; Cope and Hills, 1988). Burdge and Robertson (1990) have reviewed several examples of how Public Involvement (PI) fits within the SIA process. One PI technique is questionnaire surveys, including community surveys, community leader studies, and synchronized policy issue studies. Public inputs are needed in various stages of the SIA process, especially in the formulation of alternatives, assessment, evaluation, and monitoring stages (Smith, 1984). Formulation of attitudes towards the project, perceptions of public welfare, and interest group activities can help in compiling a social profile which can be used in the decision making and planning processes. The present study employs this outline as a frame of reference for community-focussed SIA.

REIA and SIA have apparent incompatibility due to their application at different spatial scales: REIA tends to emphasize macro-regional economic growth effects whereas SIA stresses local level changes in social variables, such as, health, education, social relations and amenities. Rickson et al. (1990: 4) state that "local communities are a focus of social impact assessment because in these the costs and benefits of change are most acutely experienced". They also find that the relationships among formal organizations like government agencies, and the general public including citizen's groups, industry and business, and development firms, are vital to policy formulation and the application of impact assessment information. Effective policy formulation requires community studies emphasizing public participation and development of social theories in terms of resource conflicts and resolution, knowledge diffusion, and analysis of organizational relationships.

Despite their differences, REIA and SIA are closely related since economic and social variables originate from a common set and they overlap in some vital areas. On the one hand, many social variables are of relevance to REIA based planning. Predicted changes in employment are influenced by the derived demand for social services, future demographic changes, and future demand for infrastructure. On the other hand, SIA overlaps with regional development objectives, which have as their main elements regional employment and regional infrastructure. The most important justification and call for combining SIA and REIA stems from the need to determine the political feasibility of economically viable projects (see Mitchell, 1986; Lang, 1986).

> Regional economic impact assessment provides predictions of considerable value to social impact assessment and the two fields of impact assessment are very close: both concentrate on the distribution of positive and negative consequences of a proposal and on means of mitigating negative effects. Given that decisions will probably be made by political negotiation rather than rational analysis, objective assessment of the distribution of impacts will be influential in the process despite the theoretical propositions of the rational economist that often these distributional effects are not relevant from the national point of view (McDonald, 1990:35).

Although the variables studied in SIA are quite different from those involved in REIA, SIA can add consideration of critical political and development issues to the more narrowly economic considerations of REIA, and especially by feeding public issues, concerns and values back to the decision makers.

REIA of the Proposed Pembina Valley Water Supply Project: An Overview

The Pembina Valley proposal involves withdrawal of water from the Red and Assiniboine Rivers and a regional distribution system to be operated by Pembina Valley Water Cooperative Inc. (PVWC) (Figure 8.1). The proposed project further involves expansion of the water treatment plant located at Portage la Prairie on the Assiniboine River, and construction of water pipelines to the towns of Winkler and Morden. Water treatment plants would also be built at Morris and Letellier on the Red River with associated pipelines. The proposed projects are aimed at supplying municipal, industrial, and on-farm water and would not deliver water for the irrigation of field crops. The project will improve water services for 38,000 residents in the Pembina Valley and will cost $63 million over 10 years. PVWC argues that the project is needed to "drought-proof and sustain existing water supplies; to meet anticipated future water demands, and to remove water-based constraints to economic development" (PVWC, 1991: iv).

A draft environmental impact statement was compiled, which essentially provides a baseline study of regional economic impacts (MacMillan and Coyle, 1993; MacMillan et al., 1994). The study area for the regional impact assessment (i.e., Pembina Valley region) also covers one of the two rural municipalities selected for the community-focussed social impact study (Figure 8.1).

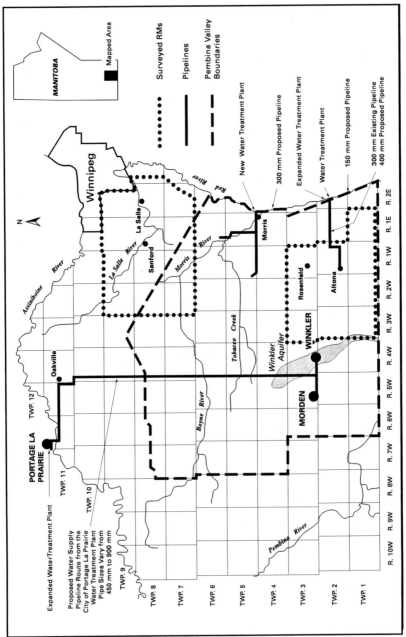

Figure 8.1: Proposed Pembina Valley Regional Water Scheme

The report prepared by PVWC (1991) points to rising long-term demand for water. On the basis of 1981-86 census figures, the cooperative forecasts an increase in the Pembina Valley population from 38,300 in 1986 to 109,000 in 2040. Most of this increase will occur in urban areas, slated to experience a 320 percent increase in population to 2040, with most of the growth in larger centers such as Winkler, Morden, Carman, and Altona (PVWC, 1991: 10-11).

The economic impact of the PVWC proposal is estimated to be immense and positive. In addition to 263 person-years of direct construction employment in the first ten years of the project ($63 million expenditure), the study predicts a further 195 person-years of indirect economic activity employment ($58 million) (PVWC, 1991: 94). MacMillan and Coyle (1993) and MacMillan et al. (1994) have assessed the local and extra-regional components of regional economic benefits expected from the project. They have identified potential regional output, income, and employment benefits from water service infrastructure investment. In their assessment, the investigators found Manitoba to be a competitive location and the returns so large that opportunity costs were outweighed. In order to cite an instance, MacMillan et al. (1994) have noted that Manitoba's cattle and hog producers possess some competitive advantages over producers in other prairie provinces, according to tax filer data.

A rapid expansion of manufacturing in the Pembina Valley area, encompassing printing, farm machinery, recreational vehicles, plastic, construction materials, and food processing, especially vegetable oil seed meal and oil production, has been recorded by MacMillan et al. (1994). The Pembina Valley appears to be strongly competitive at both the national and international level in these areas, according to the region's 1989 annual sales of manufacturing commodities. Assuming a 10 percent interest rate in discounting, the present value for all the direct and indirect value added due to growth in manufacturing sectors in the Pembina Valley region over the first 20 years of the 30-year engineering project design life was calculated at $1,494.56 million (Table 8.1). The study predicted a large potential loss without the implementation of the proposed projects.

Table 8.1
Present Value of Canadian Value Added At Risk Without Additional Pembina Valley Water Supply, 1991-2010 (1984 base) (in million dollar)

Location	Direct Value Added	Indirect Value Added	Total	Percent
Pembina Valley Region	420.38	-	420.38	28.13
Rest of Manitoba	207.11	4.70	211.81	14.17
Rest of Canada	110.20	752.17	862.37	57.70
Canada	737.69	756.87	1494.56	100.00

In view of these economic and employment benefits, the opportunity costs are thought to be low but have not been estimated. The potential economic displacement effects due to the diversion of funds to the proposed project will likely be outweighed by the immense magnitude of output, value added and employment benefits. A strong competitive advantage of the region over the rest of the country and many foreign countries (especially for some selective manufacturing and agricultural value added commodities) will more than compensate for any opportunity costs.

A Critique of the REIA Application to Pembina Valley Project

The proposal of the Pembina Valley water supply project suffers from several shortcomings related to an "engineering-structural approach" to water utility design and also from limitations of aggregated economic assessment methods. These qualifications can be grouped under four headings:

Economic Concerns

The Pembina Valley REIA is able to predict significant local economic growth on the back of the water project expenditures because water is seen as a catalyst to population growth. But the catalytic effect needs to be demonstrated. Is there a direct correlation between water provision and urban and industrial development? Do Manitoba's industries need treated, piped water? More significantly, the population growth estimates used in the REIA have been criticized (Winnipeg Free Press, 1992:A6). To say the least, a 70.58 percent increase in the Pembina Valley region is overly optimistic. Population in Rhineland RM, central to the Pembina Valley region, fell from 4,550 in 1971 to 4,150 in 1991, despite modest growth in the few towns. Indeed population growth in Manitoba has been slow (6.4 percent between 1981 and 1991) and concentrated in Winnipeg. If the province continues to add just 65,700 persons a decade as it did in the 1980s, or 21,956 persons per inter-censal period as it did during 1991-1996, then the REIA is arguing that Pembina Valley region will capture the lion's share of the province's population increase, outcompeting Winnipeg and rural municipalities closer to Winnipeg (e.g., MacDonald R.M. or Selkirk) which have experienced above average growth rates in recent years.

The Pembina Valley project has already been viewed as a "water grab" from the Assiniboine River. But, implicitly, the REIA's predictions indicate that the project is also an "urbanization grab". By using potential provincial and federal government development funds available for water projects, the interests behind the project hope to channel urban growth south of Winnipeg into the Pembina Valley. This motivation has not been specified in the REIA.

Social Issues and Concerns

A vital public policy and planning concern must be the social impacts of the project, especially upon people and their lives. A recent study on impact assessment has asserted that an effective attempt must be, at least partially, "politically oriented" rather than technically oriented (see Craig, 1990). It underscores the importance of PI in the project decision-making process whereas the scope for PI in regional economic analysis is nominal.

Water supply is bound up in quality-of-life issues and not just economic growth. The achievement of urban lifestyle standards in rural communities is at issue. To address these concerns impact assessment must, necessarily, gauge public perception of the project over and above the apparently objective measures of REIA.

Also, since REIA is concerned with the aggregated features, the local-level effects are generalized and shaped in unrecognizable forms. The regional benefits from projects may involve redistribution of wealth and economic opportunities, and thus growth in one community could take place at the expense of the other communities (see McDonald, 1990). Knowing the distribution of impacts is vital for decision makers, and community-level studies ought to be part of impact assessment (see Chapter 3 for a discussion of the PI techniques used in the case).

Location as a Factor and Intra-Regional Variation

Within the Pembina Valley region there are varied economic circumstances. Some communities have recently taken advantage of urban growth associated with Winnipeg. They have benefitted greatly from increased manufacturing and service activity associated with urban Winnipeg, and their real estate markets are booming on the back of an influx of urban commuters. In contrast, communities located far from Winnipeg's orbit have had to garner economic growth from farm diversification and an expansion of food processing. At the very least, this means that the REIA for the Pembina Valley water project cannot be used as a baseline for other rural communities. The economic diversity of rural Manitoba cuts across this kind of transition. It is necessary to differentiate between the RMs influenced by Winnipeg's urban growth and those further away that are experiencing rural decline. The economic impacts in peri-urban areas and declining rural communities are likely to be substantially different.

The provision of improved water services has been an ongoing activity in the Pembina Valley region. RMs have been limited in their attempts to meet consumer demands by their varied access to surface water, their local revenues, and access to federal and provincial funds to meet the high capital costs of water treatment and pipeline facilities. In some cases the benefits from water pipeline provision are already manifest. In locating future developments, it is important to determine the trade-offs between maximizing regional gains and retaining or creating local opportunities.

Externalities, and Ecological Costs

The claimed regional economic benefits from the Pembina Valley water improvement project should be considered cautiously. The economic definition of gains is narrow, and the associated benefit-cost analysis is limited since the ecological costs have not been accounted. Most REIA tend to factor these costs as externalities and thus keep them outside the benefit-cost analysis. Yet, in an analysis of water-service development, ecological costs and issues must be a principal concern. In particular, if a supply constraint prevails in a given watershed or drainage basin, as in fact it does in most of southern Manitoba, the opportunity costs involved in delivering water supply to a few locations and not others, and the ecological costs associated with overdraw on limited resources, may prove to be substantial.

In this case, consideration of the economic impacts only in terms of economic optimization may not be effective. The ecological costs should be accounted for to estimate the actual net benefits that would accrue from the proposed project. The physical supply constraint itself can impose restriction on further utilization of natural resources. Even when physical limitations do not impede improvement on the supply side, other ecological costs may emerge. Southern Manitoba's surface water has largely been tamed, often within concrete walls and pipes. The specific parameters of the effects of urban and industrial pollution are unknown as are the impacts on wildlife. The ecological costs should be accounted for, and, when they are, estimates of the actual net benefits that are to accrue from the proposed project will be considerably reduced.

In assessing the feasibility of the proposed Pembina Valley water project, both the surface water conditions in the Red and Assiniboine River basins as well as the ground water reserves in the related water basins require a critical appraisal. This evaluation should form a basis for ecological knowledge. In other words, the economic optimization envisioned in the REIA may neither allow preservation of ecological amenities nor reflect the actual net long-term gains from water supply projects. Perhaps too, they are apparent in the lack of interest in local economic and social impacts. After all the REIA predicts strong regional impacts, but says little about local benefits.

SIA of Water Supply Improvements in Rural and Rural-Urban Fringe Areas

Piped Water Provisions in Rhineland and MacDonald RMs: A Supply-Side Response

Demands for improved water services are socially driven. Increased affluence in the post-war era led to rising expectations, and rural communities demanded new and better services, especially an improved highway network, better schooling and medical facilities and improved water services. In the last two decades, nevertheless, the impetus behind improved rural services has faltered. Rural depopulation and decline, farm amalgamation and the slow demise of the family farm have all reduced the relative buying power of rural areas. In addition, governments' budgetary problems and demands for a reduced service role have translated into restructured and diminished public-service provision.

Governments have responded to demands for improved water services. The supply response has involved many different initiatives with various partnerships among different levels of government as well as water users. Between 1972 and 1991, the Alberta, Saskatchewan and Manitoba governments implemented a series of infrastructure programs at the municipal level in association with the federal government. The two major federal agencies financing and executing the community water infrastructure projects are the Prairie Farm Rehabilitation Administration (PFRA) and the Department of Regional Economic Expansion (DREE). Their activities in the field are relatively recent; however, only a few community water supply systems have been completed in rural Manitoba. Two finished pipeline projects, in Rhineland and MacDonald municipalities, were selected for study.

Differences in local fiscal circumstances and economic

and population growth rates are reflected in different patterns of water pipeline provision. Water services in Rhineland RM have been developed on a piecemeal basis from as early as 1976 as residents called for improved services. The Rhineland regional water system consists of ten separate pipeline systems which together supply 802 service connections (Figure 8.2). Four of these lines are administered by non-profit co-operatives and serve 330 rural households. The remaining six pipelines are administered by the Rhineland RM. Total costs of about $6.3 million have been widely spread over the years 1976 to 1989, with the peak expense of $1 million falling in 1992. About 36 percent of the costs were borne by PFRA another 44 percent by the municipality, residents and local co-operatives, and the remaining 20 percent by the Manitoba government largely through the Manitoba Water Services Board. The result is a decentralized system, partly in private hands, and largely catering to the needs of dispersed rural households (Figure 8.2). Despite these investments, the population of the RM has not grown and consequently the economic impact of water provision, while substantial, could be said to be limited.

In contrast, water improvements in MacDonald RM only began in the mid 1980s and were co-ordinated by the council. Pipelines were actively promoted by the Macdonald RM council beginning in 1984. A treatment plant at Sanford, drawing water from the Assiniboine River, was running in 1989 (Figure 8.3). As sufficient local interest develops, water pipeline connections to the Sanford plant are extended to new communities. So far, Domain, Oak Bluff, Starbuck, Osborne and surrounding rural households have been connected to the system. Improved water service has therefore been concentrated in the northeastern section of the municipality (Figure 8.3).

Altogether, the water system cost over $9 million during the period 1989 to August 1993. PFRA contributed $2.3 mil-

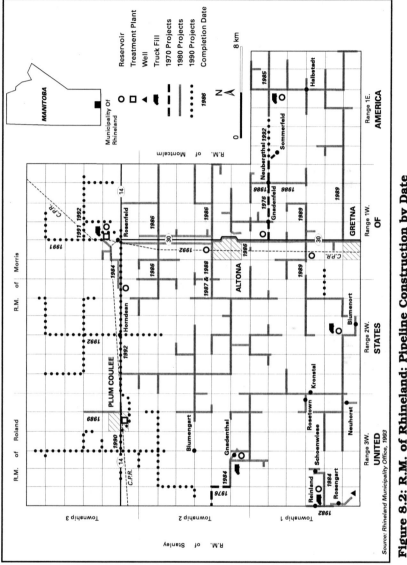

Figure 8.2: R.M. of Rhineland: Pipeline Construction by Date

Source: Rhineland Municipality Office, 1993

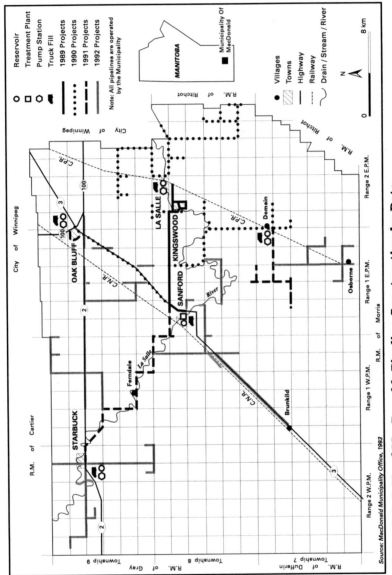

Figure 8.3: R.M. of MacDonald: Pipeline Construction by Date

Source: MacDonald Municipality Office, 1993

lion, the Manitoba Water Services Board $2.5 million and the municipality $4.5 million. The MacDonald system is under municipal management and control, is relatively capital intensive, is centralized on the Sanford treatment plant, and largely serves the urbanizing northeastern sections of the municipality. Indeed the system has been created because of the growth and revenue potential of non-farm activities on the edges of Winnipeg. This helps to explain the late (i.e., 1989) start of the water service improvement in this municipality. But it also relates to population and economic growth in the municipality. In MacDonald RM, improved water services have had substantial impacts.

The Survey Methods

The impacts, both perceived and actual, at the local level were studied using a sample of households in the two selected municipalities. The sampling frame of the study produced a total of 1,260 MacDonald RM households and 1,099 Rhineland RM households. Among these, the number of households having the water pipeline service facilities (i.e., target group) were 810 and 745, respectively, and the size of the control groups (i.e., households without pipeline connections) were 450 and 354, respectively.

Considering the significant variation within the target and control groups, in terms of farm and non-farm economic organization, further stratification of each group was necessary. Based on a random samplings procedure, a total of 1,200 households were mailed a questionnaire survey. The survey was carried out in the summer months of 1993. With a 25 percent response rate, a total of 301 responses was received: 173 from the water pipeline service users (WPSU) and 128 from the control group. The resulting distribution of respondents by economic activity was as follows: WPSU sample consisted of 64 farm and 109 non-farm households and the control group consisted of 49 farm and 79 non-farm households.

Community Level Social Impacts

The community-based questionnaire survey was made broad enough so that all relevant economic, social, community-developmental, and organizational aspects of water pipeline service provision could be assessed. In this study, only results of the analysis dealing with the most significant variables associated with SIA are reported. First, the economic multiplier effects are examined; second, the community-based social impacts are assessed; and finally, public attitudes towards improved water services are analyzed. The details of other SIA variables and the pertinent findings are available elsewhere (Haque and Winder, 1994; 1995).

Effects on Community and Local Economy

The relationships between infrastructure and development are debatable issues and so is the role of water service facilities in development. Many studies confirmed that water service facilities tend to "follow" development activities (Ashton and Bayer, 1983; Consulting and Audit Canada, 1992; Livingstone and Campbell, 1992; World Bank, 1994). However, along with many supply-side advocates, MacMillan et al. (1990; 1992) and Pembina Valley Water Cooperatives Inc. (1992) regard water service provision as a catalyst to non-farm activities, including suburban housing and infrastructural development.

Isolating the impacts of piped water services may be difficult. An initial step is to ask rural residents about the repercussions of pipe connection. Development of new farm activities like enlarged livestock operations, poultry farming, increased crop diversity, and the addition of commercial activities to the farmstead may be encouraged. Other effects are hidden inside the rural households themselves, offering better quality of life and access, and options for associated improvements in amenities and appliances. If these views are well-founded, there may be potential "forward" and "backward" linkages from improved water service provision.

The questionnaire elicited responses on the effects of pipeline provision on community development and the local economy. Primary effects were anticipated in terms of population change, diversified farm activities, and industrial and commercial growth. However, the survey responses reveal that the direct effects of pipeline-service facilities at the community level were limited (Tables 8.2 and 8.3). Increasing population size was thought to be an effect of pipeline provision by 43 percent of respondents (Table 8.2). However, a marked variation exists between the two study municipalities. Almost two-thirds of MacDonald RM respondents recognized a relationship between population increase and piped-water service, whereas only one-quarter of Rhineland respondents did (Table 8.2). These evaluations are realistic. The Rhineland population has not been growing. Location matters here: pipelines have different impacts depending on where they are built.

Table 8.2
Direct Effects of Pipeline Services on Population Change

Change Characteristics	MacDonald RM			Rhineland RM			Study Area		
	WP[1] n=86	CG[2] n=74	TS[3] n=160	WP n=87	CG n=54	TS n=141	WP n=173	CG n=128	TS n=301
Increased	63%	61%	62%	25%	18%	23%	44%	42%	43%
No Change	37%	39%	38%	75%	82%	77%	56%	58%	57%

[1]WP = WPSU Sample
[2]CG = Control Group
[3]TS = Total Sample

Table 8.3
Direct Effects of Pipeline Services on Community Economy,
Percentage Distribution*

Change Characteristics	Farm Activities			Industry and Commerce		
	WPSU Sample n=173	Control Group n=128	Total Sample n=301	WPSU Sample n=173	Control Group n=128	Total Sample n=301
Increased	29%	34%	31%	22%	25%	23%
No Change	71%	65%	68%	78%	75%	77%
Decreased	1%	1%	1%	-	-	-

*Multiple response possible.

Respondents reported few effects from pipeline services on the local economy (Table 8.3). The majority found no correlation between pipeline provision and community economic development. However, this view was most prominently held by the WPSU sample group. A lower proportion of the WPSU sample found a visible effect of pipelines on farm activities or industrial and commercial development than those not yet connected. These differences may be attributed to the varied experiences of the households. Those awaiting connection perceive water pipelines making a significant contribution to farm and non-farm activities.

Of the 173 WPSU sample households, only three reported that they started a new commercial venture since pipeline connection (i.e., 2 percent). So, while there are cases where the pipeline connection indeed prompted decisions to commence businesses, they are few in number. Only one business-household hired more employees after the pipeline connection.

Users also assert a positive correlation between population retention or an increase (through in-migration) and the quality and convenience of water supply. About 16 percent of the current pipeline users in MacDonald RM in-migrated to the RM after the pipeline infrastructure (i.e., since 1989). The respective figure for the RM of Rhineland is 10 percent but this has occurred over a longer period, 1976-1993. Among these recent arrivals to MacDonald RM, 85 percent considered piped water supply facility as an "important" or "very important" variable in their location decisions. In Rhineland RM, the availability of piped water was a less important influence upon migration: only 38 percent of the in-migrations considered this variable positively. These variations can be attributed to the different potentials for urbanization in the two RM's, and one must ask whether the community development effects are primarily a result of pipeline provision. Cutting across the effects of the pipelines are the different development potentials in each community.

Benefits to Life Styles and "Quality of Life"

The WPSU sample experienced many positive changes in addition to benefits from economic cost-reduction in household chores. Reception of "better drinking water" from pipeline service facilities benefitted the majority of the current users. More than 60 percent of the WPSU sample indicated that they obtained a better quality of drinking water after the pipeline connection. Connection to piped water has allowed the users to make significant changes in household amenities, most of which are associated with lifestyle changes. The number of household amenities and appliances has significantly increased since pipeline connection. The number of washing machines, dishwashers and hot tubs has risen by more than 45 percent.

Piped water supply brings about more leisure time and provides convenience. It also contributes to the relief of stress. More than 44 percent of pipeline users found a positive correlation between piped water supply and relief of stress (Table 8.4). This is not surprising, given the labor and stress associated with trucking and storing water in drought-prone prairie farm districts. Health conditions, however, are not as affected by piped water supply: according to the current users only 19 percent thought they experienced improvements in health due to piped water (Table 8.4).

Table 8.4
Changes in "Quality of Life" Since Pipeline Connection (WPSU Sample), Percentage Distribution*

Change Characteristics	"Quality of Life" Items				
	Convenience	Leisure Time	Enjoyment of Property	Health	Relief of Stress
Much Improved	59%	7%	15%	7%	13%
Improved	33%	35%	41%	12%	31%
Same (No Change)	9%	57%	44%	82%	54%
Worse	-	1%	1%	-	1%

*Multiple response possible.

Pipeline water services have significantly improved household water supply to both farm and non-farm households (84 and 93 percent respectively). Such improvements in water supply have helped keep rural dwellers in their present communities and/or allowed them to commute to urban work places. Among non-farm households of the WPSU sample, 62 percent indicated that the piped water supply allowed them to live in the countryside and commute. This was a much higher percentage than for farm households (only 26 percent). One quarter of the farm household sample thought that piped water has facilitated enlargement of farm operations.

Change in Water Use

Significant shifts in the patterns of water use among both farm and non-farm sample households are discernable after the pipeline connection. For instance, more of the sample households use water in sprinkling their lawns, garden and yards now than before the pipeline connection. Two farmsteads have reported that now they use more than three-quarters of their water in livestock raising, whereas none used such a high percentage share prior to pipeline services. Overall, changes in water use indicate a gradual diversification in household activities and economic organization, but reveal no dramatic shifts.

Adverse Effects

The survey contained both "open ended" and closed questions to capture the adverse effects of pipeline infrastructure at the household level. Three types of problems were identified by the WPSU respondents: (i) increases in property tax; (ii) rising home insurance costs; and (iii) trouble with septic tank, field and well water. However, only rising property taxes were identified as a problem by a considerable proportion of the pipeline users (45 percent; Table 8.5). Property tax increases are primarily attributed to an increase in property value. Similarly, rising home insurance costs are chiefly caused by the increased property values. This is confirmed by the significant difference in property tax increases between MacDonald and Rhineland (Table 8.5). Only four percent of the WPSU respondents reported an increase in problems with septic tank, field or well associated with piped water supply.

Table 8.5
**Adverse Effects of Pipeline Connection on Household
Economy and Environment (WPSU Sample), Percentage
Distribution***

Adverse (unintentional) effects of pipeline connection	MacDonald RM n=86	Rhineland RM n=87	Study Area n=173
Property tax has increased	53%	38%	45%
Insurance costs have increased	11%	10%	10%
Problems with septic tank, field and well water have increased	5%	3%	4%

*Multiple response possible.

Community Attitudes Towards Water Infrastructure Projects

Although the respondents were quite divided about local social impacts, they were nevertheless wholly in favour of water service provision. They expressed a high level of satisfaction with the services provided and anticipated future expansion of pipeline services. Rhineland and MacDonald residents also had clear views on the costs and funding arrangements for water projects.

Level of Satisfaction

A high degree of satisfaction among the piped water users, in terms of improvements in quality of life, convenience, time saving and cost-effectiveness, is revealed in the survey data. Residents offered qualitative information on the utility of piped water in a voluntary section in the questionnaire. The comments of the WPSU sample consisted largely of evaluative notes on: (i) utility or satisfaction; (ii) costs and fees; and (iii) water quality and taste. In total, 19 WPSU respondents included voluntary comments, expressing their satisfaction with the pipeline connection and services. They assessed satisfaction primarily in terms of convenience, and lifestyle. One farmer noted:

> I am very happy with the pipeline as it saves me time and money over hauling my own water. Trucking water in bad weather was both time consuming and dangerous. Quality of water I receive is now very good and I have never been without water pressure since I have hooked up.

Another farm dweller wrote,

> It is just great. No more Sunday morning emergency trips to pick up water because we just ran out half way through a shower or half way through the dishwasher cycle. A real great convenience.

This simple impact should not be underestimated. It is at this personal level that the demands for treated, piped water can best be understood. Indeed, pipeline water supply has greatly reduced the anxiety of rural inhabitants, and materially as well as psychologically improved their lot.

Current and Future Needs

The majority of both WPSU sample and control group respondents felt that the existing pipeline infrastructure is sufficient to meet the current and future needs (95 and 90 percent respectively). There is no noticeable variation in the assessment by the WPSU sample and the control group, and thus a pattern of uniformity can be asserted. About 71 percent of the entire sample foresee an increasing demand for piped water facilities in their communities in the next decade. As one might expect, the control group perceives a significantly higher future demand than that of the WPSU sample.

A considerable proportion of the survey respondents also foresee a need to expand or modernize their community's municipal water supply facilities in the next decade (i.e., 40 percent) (Table 8.6). A conspicuous variation in this response between the MacDonald and Rhineland residents emerged. About 52 percent of all sample households in the RM of MacDonald responded affirmatively to the relevant question whereas the respective percentage in the RM of Rhineland was only 25 (Table 8.6). This reflects the more limited pipe network in MacDonald RM. The future demand for piped water, as expressed by the respondents, is likely to be higher in the communities closer to Winnipeg than in more distant areas. Overall, the survey data indicate general satisfaction with the current infrastructural network and services. However, future demand for piped water service facilities is expected by the majority of the rural inhabitants.

Table 8.6
Perception of Future Needs of Water Services,
Percentage Distribution

Location	"Foresee a need to expand or modernize my community's municipal water facilities in the next decade"		
	WPSU Sample n=173	Control Group n=128	Total Sample n=301
RM of MacDonald	51%	55%	52%
RM of Rhineland	18%	38%	25%
Study Area	35%	48%	40%

Cost Procurement

Many of the control-group respondents found the installation and connection fee too high, and unaffordable. One farmer commented:

> Initial cost to bring water pipeline one and half miles to my farm is just too great and not justifiable at the present - a grant should be made available.

The majority of the control group is of the opinion that public institutions, with an arrangement for sharing the installation cost, should be responsible for undertaking the infrastructure projects. It appears that the majority would like to see the municipal government responsible for water pipeline installation - cost procurement wise (53 percent) (Table 8.7). Similarly, about 42 and 31 percent would prefer the provincial and federal governments respectively for performing the above role. However, only 27 percent of respondents feel that it is a private responsibility.

Table 8.7
Responsibility for Pipeline Installation (Control Group)*

Response	"In your opinion, who should be responsible for installing a pipeline to your property?"	
	Number n=128	Percentage
Federal Government	40	31
Provincial Government	54	42
Municipal Government	68	53
Cooperative	21	16
Private Owners	35	27

*Multiple response possible.

Questions concerning cost procurement and its distribution were put forward both to the WPSU sample and the control group. Altogether 89 percent of the entire sample favor some kind of user fee for piped water service; more than 60 percent of both the WPSU sample and control group would prefer "entirely user fee" or "primarily user fee" arrangement for piped water services. Interestingly, more of the control group respondents prefer an "entirely user fee" than the WPSU sample, whereas many of the latter group prefer a "primarily user fee" option. This is reflected in the chi-square test which shows a significant difference in preference between the WPSU sample and the control group ($p < 0.05$). Overall, it is indicated that the present and potential piped water consumers do not prefer a higher magnitude of subsidy from the public institutions. However, residents recognize that supports from all levels of government are required if projects are to be built in municipalities. This seems realistic given the high, initial capital costs.

A Concluding Commentary

In the case of Canadian prairie water service improvement projects, a simple SIA reveals limitations to the REIA approach, and thus indicates SIA as an important complement to REIA. This study reveals that, because of the inherent inadequacies of the REIA approach, the analysis is heavily biased towards economic and macro-regional dimensions. Consequently, although MacMillan and Coyle (1993) and MacMillan et al. (1994) applied REIA to the case of Manitoba appropriately, their scope was limited by the inherent shortcomings of REIA. The REIA of the proposed Pembina Valley water supply project predicts that the project will generate immense economic multipliers both within and outside the region. While construction itself would contribute to the regional economy, water service provision was hypothesized as a catalyst to both farm and non-farm activities. Experience in two rural municipalities, however, challenges this notion. Survey results and interviews with key-informants in the RMs of MacDonald and Rhineland reveal no industrial/commercial and employment spillovers resulted from piped water supply facilities. The community-based SIA here suggests that the macro-economic benefits portrayed in REIA may not be realized at the micro-regional or community level, and indeed may be heavily overstated.

Improved water supply provision in rural areas, nonetheless, plays some crucial community development roles: in attracting new immigrants and retaining the existing population; and by providing convenience, access to better life-styles, and more leisure time, for what is an aging population. In a period of general decline in Canadian rural population and economy, viable infrastructural projects are of vital importance to the local communities. The political support to these initiatives would stem from social rather than direct economic factors. The SIA presented in this study has demonstrated unanimous support for improved water supply provisions through infrastructure development projects. The survey indicates, too, that residents have well-founded knowledge of social and economic impacts. Their views should be treated with respect.

Comparison of the REIA and SIA findings raises troubling questions. The PVWC's consultants neglect the social reasons for treated, piped water provision: convenience, improved life-styles, and relief of stress. Instead, their analysis points to economic growth on a grand scale. Neither the local impacts of growth (industrialization and urbanization, loss of farmland, etc.), nor the opportunity costs for other communities, nor the spatial distribution of benefits are treated seriously.

The key question is who is planning for what? REIA focuses planning on regional economic growth issues. The winners and losers in the proposed allocation of resources are not identified. What is important is the aggregate outcome. Yet residents are unable to identify spinoff effects in their communities. Few jobs are actually generated from this investment, especially in local communities. If the planning goal is job creation, then other investments might be better bets. Indeed, the planning requirements for a REIA give a message to community groups anxious for piped water provision that the proper justification for a treated plant and pipe network is overall growth in wealth, and job generation outside the community. Even from an economic point of view, there is no requirement to indicate ways to enhance local capture of economic impacts.

This peculiar situation is reflected in the nature of the REIA done for the Pembina Valley. All of the salient allocation issues are no more than implicit in the report. Other communities might well regard this proposal as a water and finance grab by Pembina Valley. The REIA ignores this but offers no comprehensive basis for planning water resource allocation and enhancement. The SIA goes someway to reflect the limited assumptions of the REIA and thus to place other issues — especially life-style issues — front and center. But even it does not go far enough. Perhaps most worrying of all is the silence in both REIA and SIA on the subject of environmental and resource issues. Can there be an expectation of residents to identify environmental concerns and impacts associated with piped water provision? Can there be a desire for REIA to deal with ecological costs? The planning process will have to come to terms with this.

This study underscores the need for an integration between REIA and SIA in the impact assessment process. Neither one alone is sufficient to offer a thorough analysis of the effects of project implementation. As regional economic impact assessment provides predictions of significant elements of social impact assessment, the latter also offers crucial political insights required in the decision-making process. For the process of negotiation to be efficient, both regional and social impact information should be available.

Acknowledgements

The author thanks the Ministry of Rural Development, Government of Manitoba for funding this research; Richard Rounds, Director, Rural Development Institute, Brandon for his logistical and administrative contributions; Gordon Winder, University of Auckland at Tamaki, New Zealand, for his inputs in conducting the research; Molly Parvin for her assistance in data management and processing; and, Darren Stanger for his assistance in preparing the map.

References

Ashton, W.J. and Bayer, M.B. (1983) "Water supply and urban growth planning: a partnership," *Water Resources Bulletin*, 19: 779-784.

Bisset, R. (1983) "A critical survey of methods for impact assessment," in O'Riordan, T. and Turner, R.K. (eds.), *An Annotated Reader in Environmental Planning and Management*, Oxford, UK: Pergamon, 168-186.

Burdge, R.J. and Robertson, R.A. (1990) "Social impact assessment and the public involvement process," *Environmental Impact Assessment*, 10: 81-90.

Caldwell, L.K. (1988) "Environmental impact analysis: origins, evolution, and future directions," *Impact Assessment Bulletin*, 6: 75-83.

Carley, M.J. and Bustelo, E.S. (1984) *Social Impact Assessment and Monitoring*, Boulder, CO: Westview Press.

Consulting and Audit Canada (1992) *Evaluation Study of the Agricultural Community Water Infrastructure Program*, Ottawa, ON: Ministry of Supply and Services.

Cope, D. and Hills, P. (1988) "Total assessment: myth or reality?," in Clark, M. and Herington, J. (eds.), *The Role of Environmental Impact Assessment in the Planning Process*, London, UK: Mansell, 174-193.

Craig, D. (1990) "Social impact assessment: politically oriented approaches and applications," *Environmental Impact Assessment Review*, 10: 37-54.

D'Amore, L.J. (1978) "An overview of SIA," in Tester, F.J. and Mykes, W. (eds.), *Social Impact Assessment Theory and Method and Practices*, Calgary, AB: Detselig, 366-373.

Doern, G.B. and Phidd, R.W. (1983) *Canadian Public Policy: Ideas, Structure, Process*, Toronto, ON: Methuen.

Finsterbusch, K. (1980) *Understanding Social Impacts*, Beverly Hills, CA: Sage Publishers.

Finsterbusch, K. and Wolf, C.P. (eds.) (1977) *Methodology of Social Impact Assessment*, Stroudsburg, PA: Hutchinson and Ross.

Finsterbusch, K., Llewellyn, L.G. and Wolf, C.P. (eds.) (1983) *Social Impact Assessment Methods*, Beverly Hills, CA: Sage Publishers.

Flynn, C.B., Flynn, J.H., Chalmers, J.A., Pijawka, D. and Branch, K. (1983) "An integrated methodology for large scale development projects," in Finsterbusch, K., Llewellyn, L.G. and Wolf, C.P. (eds.), *Social Impact Assessment Methods*, Beverly Hills, CA: Sage Publications.

Hamilton, J.R. et al. (1991) "Economic impacts, value added, and benefits in regional project analysis," *American Journal of Agricultural Economics*, 73: 334-344.

Haque, C.E. and Winder, G. (1994) "Provision of water services and infrastructure planning in rural Manitoba: a regional (EIA) and social impact assessment (SIA)," A paper presented at the Annual Meeting of the Canadian Association of Geographers, Prairie Division, Minot, North Dakota, September 30 - October 1.

_____ (1995) *Impact Assessment of Rural Water Systems: An Evaluation of Regional Water Services in Rhineland and MacDonald*, Brandon, MN: Rural Development Institute.

Lang, R. (1986) *Integrated Approaches to Resource Planning and Management*, Calgary, AB: University of Calgary Press.

Leistritz, F.L. and Murdock, S.H. (1981) *The Socioeconomic Impact of Resource Development: Methods for Assessment*, Boulder, CO: Westview Press.

Livingstone, A.J. and Campbell, I.A. (1992) "Water supply and urban growth in southern Alberta: constraint or catalyst?," *Journal of Arid Environments*, 23: 335-359.

MacMillan, J., Chorney, B., Coyle, B. and Grunau, S. (1990) *Pembina Valley Water Task Force Study: Economic Assessment*, Research Report, Winnipeg, MN: Department of Agricultural Economics, University of Manitoba.

MacMillan, J. and Coyle, B.T. (1993) *Regional Economic Evaluation Methodology: The Pembina Valley Water Supply Project*, Working Paper No. 93-2, Winnipeg, MN: Department of Agricultural Economics and Farm Management, University of Manitoba.

MacMillan, J. and De Matos, G. (1992) *Manitoba/Western Canada Red Meat Industries: Strategies and Impact Analysis*, Winnipeg, MN: Manitoba Red Meat Forum.

MacMillan, J., Johnson, G., Kraft, D., Power, M. and Dragojevic, I. (1994) "Trade policies and impact assessment: the Manitoba Pembina Valley water supply project," *Impact Assessment*, 12: 153-173.

McDonald, G.T. (1990) "Regional economic and social impact assessment," *Environmental Impact Assessment Review*, 37: 25-36.

Mitchell, B. (1986) "The evolution of integrated resource management," in Lang, R. (ed.), *Integrated Approaches to Resource Planning and Management*, Calgary, AB: University of Calgary Press, 13-26.

Pembina Valley Water Cooperative Inc. (PVWC) (1991) *Pembina Valley Regional Water Supply Draft Environmental Impact Statement*, Altona, MN: Pembina Valley Development Corporation.

Pembina Valley Water Cooperative Inc. (1992) *Environmental Impact Statements for the Pembina Valley Water Supply Proposal*, Winnipeg, MN: Dillon Consulting Engineers, Planners and Environmental Scientists.

Rickson, R.E. et al. (1990) "Social impact assessment: knowledge and development," *Environmental Impact Assessment Review*, 37: 1-10.

Smith, G.L. (1993) *Impact Assessment and Sustainable Resource Management*, New York, NY: John Wiley and Sons, Inc.

Smith, L.G. (1984) "Public participation in policy making," *Geoforum*, 15: 253-59.

Tester, F.J. and Mykes, W. (eds.) (1981) *Social Impact Assessment: Theory, Method and Practice*, Calgary, AB: Detselig.

Vig, N.J. and Kraft, M.E. (eds). (1990) *Environmental Policy in the 1990s*, Washington, DC: C.Q. Press.

Winnipeg Free Press (1992) "Living in the valley," January 2, A6.

World Bank (1994) *World Development Report 1994: Infrastructure for Development*, New York, NY: Oxford University Press.

Section 3

Examining the Context of Environmental Assessment

Chapter 9

Differentiation and Integration in the EIA Planning Process

David P. Lawrence
Lawrence Environmental

The chapter seeks to transcend the competing negative propensities in environmental impact assessment (EIA) practice to ignore context in the quest for standardized approaches or to view each EIA as a unique endeavour that cannot draw upon past and parallel experiences.

A recurrent concern with the state of EIA practice, at both the regulatory and applied levels, has been the need for consistency. This concern has arisen from a high degree of variability in regulatory requirements (often for the same proposal type) and in the content of individual EIA documents. These differences often are not warranted by contextual variations or by the legitimate differences in interpretation and perspective inevitable in a rapidly evolving field of theory and practice. As a consequence there has been a call for the harmonization of requirements and the standardization of report formats, procedures, methods and, in some cases, even alternatives and criteria. The concerns that have led to the call for harmonization and standardization are valid. However, the suggested solutions could be even more problematic. Somewhere between the two extremes of standardized EIA regulatory requirements, procedures and products and the view that EIA in each jurisdiction and for each proposal is unique is the fertile middle ground that should be the focus of EIA planning process design. It is a middle ground that should be approached with great care.

This issue of balancing differentiation and integration in EIA planning process design is approached in this chapter through a series of contextual categories - environment type, proposal type, proponent type, public type and setting type. In each case, examples of major distinctions are identified that might warrant differences in EIA planning process design at the regulatory and applied levels. Having indicated the need to respect differences, consideration then is given to the potential for spanning boundaries and transcending differences. The analysis concludes with general lessons regarding balancing differentiation and integration in EIA.

Environment Type

EIA is generally viewed as encompassing three major subfields - ecological, social and economic impact assessment. Social and economic impact assessment are sometimes combined as the human environment or as socio-economic impact assessment (McDonald, 1991). The similarities and differences among these subfields are important to EIA planning process design considerations. Given the need to integrate ecological, social and economic perspectives in EIA, transcending differences are even more important.

The three EIA subfields share a common aim - to broaden planning and decision making beyond narrow technical and economic concerns (Craig, 1990). The major steps in the EIA planning process for each do not differ appreciably (Interorganizational Committee, 1995) nor do the major impact dimensions (e.g., positive - negative, scale, extent, duration, intensity, severity) (McDonald, 1991; Interorganizational Committee, 1995). There are many parallels in the issues addressed (e.g., threatened, rare and endangered species, vulnerable human populations) (Interorganizational Committee, 1995) and all require institutional arrangements to ensure implementation.

The three subfields, however, address different variables and have a different disciplinary knowledge base (Leistritz, 1994; Interorganizational Committee, 1995). Major differences exist in the perspectives and conceptual tools used by the natural and social sciences. The social sciences tend to be more discursive and critical and less predictive and explanatory than the natural sciences (Burdge and Vanclay, 1996). This latter difference, coupled with the complexity of social and economic systems (i.e., multi-finality - the same inputs often produces different results), make it especially difficult to predict impacts on social and economic phenomena (Thompson and Williams, 1990; Finsterbusch, 1995).

Social phenomena react in different ways to change, and the prospect of change, than do natural phenomena. The social and economic environment reacts in anticipation of change and can adapt in reasoned ways to changing circumstances (Interorganizational Committee, 1995). Reality can be socially constructed through perceptions, attitudes and values (Interorganizational Committee, 1995). Social impact analysis must address cultural differences (Nesbitt, 1990; Edelstein and Kleese, 1995; Burdge and Vanclay, 1996), social equity implications, especially with regard to marginalized and disenfranchised parties (Dale and Kennedy, 1981), and political - economic impacts (Rickson et al., 1990).

Although the three subfields generally share common EIA institutional arrangements, social impacts tend to be less well entrenched in public and private planning processes and have less decision-making influence (Interorganizational Committee, 1995). A greater effort may be required to ensure such concerns receive adequate consideration.

While differences among ecological, social and economic variables and analysis methods must be appreciated, a greater integration of these subfields within the EIA planning process is also desirable, beginning with a sound understanding of the interconnections among proposal components, among environmental components within disciplines (McDonald and Brown, 1995) and between individual environmental components and individual proposal components. The integration of environmental and proposal components should culminate in the integration of EIA within the proposal planning process (Armour, 1990).

Major interactions among disciplines next can be identified and implications addressed - an interdisciplinary analysis (Stefanovic, 1996). More subtle and less direct interactions can then be explored (Westman, 1985). Still more systematic interdisciplinary analyses require a modified planning process (e.g., adaptive environmental assessment) (Holling, 1978; Regier, 1985; Geisler, 1993), the explicit assessment of cumulative environmental effects (Shoemaker, 1994) and the incorporation of sustainability ends and means (Sadler, 1995). Disciplinary boundaries should be progressively spanned with this process. Ideally what should emerge is a truly transdisciplinary analysis. Transdisciplinary synthesis transcends interdisciplinary integration by fully addressing interconnections and by establishing a new meta-level of discourse (Klein, 1990; Stefanovic, 1996).

Proposal Type

The most common proposal type distinction in EIA concerns project type. Examples include linear transportation and utility systems, airports, transit systems, waste management facilities, water resource facilities, mines and energy projects. Until recently, for example, there were different EIA requirements in British Columbia for different project types - major industry, energy and mining. EIA requirements in Canada now apply across project types. Generic guidelines have been formulated for various project types in some jurisdictions (Canada, Ontario, Quebec). Generic guidelines, by project type, can focus on the analysis of alternatives, impacts, mitigation measures and issues. Care must be taken to ensure that sufficient flexibility is retained to address project and site-specific issues and concerns. Important lessons can be drawn from experience with similar projects in similar settings (Egre and Senecal, 1990; Dickman, 1991; Rhodes, 1993; Sadar and Dirschl, 1996).

A further distinction can be drawn between project level EIA and the application of EIA to policies, programs and plans. The latter is often referred to as strategic environmental assessment (SEA) as outlined in Chapter 7. (See also Therivel et al., 1992; Sadler, 1996). The related field, technology assessment (TA), addresses the effects on society that occur when a technology is introduced, extended or modified (Coates, 1976). The similarities and differences between EIA and SEA parallel those between EIA and TA.

SEA and TA involve more than the simple extension of EIA procedures, requirements and methods, largely developed at the project level. The very limited application of EIA requirements in Canada beyond the project level is not an accidental oversight. It reflects important differences and significant barriers, as Novakowski and Wellar address (Chapter 7). Nevertheless, public and private decision making at all levels should be broadened to systematically anticipate and evaluate social, economic and ecological consequences (Craig, 1990; Porter, 1995; Partidario, 1996). Institutional arrangements that address such concerns also will be necessary.

Although such reforms are desirable, it does not necessarily follow that SEA is the appropriate instrument for broadening the decision-making basis of policies, plans and programs. Other instruments, such as environmental planning and management, may be as or more appropriate, providing that they require the consideration of social, ecological and economic concerns and consequences and that they consider the perspectives of interested and affected parties. Thus, in addressing the differences between EIA and SEA (and the potential for their integration) in the balance of this section, the phrase "or its equivalent" could be attached to all references to SEA.

Project level EIA can offer SEA and TA many insights, procedures and methods, providing the implications of operating at different decision-making levels are appreciated. Ultimately, EIA, SEA and TA should be integrated, together and within still broader frameworks.

EIA at the project level (referred to as EIA in the balance of this chapter) addresses physical projects and activities. An EIA decision determines whether a project will or will not be undertaken. The ultimate product of a SEA (used to refer to both SEA and TA in the balance of this chapter) is a decision or a series of decisions (Partidario, 1996).

The EIA planning process usually is initiated by a decision - the identification of a need or opportunity that may be fulfilled by a physical project. It also ends, with the exception of post-approval monitoring, with a decision regarding whether a project should or should not proceed. SEA focuses on emerging issues and problems. Hence it is more proactive (Therivel et al., 1992). SEA is more properly characterized as a continuous series of decisions (Coates, 1990; Lerman, 1994; Partidario, 1996). This continuity of SEA decision making makes it difficult to bound the SEA planning process. When, for example, does the policy-making and program formulation process begin and end (Ortolano and Shepherd, 1995)?

Other EIA versus SEA differences include:

- The SEA planning process is less clearly defined, less formally structured and more open-ended (Smith, 1993; Lerman, 1994; Porter, 1995).

- The SEA planning process is necessarily more uncertain (Ortolano and Shepherd, 1995) and consequently more adaptable (Partidario, 1996).

- SEA alternatives often are more difficult to identify (Therivel et al., 1992). SEA usually embraces a wider range of choices, although the no-action alternative is rarely considered (Coates, 1990; Lerman, 1994). SEA alternatives tend to overlap (i.e., rarely mutually exclusive) to a greater degree with permutations and combinations of alternatives emerging as the planning process evolves.

- The temporal and spatial area of application with SEA is generally much greater (Therivel et al., 1992; Therivel, 1993).

- SEA usually encompasses a wider range of issues and publics (Therivel, 1993; Porter, 1995).

- SEA must consider impacts on related policies and decision-making areas.

- With SEA, impact management can be undertaken in a more proactive and systematic manner (Therivel et al., 1992).

- The level of detail necessarily is broader with SEA (Tywoniuk, 1990).

- SEA is more concerned with and suited to addressing cumulative, indirect and time delay impacts as well as sustainability-related issues (Therivel et al., 1992; Therivel, 1993; Kennett and Perl, 1995).

- SEA methods tend to be more theoretical and less fully developed and accepted (Porter, 1995). The range of disciplines involved in SEA tends to be narrower (Therivel,

1993; Partidario, 1996).

- The SEA planning process tends to be less formal, more political and less open to public involvement (Therivel et al., 1992; Partidario, 1996). Concerns with confidentiality often are used to preclude or limit stakeholder involvement, until very late in the planning process.

- SEA is institutionalized to a much lesser extent, as is readily evident in EIA requirements in Canada.

- The SEA planning process more frequently involves multiple agencies (i.e., co-proponents) and levels of government (Partidario, 1996). As a result, channels of communications among agencies and levels of government are more important.

These differences should be reflected in the planning process. This accords with the view that EIA theory building should be pluralistic and contingent. Notwithstanding such differences, the over twenty years of EIA theoretical development and experience can still be highly instructive for SEA.

Boundary spanning is especially important at the regulatory level. To take the Canadian example, the current structure seems to be largely an amalgam of:

- EIA and a very restricted form of SEA, as represented by a statement of environmental implications for major new policies and programs at the federal level.

- EIA and no, or very occasional SEA, as evident in most provinces.

- EIA and SEA as separate systems with very limited interconnections. Ontario, with largely separate EIA planning and SEA (the Environmental Bill of Rights)

(Ontario, 1990) systems, is a case in point.

The integration of EIA and SEA could begin with a commitment to apply a consistent set of environmental and sustainability principles and criteria to existing and new policies and programs. A more formal and systematic SEA procedure then could be initiated in each jurisdiction. EIA and SEA experiences in other jurisdictions (Therivel et al., 1992; Therivel, 1993; Wood, 1995; Partidario, 1996) would be instructive in this endeavour. Obvious overlaps and omissions between the two systems could be identified (Richardson, 1994), as the first step toward harmonization (Kennett and Perl, 1995; Partidario, 1996). Some jurisdictions may elect to proceed with a single EIA/SEA system, perhaps with separate subsystems. Alternatively, they may prefer a process of gradual convergence (European Bank for Reconstruction and Development, 1995).

SEA should frame EIA (Lichfield, 1996). Both should be based on sustainability (Therivel et al., 1992). The policies, programs and plans that emerge from the SEA process should establish the terms of reference for EIA projects. SEA can address need and most alternatives to a proposed project. The geographic scope of any site search process can be narrowed, an environmental data base can be provided and a policy context can be established. A SEA also can identify generic impacts and mitigative measures, address cumulative and sustainability impacts and provide a broader impact management system (Wood and Dejeddour, 1990; Johnston and Madison, 1994; Rivas et al., 1994; Kennett and Perl, 1995; McDonald and Brown, 1995; Sadar and Dirschl, 1996).

The framing of EIA within SEA next can be formalized into a hierarchical or tiered system. An EIA would be triggered by specific SEA requirements (e.g., a project proposal of a certain type, scale or location) (Partidario, 1994). Areal planning then can be added at the regional, community and development control levels (Tywoniuk, 1990; Johnston and Madison, 1994; Lerman, 1994; Conacher, 1994/1995). A blended approach can assess the compatibility of existing and proposed facilities with environmental protection requirements (i.e., environmental integration assessment) (Lachavanne, 1991). Further extensions can encompass such related fields as risk assessment, technology assessment, resource management (Dunster, 1990; Williams, 1990) and environmental quality control (Coates, 1976, 1990; Marshall et al., 1985; Grima et al., 1986; Vig, 1992; Arquiga et al., 1992, 1994; Carpenter, 1995; Margerum and Born, 1995; Porter, 1995; Wyant et al., 1995).

As the integration process proceeds, components will be redefined (Mayda, 1996). Sustainability goals and objectives and ecosystem planning (Brocking, 1994; Kay and Schneider, 1994) and management principles (Slocombe, 1993) can guide and structure integration efforts (Smith, 1993). Strategic interventions (Conacher, 1994/1995; Treweek, 1995) will be required. Non-hierarchical network-based institutional structures, with flexible and permeable boundaries (Marshall et al., 1985; Partidario, 1996) can better manage complex, rapidly changing environmental and social systems than rigid hierarchical, bureaucratic structures. Such structures also can respect valid differences among proposal types. Ultimately, environmental management systems should be nested within, and responsive to, national environmental strategies (Kuusinen et al., 1994) and global and international environmental perspectives and institutional arrangements (Wood and Dejeddour, 1990; Malik, 1995; Sandford, 1996).

Strategic and structural harmonization initiatives, as described above, will face significant institutional barriers (Caldwell, 1994). They also will encounter perspectives that fundamentally conflict (e.g., ecocentric versus anthropocentric) (Bell, 1994). Because such conflicts are not fully reconcilable, difficult and controversial positions will need to be taken if the full potential of such systems is to be realized.

Proponent Type

EIA requirements in Canada, with the exception of Ontario, are triggered by project type rather than proponent type. EIA planning process design should still be sensitive to proponent-type differences. Small municipalities and native bands, for example, have limited resources and expertise. Involvement in a costly and protracted EIA planning and approval process can represent a major hardship.

There are also significant differences between public and private proponents. A private proponent, who operates on the basis of market opportunity rather than public need, will only commence a process if convinced of economic and technical feasibility; will only consider services within its current and anticipated future mission statement; requires an economic return of investment; will tightly circumscribe its exposure to economic risk; and, will require sufficient certainty to flexibly respond to changing conditions relative to marketplace competitors. Also, a private proponent can not expropriate land, ensure that the sale price of land is at market value, or modify regulatory requirements if necessary to achieve its purposes. These characteristics will determine if and when a private sector proponent initiates an EIA planning process, what are considered reasonable alternatives, the economic factors used to screen and compare alternatives and to predict and to manage impacts, the public involvement methods applied (e.g., limits to which it will share decision making), and impact management choices and commitments.

At a broader level, strict boundaries among proponent types are becoming less relevant. Environmental management is a multistakeholder process involving the public sector, the corporate sector, non-government organizations and the public. Public - private partnerships are more common.

SEA, area-wide EIA and cumulative impact assessment usually involve multiple proponents and a diverse array of stakeholders. Harmonizing environmental requirements among government levels, if legitimate differences are respected, can avoid duplication, address omissions and ensure consistent and complementary efforts. Multistakeholder mechanisms (e.g., round tables, commissions, trust partnerships) may facilitate cooperative environmental management approaches.

The public sector is charged with defining and protecting the public interest. EIA proposals should be evaluated against public policies and priorities, potentially defined through SEA. EIA requirements, that apply to any proponent type, should be specified. Supplementary requirements may be needed for particular proponent types and/or adjustments and interpretations may be required to reflect legitimate differences among proponent types. These adjustments should be made explicit and should be applied consistently.

Public Participation Perspectives and Types of Publics

Public and agency involvement in the EIA planning process is both desirable and necessary. Arguably, the public has a right to be involved in decisions that interest and affect them, consistent with democratic principles (Gibson, 1975; Priscoli and Homenuck, 1986; Howell et al., 1987). Public and agency involvement is of value both in its own right (e.g., greater public understanding and involvement in public life, fosters self expression, environmental sensitivity and leadership development) and in an instrumental sense (e.g., contributes substantive knowledge, identifies public concerns and values, assists in EIA interpretations and evaluations, provides a check on government and private action, facilitates consensus building and conflict resolution) (Pateman, 1970; Hadden et al., 1981; Priscoli and Homenuck, 1986; Howell et al., 1987; Hyman et al., 1988;

Praxis, 1988).

The choice of method for involving agencies and the public is more open to debate, as established in Section 1 of this book. The EA planning process should select and adapt public consultation methods to match the characteristics, needs and desires of interested and potentially affected segments of the community.

Public consultation methods tend to be depicted in hierarchical structures (Parenteau, 1988; Sinclair and Diduck, 1995), often based on distinctions drawn from urban and regional planning literature (Arnstein, 1969). The lowest level of this structure is usually identified as non-participation (i.e., either a closed planning process or deliberate manipulation). This level is unacceptable. At the next level the public is informed and educated - information flows out to the public. Public consultation, the next level, involves a dialogue (an exchange of information, perspectives and positions) between the proponent and interested and potentially affected members of the public. Decision-making authority continues to reside with the proponent. Public involvement occurs periodically, usually just prior to and subsequent to major decision points. The remaining levels represent degrees of citizen control ranging from a partnership, through delegated power and up to full citizen control. Extended public involvement or joint planning is the rule, and frequent use is made of conflict resolution and consensus building techniques.

Conflicting perspectives often emerge between those viewing forms of citizen participation short of citizen control in a pejorative manner (i.e., tokenism), and those agreeing with informing and consulting the public but who consider sharing or delegating authority to the public as unreasonable and unwarranted (Gagnon et al., 1993). These conflicting positions are not fully reconcilable. To some degree, they reflect different political economic perspectives (Dale and

Lane, 1994).

Nevertheless, there is some middle ground. A valid role for education, consultation and shared decision making in the EIA planning process can be acknowledged (Chapter 3). Different methods will be appropriate for different proponents, settings and proposal types and for different stages in the planning process. Misrepresentation, the absence of public consultation, and limiting public participation to the one way transmission of information is unacceptable. Various forms of shared decision making, citizen advisory committees for example, have had a better record in securing higher levels of public acceptance and in obtaining proposal approval (Landre and Knuth, 1993). An increased emphasis on public consultation and, especially shared decision making, is more consistent with minimizing social impacts, opening up the EIA planning process, and facilitating more effective planning and decision making.

The EIA planning process design should anticipate and be responsive to the concerns, interests and preferences of potentially affected publics. A particular effort is needed to meet the needs of culturally distinct groups, more vulnerable groups and individuals and groups and individuals likely to experience the most severe impacts. This concern can be addressed to some extent at the regulatory levels (e.g., special provisions for First Nations involvement, participant funding), but should be extended to the applied level. Examples of potentially affected publics include: directly and indirectly affected or interested individuals, groups and organizations; citizen groups; local and province-wide interests groups; community leaders and key informants; segments of communities based on variations in traditions, lifestyle and institutions; elected representatives; and the media. Public participation methods should be designed and applied to meet the varying needs of each public, appreciating that different interests will be represented at different stages in the EA planning process.

Resource planning and management is instructive regarding how a contingent approach to public participation in EIA planning process design can be transcended (Duffy et al., 1996). Innovative approaches to multi stakeholder involvement (e.g., round tables, environmental networks, environmental commissions) (Kofinas and Griggs, 1996; Wilson et al., 1996), and experimental approaches to the devolution of authority (Taylor and Wilson, 1994) (e.g., co-management agreements, local stewardship councils) (Berkes et al., 1991; Harris, 1991; Pinkerton, 1993, 1996; Lerner, 1994; Hawkes, 1996) point to the considerable potential of shared decision making to build consensus and resolve conflicts across stakeholders (Flynn and Gunton, 1996). Again, innovative approaches must overcome significant institutional barriers (Caldwell, 1994) and confront major value and ethical divisions (Clow, 1992; Grant, 1992; Howlett, 1992; Bell, 1994; Lerner, 1994).

Setting Type

Also, setting should be considered in EIA planning process design. Still, many elements of the EIA planning process will apply regardless of setting, including the overall role and purpose of the process, major process steps and activities, environmental components and impact dimensions, major assessment methods and some form of institutional arrangement (Burdge, 1991). However, consideration should be given to the implications of state type (developed versus developing, newly industrialized or central and eastern Europe) (Balaban, 1994), region type (remote, rural, urban fringe, suburban, urban) (Jin et al., 1992; Richards, 1992; Leitmann, 1993; Reed, 1994; Rickson et al., 1995) and local setting characteristics.

In developing or third world countries, for example, significant cultural and religious differences need to be considered (Burdge, 1991; Edelstein and Kleese, 1995; Kennett and Perl, 1995; Wood, 1995). The cultural impacts associated with the introduction of certain new technologies can be especially severe (Yap, 1990). EIA-related expertise, skills and resources may be limited (Brown et al., 1991; Tongcumpou and Harvey, 1994; Kakonge, 1994, 1995). Limited baseline environmental data (Kennett and Perl, 1995) and secondary sources may be available (Brown, 1990; Wood, 1995). Supplementary funding, capacity building within local institutions, training and a strict scoping of impacts may be required (Wood, 1995). A much heavier reliance on indigenous knowledge, non-government organizations and participatory research techniques also may be necessary (Brown, 1990; Yap, 1990; Burdge, 1991; Appiah-Opuku, 1994; Kakonge, 1995).

Barriers to EIA in third world countries can be substantial. EIA requirements are often initiated because of the insistence of development assistance agencies rather than as a result of indigenous demand (Wood, 1995). Industrial development and urban infrastructure are often viewed as acceptable and desirable (Tongcumpou and Harvey, 1994), with a consequent focus on management options (Fuggle, 1990). Private sector developers are frequently unreceptive to EIA (Yap, 1990; Vizayakumar and Mohapatra, 1991). There may be a lack of political will (Wood, 1995). Public institutions are sometimes less open (Vizayakumar and Mohapatra, 1991; Kakonge and Imebove, 1993) and governments can be paternalistic and authoritarian (Fu-Keung, 1991). There is often less of a public involvement tradition, that can be further inhibited by illiteracy and poverty (Brown et al., 1991; Tongcumpou and Harvey, 1994; Wood, 1995).

The EIA characteristics and barriers highlighted above are far from uniform across third world countries. What is evident is the need for EIA process modifications to accommodate cultural setting differences. Integration of EIA into project design and implementation is crucial (United Nations Environment Programme, 1988). Given the potential for implicit, inappropriate assumptions, it is generally best if lead roles are assumed by individuals with a substantial and long-term understanding of and experience in such settings.

The matching of EIA planning process to different settings should proceed in stages. First, state-type characteristics (e.g., newly industrialized) should be considered followed by an analysis of applicable jurisdiction characteristics. In the latter case, all potentially applicable regulatory requirements, policies and priorities should be anticipated and satisfied. Interconnections with related decision-making areas also should be addressed.

Region-type characteristics (e.g., resource communities) next should be considered. A regional and community study area profile should then be undertaken, focusing on characteristics with the potential to influence and constrain available choices. Further refinements should be introduced as the geographic focus of the planning process narrows, culminating in a systematic profile of local setting. Again, particular consideration should be given to attributes that might affect EA planning and decision-making processes.

A sound understanding of potential setting implications is best acquired in an open planning process characterized by an ongoing dialogue with all stakeholders. Valuable lessons and insights also can be obtained through the systematic consideration of comparable proposals in comparable settings.

Transcending setting type differences is questionable if the aim is to develop a generic EIA planning process suitable for any and all settings. Instead, EIA should be guided by sustainability goals. It should also be sensitive to ecosystem boundaries and characteristics, cognizant of potential cumulative effects and directly linked to other forms of environmental management. An enlarged spatial perspective, especially with regard to indirect connections to and from other environmental systems, will be especially important.

Combinations of Factors

The various factors that can and should influence EIA planning process design are not mutually exclusive. Varying combinations of environment, proposal, proponent, setting, and public types, should be considered. Although differences should be appreciated, barriers and boundaries should be spanned and transcending frameworks formulated and applied.

Conclusions

The preceding analysis underscores the difficult task facing EIA practitioners of respecting and yet transcending contextual differences in planning process design and execution.

Differences, and the implications of differences, between environment, proposal, proponent, public and setting types should be acknowledged and addressed. This suggests both generic guidelines, for each set of contextual categories, and individual adjustments, at both the regulatory and applied levels, to reflect unique circumstances. Although contextual differences should be acknowledged, care must be taken to avoid the trap of ascribing all differences among regulatory requirements and individual EIA planning processes and documents to contextual differences. The "learning curve" with EIA is already too gradual because of a failure to adequately draw upon the knowledge available from comparable situations.

At the same time, it is reasonable and necessary to identify core EIA attributes and minimum requirements that should cut across categorical differences. Interconnections within and among categories need to be identified and explored. This procedure is akin to moving from multidisciplinary to interdisciplinary analysis (Stefanovic, 1996). Categorical differences should be transcended through the identification and application of sustainability-based principles and criteria and through integration within broader conceptual frameworks. Such initiatives should encompass both alternative institutional arrangements and planning process modifications. These reforms are comparable to moving from interdisciplinary to transdisciplinary synthesis (Bartoft 1985; Stefanovic 1996). The danger with initiatives in this area is the potential for formulistic approaches to EIA practice that are insensitive to context and that inhibit innovation.

The balancing of the competing needs for differentiation and integration in EIA planning process design is likely to require evolving, partially-integrated, processes and structures. External, albeit permeable, boundaries should be delineated, core principles should be identified, valid differences (and their implications) should be appreciated and interconnections among components should be determined and explored. This dynamic process of integration and differentiation pertains to both EIA and to interrelationships between EIA and related fields of theory and practice.

The barriers to changing current modes of operation, among disciplines and professions and within institutional structures, are substantial. Although such barriers are surmountable, the potential for changing EIA-related structures, procedures and documents along the lines described above will be greater if gradual refinements are made to existing institutional arrangements and if bottom-up and lateral communications and participation is favoured over top-down directives. As in society at large, multiple, often conflicting, perspectives will and should remain. This need for diversity, however, does not absolve EIA practitioners from their responsibility to take valued-based, often controversial, positions in support of a sustainable society and environment.

References

Appiah-Opuku, S. (1994) "Theoretical orientations of environmental assessment in Canada," *Environments*, 22: 103-110.

Armour, A. (1990) "Integrating impact assessment in the planning process: from rhetoric to reality?," *Impact Assessment Bulletin*, 8: 3-15.

Arnstein, S.R. (1969) "A ladder of citizen participation," *Journal of the American Institute of Planners*, 35: 216-224.

Arquiaga, M.C., Canter, L.W. and Nelson, D.I. (1992) "Risk assessment principles in environmental impact studies," *The Environmental Professional*, 14: 204-219.

Arguiga, M.C., Canter, L.W. and Nelson, D.I. (1994) "Integration of health impact considerations in environmental impact studies," *Impact Assessment*, 12: 175-198.

Balaban, V. (1994) "Introduction to the special issue - environmental decision making in central and eastern Europe," *Environmental Impact Assessment Review*, 14: 75-79.

Bartoft, H. (1985) "Dwelling in nature," in Seamon, D. and Mugerauer, R. (eds.), *Dwelling, Place and Environment: Towards a Phenomenology of Person and World*, New York, NY: Columbia University Press, 281-302.

Bell, A. (1994) "Non-human nature and the ecosystem approach: the limits of anthropocentrism in Great Lakes management," *Alternatives*, 20: 20-25.

Berkes, F., George, P. and Preston, R.J. (1991) "Co-management: the evolution in theory and practice of the joint administration of living resources," *Alternatives*, 18: 12-19.

Brocking, S. (1994) "Visions of nature and society: a history of the ecosystem," *Alternatives*, 20: 12-19.

Brown, A.L. (1990) "Environmental impact assessment in a development context," *Environmental Impact Assessment Review*, 37: 135-144.

Brown, A.L., Hindmarsh, R.A. and McDonald, G.T. (1991) "Environmental assessment procedures and issues in the Pacific-Southeast Asia Region," *Environmental Impact Assessment Review*, 11: 143-156.

Burdge, R.J. (1991) "The benefits of social impact assessment in third world development," *Environmental Impact Assessment Review*, 10: 123-134.

Burdge, R. J. and Vanclay, V. (1996) "Social impact assessment: a contribution to the state of the art series," *Impact Assessment*, 14: 59-86.

Caldwell, L.K. (1994) "Disharmony in the Great Lakes Basin: institutional jurisdictions frustrate the ecosystem approach," *Alternatives*, 20: 26-31.

Carpenter, R.A. (1995) "Risk assessment," *Impact Assessment*, 13: 153-188.

Clow, M. (1992) "Round tables taken with a grain of salt," *Alternatives*, 19: 29-30.

Coates, J.F. (1976) "Technology assessment - a tool kit," *Chemtech*, June: 372-383.

_____ (1990) "Impacts we will be assessing in the 21st century," *Impact Assessment Bulletin*, 9: 9-26.

Conacher, A.J. (1994/1995) "The integration of land use planning and management with environmental impact assessment: some Australian and Canadian perspectives," *Impact Assessment*, 12: 347-372.

Craig, D. (1990) "Social impact assessment: politically oriented approaches and applications," *Environmental Impact Assessment Review*, 10: 37-54.

Dale, A.P. and Lane, M.B. (1994) "Strategic perspectives analysis: a procedure for participatory and political impact assessment," *Society and Natural Resources*, 7: 253-268.

Dale, N. and Kennedy, S. (1981) "Towards a socially relevant process of impact assessment," in Tester, F.J. and Mykes, W. (eds.), *Social Impact Assessment*, Calgary, AB: Detselig Enterprises, 43-54.

Dickman, M. (1991) "Failure of an environmental impact assessment to predict the impact of mine tailings in Canada's most northerly hypersaline lake," *Environmental Impact Assessment Review*, 11: 181-193.

Duffy, D. M., Roseland, M. and Gunton, T.I. (1996) "A preliminary assessment of shared decision-making in land use and natural resource planning," *Environments*, 23: 1-16.

Dunster, J.A. (1990) "Integrating environmental assessment with forest planning: the province of Ontario example," *Impact Assessment Bulletin*, 8: 119-130.

Edelstein, M.R. and Kleese, S.A. (1995) "Cultural relativity of impact assessment: native Hawaiian opposition to geothermal energy development," *Society and Natural*

Resources, 8: 19-34.

Egre, D. and Senecal P. (1990) "Resettlement studies and human EIA at water control projects," *Impact Assessment Bulletin*, 8: 5-18.

European Bank for Reconstruction and Development (1995) "The case for 'soft' harmonization," *Environmental Impact Assessment Review*, 15: 289-294.

Finsterbusch, K. (1995) "In praise of SIA," *Impact Assessment*, 13: 229-252.

Flynn, S. and Gunton, T. (1996) "Resolving natural resource conflicts through alternative dispute resolution: a case study of the Timber Fish Wildlife Agreement in Washington State," *Environments*, 23: 101-112.

Fuggle, R.E. (1990) "Integrating environmental management: an appropriate approach to environmental concerns in developing countries," *Impact Assessment*, 8: 31-46.

Fu-Keung, D. (1991) "Difficulties in implementing social impact assessment in China: methodological considerations," *Environmental Impact Assessment Review*, 10: 113-122.

Gagnon, C. Hirsch, P. and Howlitt, R. (1993) "Can SIA empower communities?," *Environmental Impact Assessment Review*, 13: 229-254.

Geisler, C.C. (1993) "Rethinking SIA: why ex ante research isn't enough?," *Society and Natural Resources*, 6: 327-338.

Gibson, B. (1975) "The value of participation," in Elder, P.S. (ed.), *Environmental Management and Public*

Participation, Toronto, ON: Canadian Environmental Law Research Foundation, 7-39.

Grant, J. (1992) "Round tables and the role of business," *Alternatives*, 19: 30-33.

Grima, A.P., Timmerman, P., Fowle, C.D. and Byer, P. (1986) *Risk Management and EIA: Research Needs and Opportunities*, Canadian Environmental Assessment Research Council, Ottawa, ON: Ministry of Supply and Services.

Hadden, S., Chiles, J., Ansejionu, J. and Cerny, K. (1981) *High Level Nuclear Waste Management*, Austin, TX: Energy and Natural Resources Advisory Council.

Harris, J. (1991) "Temagani Stewardship Council: an interview with Mary Laronde," *Alternatives*, 17: 7-8.

Hawkes, S. (1996) "The Gwaii Haanes Agreement: from conflict to consensus," *Environments*, 23: 87-100.

Holling, C.S. (1978) (ed.) *Adaptive Environmental Assessment and Management*, Toronto, ON: John Wiley and Sons.

Howell, R.E., Olsen, M.E. and Olsen D. (1987) *Designing a Citizen Involvement Program*, Corvallis, OR: Western Rural Development Center, Oregon State University.

Howlett, M. (1992) "Differences of opinion: round tables, policy networks and the failure of Canadian environmental strategy," *Alternatives*, 19: 25-28.

Hyman, E.L., Stiftel, B., Moreau, D.H. and Nichols, R.C. (1988) *Combining Facts and Values in Environmental Impact Assessment*, Boulder, CO: Westview Press.

Interorganizational Committee on Guidelines and Principles for Social Impact Assessment (1995) "Guidelines and principles for social impact assessment," *Environmental Impact Assessment Review*, 15:11-44.

Jin, X., Hui, K. and Porter, A.L. (1992) "Urban economic development on a grand scale: impact assessment," *Impact Assessment Bulletin*, 10: 79-88.

Johnston, R.A. and Madison, M.E. (1994) "Tying mitigation requirements to local general plans," *Environmental Impact Assessment Review*, 14: 61-74.

Kakonge, J.O. (1995) "Dilemmas in the design and implementation of agricultural projects in various African countries: the role of environmental impact assessment," *Environmental Impact Assessment Review*, 15: 275-285.

_____ (1994) "Monitoring of environmental impact assessments in Africa," *Environmental Impact Assessment Review*, 15: 275-285.

Kakonge, J.O. and Imebove, I.A. (1993) "Constraints on implementing environmental impact assessment in Africa," *Environmental Impact Assessment Review*, 13: 299-310.

Kay, J.J. and Schneider, E. (1994) "Embracing complexity: the challenge of the ecosystem approach," *Alternatives*, 20: 32-46.

Kennett, S.A. and Perl, A. (1995) "Environmental impact assessment of development-oriented research," *Environmental Impact Assessment Review*, 15: 341-360.

Klein, J.T. (1990) *Interdisciplinarity: History, Theory and Practice*, Detroit, MI: Wayne State University.

Kofinas, G. and Griggs, J. (1996) "Collaboration and the B.C. round table: an analysis of a "better way" of deciding," *Environments*, 23: 17-40.

Kuusinen, T., Lesperance, A. and Bilyard, G. (1994) "Toward integrated strategies for achieving environmental quality," *The Environmental Professional*, 16: 22-27.

Lachavanne, J.B. (1991) "The environmental integration study (eis): an essential adjunct to the environmental impact study (eis)," *Impact Assessment Bulletin*, 9: 89-98.

Landre, B.K. and Knuth, B.A. (1993) "Success of citizen advisory committees in consensus-based water resources planning in the Great Lakes Basin," *Society and Natural Resources*, 6: 229-258.

Leistritz, F.L. (1994) "Economic and fiscal impact assessment," *Impact Assessment*, 12: 305-318.

Leitmann, J. (1993) "Rapid urban environmental assessment: toward environmental management in cities of the developing world," *Impact Assessment*, 11: 225-260.

Lerman, P. (1994) "Physical planning linked to EIA: a method for processing knowledge that promotes sustainability and efficient procedures," *Third EU (European Union) Workshop on EIA, Methodology and Research*, Delphi, Greece: European Community, Director General XI, 173-176.

Lerner, S. (1994) "Local stewardship: training ground for an environmental vanguard," *Alternatives*, 20: 14-19.

Lichfield, N. (1996) *Community Impact Evaluation*, London, UK: UCL Press Limited.

Malik, M. (1995) "Environmental procedures of international-al organizations: a preliminary evaluation," *The Environmental Professional*, 17: 93-102.

Margerum, R.D. and Born, S.N. (1995) "Integrated environmental management: moving from theory to practice," *Journal of Environmental Planning and Management*, 38: 371-392.

Marshall, D, Sadler, B., Sector, J. and Wiebe, J. (1985) *Environmental Management and Impact Assessment: Some Lessons and Guidance for Canadian and International Experience*, Hull, PQ: Federal Environmental Assessment Review Office.

Mayda, J. (1996) "Reforming impact assessment: issues, premises and elements," *Impact Assessment*, 14: 87-96.

McDonald, G.T. (1991) "Regional economic and social impact assessment," *Environmental Impact Assessment Review*, 10: 25-36.

McDonald, G.T. and Brown, L. (1995) "Going beyond environmental impact assessment: environmental input to planning and design," *Environmental Impact Assessment Review*, 15: 483-496.

Nesbitt, T.H.D. (1990) "Environmental planning and environmental, social IA methodology in the cross-cultural context," *Impact Assessment Bulletin*, 8: 33-44.

Ontario (1990-1993) *Environmental Bill of Rights* (R.S.O. 1990) c.E.18. and (R.S.O. 1993), c.27, *Classification of Proposals for Instruments* (O.Reg. 681/94), *General Regulation* (O. Reg. 73/94).

Ortolano, L. and Shepherd, A. (1995) "Environmental impact assessment: challenges and opportunities,"

Impact Assessment, 13: 3-30.

Parenteau, R. (1988) *Public Participation in Environmental Decision-Making,* Federal Environmental Assessment Review Office, Ottawa, ON: Ministry of Supply and Services.

Partidario, M.R. (1996) "Strategic environmental assessment: key issues emerging from recent practice," *Environmental Impact Assessment Review,* 16: 31-56.

Pateman, C. (1970) *Public Participation in Environmental Decision-Making,* Federal Environmental Assessment Review Office, Ottawa, ON: Ministry of Supply and Services.

Pinkerton, E.W. (1993) "Co-management efforts as social movements: the Tin Wis coalition and the drive for forest practices legislation in British Columbia," *Alternatives,* 19: 33-46.

_____ (1996) "The contribution of watershed-based multi-party co-management agreements to dispute resolution: the Skeena Watershed Committee," *Environments,* 23: 51-68.

Porter, A.L. (1995) "Technology assessment," *Impact Assessment,* 13: 135-152.

Praxis (1988) *Public Involvement - Planning and Implementing Public Involvement Programs,* Calgary, AB: Praxis.

Priscoli, J.D. and Homenuck, P. (1986) "Consulting the public," in Lang, R., *Integrated Approaches to Resource Planning and Management,* Calgary, AB: University of Calgary Press, 67-80.

Reed, M.G. (1994) "Locally responsive environmental planning in the Canadian hinterland: a case study in northern Ontario," *Environmental Impact Assessment Review*, 14: 245-270.

Regier, H. A. (1985) "Concepts and methods of AEAM and Holling's 'science of surprise'," in Maclaren, V.W. and Whitney, J.B. (eds.), *New Directions in Environmental Impact Assessment in Canada*, Toronto, ON: Methuen, 43-52.

Rhodes, S.L. (1993) "The effects of the environment on aviation weather safety: meterological assessment for the new Denver Airport," *Environmental Impact Assessment Review*, 13: 63-74.

Richards, A. (1992) "Implementing a voluntary and responsive siting process in rural and urban settings," *Impact Assessment Bulletin*, 10: 89-98.

Richardson, N. (1994) "Moving toward planning for sustainability: integrating environmental assessment and land use planning in Ontario," *Plan Canada*, March 1994: 18-23.

Rickson, R.E., Western, J.S. and Burdge, R.J. (1990) "Social impact assessment: development pressures and indigenous interests in Australia," *Environmental Impact Assessment Review*, 10: 1-10.

Rickson, R.E., Lane, M., Lynch-Blosse, L. and Western, J.S. (1995) "Community environment and development impact assessment in resource dependent communities," *Impact Assessment*, 13: 347-370.

Rivas, V., Gonzalez, A., Fischer, D.W. and Cendrero, A. (1994) "An approach to environmental assessment within the land use planning process: northern Spanish experiences," *Journal of Environmental Planning and Management*, 37: 305-322.

Sadar, M.H. and Dirschl, H.J. (1996) "Generic environmental impacts from water impoundment projects in the western Canadian plains region," *Impact Assessment*, 14: 41-58.

Sadler, B. (1995) "Environmental assessment: toward improved effectiveness," *International Study of the Effectiveness of Environmental Assessment*, Interim Report and Discussion Paper, Ottawa, ON: Canadian Environmental Assessment Agency and the International Association for Impact Assessment, 58 pp.

_____ (1996) "Environmental assessment in a changing world: evaluating practice to improve performance, final report," *International Study of the Effectiveness of Environmental Assessment*, Canadian Environmental Assessment Agency and International Association for Impact Assessment, Ottawa, ON: Ministry of Supply and Services, 248 pp.

Sandford, R. (1996) "International environmental treaty secretariats: a case of neglected potential?," *Environmental Impact Assessment Review*, 16: 3-12.

Shoemaker, D.J. (1994) *Cumulative Environmental Assessment*, Department of Geography Publication Series # 42, Waterloo, ON: University of Waterloo.

Sinclair, J. and Diduck, A. (1995) "Public education: an undervalued component of the environmental assessment public involvement program," *Environmental Impact Assessment Review*, 15: 219-240.

Slocombe, D.S. (1993) "Environmental planning, ecosystem zones and ecosystem approaches for integrating environment and development," *Environmental Management*, 17: 289-304.

Smith, L.G. (1993) *Impact Assessment and Sustainable Resource Management*, New York, NY: John Wiley and Sons Inc.

Stefanovic, I.L. (1996) "Interdisciplinarity and wholeness: lessons from eco-research in the Hamilton harbour ecosystem," *Environments*, 23: 74-94.

Taylor, D. and Wilson, J. (1994) "Entering the watershed battles: forest communities seek peace through local control," *Environments*, 22: 93-102.

Therivel, R. (1993) "Systems of strategic environmental impact assessment," *Environmental Impact Assessment Review*, 13: 145-168.

Therivel, R., Wilson, E., Thompson, S., Healey, D. and Prichard, D. (1992) *Strategic Environmental Assessment*, London, UK: Earthscan Publications Ltd.

Thompson, J.G. and Williams, G. (1990) "Social assessment: roles for practitioners and the need for stronger mandates," *Impact Assessment Bulletin*, 10: 43-56.

Tongcumpou, C. and Harvey, N. (1994) "Implications of recent EIA changes in Thailand," *Environmental Impact Assessment Review*, 14: 271-295.

Treweek, J. (1995) "Ecological impact assessment," *Impact Assessment*, 13: 289-316.

Tywoniuk, N. (1990) "Integrating environmental factors into both planning and impact assessment functions," *Impact Assessment Bulletin*, 8: 275-288.

United Nations Environment Programme (1988) *Environmental Impact Assessment: Basic Procedures for Developing Countries*, UNEP, Bangkok: Regional Office for Asia and the Pacific.

Vig, N.J. (1992) "Parliamentary technology assessment in Europe: comparative evaluation," *Impact Assessment Bulletin*, 10: 3-24.

Vizayakumar, K. and Mohapatra, P.K.J. (1991) "Framework for environmental impact analysis - with special reference to India," *Environmental Management*, 15: 357-368.

Westman, W.E. (1985) *Ecology, Impact Assessment and Environmental Planning*, New York, NY: John Wiley and Sons.

Williams, D.C. (1990) "Integrating impact assessment into resource management planning: the US Bureau of Land Management," *Impact Assessment*, 8: 161-178.

Wilson, A., Roseland, M. and Day, J.C. (1996) "Shared decision-making and public land planning: an evaluation of the Vancouver Island, regional CORE process," *Environments*, 23: 69-86.

Wood, C. (1995) *Environmental Impact Assessment - A Comparative Evaluation*, Essex, UK: Longman Scientific and Technical.

Wood, C. and Dejeddour, M. (1990) "Strategic environmental assessment: EA of policies, plans and programmes," *Impact Assessment Bulletin*, 10: 3-22.

Wyant, T.G., Meganck, R.A. and Ham, S.H. (1995) "A planning and decision framework for ecological restoration," *Environmental Management*, 19: 789-796.

Yap, N.T. (1990) "Round the peg or square the hole? populists, technocrats and environmental assessment in third world countries," *Impact Assessment Bulletin*, 8: 69-84.

Chapter 10

The Appraisal of Environmental Impact Assessment Processes: Towards a 'Situated' Approach

Juliet Rowson
University of British Columbia

> Without feedback, environmental assessment remains a static, linear exercise rather than a dynamic, iterative process (Sadler, 1990:7).

In Canada, many social scientists[1], for example, W. Rees (1981, 1989), Gibson (1990, 1992, 1993), Smith (1991, 1993), Weston (1992) and Lawrence (1994, 1997), have conducted evaluations of environmental impact assessment (EIA) processes, recommending specific process improvements. These appraisals have raised important critiques of EIA procedures, and have usually been aimed (either directly or indirectly) at policy makers. In this chapter, I will argue that they have largely been written in an effort to make EIA processes more inclusive and open so that process participants are given a greater voice. Nevertheless, despite the inclusive aims of the appraisals, social scientists have conducted their evaluations largely from a scientific standpoint which has resulted in participants' views of the process under evaluation being overlooked. In particular, using a case study of the Vancouver International Airport Environmental Assessment and Review Process (EARP), it is demonstrated that the views of participants have not been considered by social scientists in their evaluations of EARP. Therefore, evaluations of EIA procedures can be regarded as being fundamentally contradictory, as social scientists advocate a more open and inclusive EIA process, while ignoring the potential contributions of participants. In the following discussion, I substantiate this criticism and propose an alternative, 'situated' method for conducting evaluations of EIA processes. This method still enables social scientists to pursue what I consider to be crucial issues of inclusiveness and openness in EIA, while addressing some of the theoretical and political problems inherent in current appraisals of EIA procedures.

The discussion unfolds as follows. First, it is illustrated how many appraisals of EIA processes in Canada have been conducted in a scientific manner. It is then suggested that a social constructionist critique of science provides insight which can be used to explain the link between scientific approaches to EIA process appraisals and the lack of consultation with process participants. From this critique emerges an alternative, 'situated' approach to process appraisal. The discussion then moves from this conceptual critique of EIA evaluations to a case study highlighting how the perspectives of participants regarding EIA mechanisms have been largely overlooked by social scientists and suggesting that their appraisals would be enriched by representing participants' views. Finally, a summary of what might be involved in a 'situated' approach to EIA process appraisal is described.

The case study selected is a review of the proposal to build a parallel runway at Vancouver International Airport which was conducted under the Canadian federal EARP. Opinions of participants in the 1989-1991 Vancouver International Airport EARP inquiry are compared with the views presented by social scientists in their appraisals of EARP to determine points of congruence and departure. The comparison of general evaluations of EARP with a specific instance of it, namely the Vancouver International Airport EARP, is not direct, and this is kept in mind in the analysis. However, this could not be avoided as the majority of social scientists' appraisals of EARP are generic and not related to a particular application of the process. In contrast, most participants attending public hearings on the environment in Canada only attend one hearing (Parenteau, 1988) and are therefore only able to evaluate a specific application of EARP, rather than the process more broadly.

A Conceptual Critique of EIA Process Evaluations

> The current orientation of EIA, despite recent re-evaluation of EARP by the federal government, remains heavily invested in the supremacy of 'data' and 'expertise', that is information validated by science and technocrats (Shapcott, 1989:60).

In the following, it is argued that Canadian social scientists have frequently attempted to adopt a scientific approach to EIA, not only in method development (for example, checklists, multi-attribute utility theory) but also in process evaluation. As Pepper (1984) argued, the term 'science' refers to the epistemology of Enlightenment Science or 'classical science' which, among other things, embodies a belief in objective analysis conducted by rational, value-neutral experts. I argue that many social science evaluators have engaged with the epistemology of science through claims to objectivity, scientific rationality and reinforcing the 'cult of the expert' in an effort to legitimate their views of EIA processes.

There are two kinds of evaluative studies of EIA processes that have adopted the scientific assumptions of rationality and objectivity. First, W. Rees (1981) and W. Rees and Boothroyd (1987) evaluated EARP by comparing its achievements in 'reality' against its stated objectives. This approach assumes that EIA is a rational process (J. Rees, 1990). Second, King and Nelson (1983), CEARC (1988), Parenteau (1988), W. Rees (1989), Gibson (1990, 1993), Smith (1991), Weston (1992) and Lawrence (1997) have evaluated Canadian EIA mechanisms using specific criteria, for example efficiency, effectiveness, and fairness. These writers have all used criteria and yet they have not acknowledged that there are any other possible criteria that could be brought to their analysis other than the ones selected. In addition, they have not recognized that there are multiple ways of evaluating an EIA process using a given criterion. As a result, the criteria are presented as objective and the social scientists have implicitly established themselves as being value-free scientifically-rational individuals whose conclusions are replicable.

Other assessors of EIA procedures have not used evaluation criteria at all, but have simply stated their own views of the process in their evaluations (for example, Lucas and McCallum, 1975; Fenge and Smith, 1986; Parkes, 1991; Gibson, 1992; Lawrence, 1994). Nevertheless, for two different reasons I would argue that such evaluations are still carried out in a scientific manner through engaging with the 'cult of the expert'. First, although I do not mean to suggest that social scientists actually believe their opinions are facts, their perspectives are presented in a way which implies objectivity. There is no acknowledgment that there are any other legitimate analyses of the process and the evaluators make no attempt to acknowledge the subjectivity of their views. By not explicitly stating that their views are opinions, albeit well argued and substantiated opinions, I would argue that social scientists are implicitly presenting their views as facts and are thus framing themselves as value-neutral experts. Social scientists could have framed their views as opinions by 'situating' themselves in the process, namely stating their relationship to the EIA process under evaluation (that is, outlining if they were participants, observers, decision makers, archival researchers and so on) and outlining their own political vision of how an EIA process ought to be. For example, if social scientists believe an EIA process should be more open and inclusive this could be stated clearly as an opinion shaping the analysis. By doing this, their opinions would not come across as objective facts, but as reasoned opinions of social scientists who are looking at the process from a particular perspective. Second, social scientists have presented their views in academic journals and conferences. These represent well respected and specialized fora from which the public are structurally excluded. By removing what I would argue should be a public debate to the realm of the expert, social scientists are implicitly framing themselves as experts.

Other social science evaluators have at least partially rejected this scientific route to EIA process appraisal. First, in his article on fairness in EARP, Emond (1983) considered fairness from multiple perspectives, including that of the proponent and intervenors, recognizing that there are plural and frequently conflicting evaluations of an EIA process. He is thus implicitly acknowledging that there is no singular, objective way in which EIA processes can be evaluated, but instead there are multiple legitimate analyses possible. Nevertheless, he does not actually solicit the opinions of anyone representing these perspectives, but presumes to 'speak for' them. Emond has thus at least partially rejected the scientific approach, and yet he appears to assume that he is value-free, that he can unproblematically put himself in the shoes of others who have very different perspectives. Second, W. Rees conducted interviews with "officials of various government departments and private interest groups" (1979: preface) in his appraisal of EARP. Although he is fairly clear about which government departments interviewees were from and the perspectives these interviewees had, the same cannot be said for the private interest groups. Not only does he omit to indicate what these interest groups stood for, but in many places, it is unclear as to whether he is presenting his own views or the views of the interest groups as the evaluation largely presents a singular perspective. By not establishing the constituency of many viewpoints represented in his evaluation, and by not presenting contrasting perspectives, he is implying a universality to the perspective being presented and thus is still reverting to a scientifically rational analysis.

Finally, FEARO (1988), Walsh et al. (1988) and Sadler (1990), appear to have rejected the assumptions inherent in the scientific approach to EIA process evaluations. Rather than producing an analysis in which it is assumed that they, as experts can produce an objective, rational evaluation of EIA processes, they have conducted evaluations by consulting with participants, recognizing that there are not one, but multiple legitimate ways in which an EIA process could be evaluated. For example, Sadler (1990:14) states:

> ... judgments about the effectiveness of public processes will vary with the role and affiliation of participants and observers. A multiplicity of actors are involved in EARP, bringing with them diverse interests, values, and abilities to pursue them. The pluralist character of the process needs to be explicitly incorporated in approaches to evaluation.

Although the majority of social scientists have adopted a scientific standpoint when conducting their evaluations of EIA processes, I am not suggesting that they believe that their evaluations have been conducted in a value-free scientifically rational manner. In fact, a review of such evaluations suggests that despite adopting such an approach, these social scientists are firmly committed to ensuring EIA processes become more inclusive and open, something I fully endorse. Nevertheless, there are two characteristics of these evaluations which embody the assumption that not only is it possible to discover the 'truth' as to the merits and demerits of a process, but that the expert social scientist is able to do this. These are firstly, the ways in which the evaluations are presented, namely the lack of acknowledgment that there are many different ways in which an EIA process could be analyzed, the style of writing used, and the language employed in the discussion and second, the fora (that is, academic journals and conferences) in which these evaluations are presented which render the debate an 'expert' one. It is argued below that the adoption of this scientific approach precludes the views of participants in an EIA process from being considered and therefore it is important that social scientists who wish to advocate a more open and inclusive EIA evaluation reject such an approach. In the following, critiques of Enlightenment Science are reviewed to establish a conceptual link between the scientific approach and the marginalization of the views of process participants and to provide an alternative way in which evaluations might be conducted.

Within the broad field of environmental decision making, two critiques of, and alternatives to, Enlightenment Science have been raised. These are from proponents of traditional ecological knowledge (TEK) and social impact assessment (SIA). Each is reviewed in turn, highlighting their strengths and weaknesses. I then suggest that the insights developed from the TEK and SIA approaches can be developed further within the social constructionist critique of science which provides a coherent method for evaluating EIA processes.

The Dene Cultural Institute (1995:343) has defined TEK as:

> the body of knowledge or natural history built up by a group of people through generations of living in close contact with nature. It includes a system of classification, a set of empirical observations about the local ecology, and a system of self-management that governs hunting, trapping, and fishing.

However, to date, TEK has not been classified as a science (Hobson, 1992) and its practitioners have often not been considered 'experts' (Dene Cultural Institute, 1995). Rather than focusing on developing quantitative data as traditional science does, TEK tends to be more qualitative (Johnson, 1992), providing large amounts of qualitative time-series information that are not readily available to conventional scientists (empirical examples are provided by Finley, 1993; Nakashima, 1990; and Freeman, 1975; 1992). TEK also conceptualizes earth as a living organism (Johnson, 1992), regarding it as a complex whole, accepting its multidimensionality (Freeman, 1992) instead of approaching the world in the reductionist fashion Enlightenment Science does. The difference in emphasis of the two approaches has led some writers (for example the Nakashima, 1990; Assembly of First Nations and the Inuit Circumpolar Conference, 1993; Pinkerton, 1993; Dene Cultural Institute, 1995) to argue that TEK should be integrated with conventional science in environmental management.

Although the TEK critique of Enlightenment Science has not been specifically developed in relation to process appraisal in EIA, its insights are applicable. Importantly, this critique challenges the privileged position of Enlightenment Science as the only route to knowledge. Yet, proponents of TEK assume that combining TEK with conventional science produces a superior scientific product rather than fundamentally challenging the position of science in society. By continuing to emphasize the value of scientific knowledge, proponents of TEK do not provide a coherent critique of, and alternative to, the scientific approach to EIA process evaluations.

Social impact assessment developed as an offshoot of EIA (Boothroyd, 1978; Wolf, 1983; Craig, 1990), and has become a means of anticipating and evaluating the effects that a proposed development will have on the lifestyle, economy, population, social structure, institutions and quality of life of those affected by the proposed project (Corbett, 1986: 5). The conventional approach to SIA is known as the technical approach (Lang and Armour, 1981; Torgerson, 1981; CEARC, 1985; Corbett, 1986; Craig, 1990) and researchers who adopt this approach assume a rational and objective

SIA process which is grounded in scientific method. The result is a narrowly-defined scope and a process conducted with minimal public input. Some SIA writers have challenged this, advocating a more political approach instead (for example, Torgerson, 1981; Craig, 1990; Burdge and Robertson, 1990; Burdge and Vanclay, 1996). The political approach assumes that SIAs cannot be carried out in a value-neutral fashion and that 'interests' lie at the heart of all decision making. As a result, analysts are encouraged to scrutinize their own values. Solicitation of the views of people who are potentially impacted by the proposed development is considered mandatory. An effort is made to keep SIAs broad in scope so they are responsive and flexible to public opinion. Advocates of the political approach to SIA frequently assume that both approaches to SIA embody political commitments to different visions of society, and argue that the technical approach tends to support dominant societal interests.

The political critique of technical SIA not only raises important problems about the scientific approach to SIA and by inference, EIA, but also provides an alternative approach to EIA process appraisals. It acknowledges that it is impossible to be value-neutral and that all evaluations are inherently political. In addition, some advocates have argued that the technical approach reinforces dominant societal interests by predominantly attending to the concerns of the advantaged. These advocates are therefore making a link between the scientific approach to SIA and the marginalization of the views of the less powerful. Nevertheless, they have not explained why the scientific approach serves the interests of the advantaged, and therefore do not provide a convincing argument for its necessary rejection.

Consequently, I will turn to the social constructionist literature which allows me to elaborate on the insights developed by the TEK and political SIA literature. Social constructionism is an offshoot of postmodernism that embodies a critical stance towards taken-for-granted ways of understanding the world (Burr, 1995:63-4). This critique has been applied to science. Burr has commented:

> What we call 'knowledge' then simply refers to the particular construction or version of the phenomenon that has received the stamp of 'truth' in our society.

In society today, it is knowledge generated by Enlightenment Science that is framed as being the truth. As Yearly (1991:120) notes, using the example of a botanist:

> I am not trying to raise doubts about botanists' knowledge or expertise. But I am aiming to throw doubt on the idea that scientific knowledge is valid simply because scientists see the world plainly. All useful seeing is skilled seeing.

In other words, social constructionists are arguing that scientific knowledge should not be the only form of knowledge that is valued in society and it is important to recognize that there are many different and valid ways of knowing. Yearly (1991) and Demeritt (1994) have noted that if this critique of science is pertinent to work done in the natural sciences, then logically it is also applicable to social science studies that are also based on similar assumptions.

Social constructionists have argued that there are inherent power relations embodied in the framing of scientific insights as the superior form of knowledge in society. Foucault has demonstrated how closely knowledge is linked to power (Racevskis, 1983:27), and today it is those who can make claims of scientific knowledge who are framed as being powerful, while others who are unable to make such claims are rendered relatively powerless and their views are deemed relatively unimportant. Feminist researchers such as Code (1988) and Smith (1990) have demonstrated in practice how concepts such as scientific knowledge have resulted in hierarchies of credibility where scientifically rational, value-neutral experts are considered to generate highly valued scientific knowledge, while those who cannot claim expert status are framed as having 'experience' which is a less valued form of knowledge. Although this hierarchy is very pervasive in our society, it is rather contradictory as scientific knowledge itself constitutes a method of organizing experience.

The insights developed by social constructionists can be applied to evaluations of EIA processes. By adopting a scientific approach, social scientists are inadvertently framing themselves as being the 'experts' and the participants in any given EIA process are framed as having 'experience'. Thus considering the views of participants is implicitly rendered unimportant because participants have experiential rather than scientific knowledge. I am *not* in any way suggesting that social scientists believe participants' views are actually unimportant, but by using the language of science to legitimate their evaluations, social scientists are inadvertently perpetuating such power relations and inequity. These power relations are then reinforced further in the Canadian policy system, where social scientists are recognized as 'experts' who advise policy makers. For example, a large number of social scientists such as Nakashima (1990), Reed (1990) and Weston (1992) have had their analyses of EIA published by the Canadian Environmental Assessment Research Council, an institution established by the Minister of the Environment to "advise government, industry and universities" on EIA. In addition, EARP panels which are composed of people "knowledgeable in the subject matter likely to be raised before the Panel" (FEARO, 1985:1) frequently contain social scientists.

Instead, social constructionists, for example Haraway (1991), have argued persuasively that knowledge should be regarded as partial and related to the situatedness of the knower. They thus challenge the very possibility of there being an objective rational perspective. The knower is situated both generally, in political, social, economic and cultural terms, as well as specifically, in relation to the EIA procedure being evaluated.

The social constructionist approach to science not only provides a useful critique of Enlightenment Science, providing a conceptual link between scientific evaluations of EIA processes and the marginalization of participants views, but through the concept of situatedness, it provides an alternative way of approaching EIA process appraisals. Using empirical research from the Vancouver International Airport EARP, in the next section I investigate the relevance of this critique to EIA process evaluations in practice.

An Empirical Critique of EIA Process Evaluations

After a brief introduction of the workings of EARP, the opinions of the process as presented by social scientists will be summarized. The Vancouver International Airport EARP and my research methods are then sketched out before participants' opinions of the Vancouver Airport EARP are reviewed. Comments made by participants will then be compared with the views of EARP made by social scientists.

EARP was aimed at evaluating the environmental (defined broadly to include socioeconomic effects) consequences of proposals in which the federal government has decision-making responsibility (Canadian Gazette, 1984) and was passed as a Cabinet Directive in December 1973. The EARP guidelines had to be followed whenever a federal government department intended to undertake a proposal of its own, or when a project was to be undertaken on federal lands, or involved federal funding (FEARO, 1987). The full procedure involved two stages, initial assessment conducted by the project proponent and a public review administered by the Federal Environmental Assessment Review Office (FEARO).

Increasingly, criticisms levelled at the process both from social scientists (for example, King and Nelson, 1983; Fenge and Smith, 1986; W. Rees and Boothroyd, 1987; Smith, 1987), and interest groups (for example, the Environmental Planning and Assessment Caucus, 1988) called for process reform. In April 1989, this call for reform was strengthened by a court ruling on the Rafferty-Alameda Dam Project (Canadian Wildlife Federation Inc. v. Canada, Minister of Environment) which set a precedent by ruling that the application of the EARP guidelines had the force of administrative law. As a result, in 1990, the Environment Minister announced a package of reforms for EARP which included the proposed Canadian Environmental Assessment Act (CEAA). This Act was passed and replaced EARP on January 19th, 1995. The focus of this paper will be on the Vancouver International Airport EARP. That the case study is based on the earlier model is of little importance since the main attributes of EARP noted above exist in the new legislation and because to date, only two public reviews have been initiated under CEAA and both are following a hearing process very similar to that of EARP.

Social Scientists' Opinions of EARP

Social scientists have posed many questions regarding EARP, but here only those issues most frequently raised will be discussed. Perhaps one of the most fundamental issues raised has been *EARP's origins in a guidelines order, not legislation.* Lucas and McCallum (1975), W. Rees (1979; 1981), Fenge and Smith (1986), FEARO (1988), Smith (1991), Weston (1992) and Gibson (1993) have noted that this lack of legal clout has meant that there has been no way to force proponents to submit their proposals to EARP and in the past proponents have avoided doing so. This situation has changed, however, with the 1989 court ruling. A related criticism is that *EARP is based on self-assessment in the initial assessment phase* (W. Rees, 1979; W. Rees and Boothroyd, 1987; Jeffery, 1991; Parkes, 1991; Smith, 1991; Gibson, 1993). Parkes (1991:10) compares this to letting the fox guard the chicken coop. This has not changed under CEAA.

The *scope of EARP* has also been criticized by W. Rees (1979, 1981), Smith (1987), W. Rees and Boothroyd (1987), Walsh et al. (1988), FEARO (1988), Sadler (1990) and Weston (1992) for being far too narrow. It has been challenged on the grounds that it is too narrow conceptually, often precluding any discussion of project need per se. In addition, it is too narrow in application, largely focusing on projects at the expense of policies. Finally, it is also too confined geographically, and, for example, the cumulative impacts of projects in a given region are not considered. The narrowness of the scope has ensured that, frequently, central questions which participants have regarding the process cannot be discussed at the public hearings.

Social scientists have also been very critical of public participation as provided for under EARP. W. Rees (1981), Rees and Boothroyd (1987), Parkes (1991), FEARO (1988) and Weston (1992) have all argued that *public participation occurs too late in the process*. Most projects do not even reach the public review stage, meaning that the majority of decisions are made without any public input. Others have critiqued public participation in the public review stage on the basis of resource inequity, arguing that, although intervenor funding is often provided for participants, such programs are not mandatory and the funding provided is insufficient (King and Nelson, 1983; Emond, 1983; Reed, 1984; Walsh et al., 1988; Sadler, 1990; Parkes, 1991).

These social scientists are clearly situated, bringing a particular perspective to their critiques. Their appraisals of EARP can be broadly characterized as arguments that the process become more inclusive and open. The argument for legislation and against self-assessment, combined with soliciting public input earlier in the procedure, would ensure greater public participation. Similarly, evaluators are arguing that there is a need to broaden the scope of EARP to promote resource equity in order to make sure that the members of the general public not only have a voice, but that their input is meaningful and they are heard by decision makers. In short, social scientists have conceptualized the general public as being marginalized in EARP, and are arguing that they should be incorporated further in the process and have more power vis-a-vis the proponent. Yet, at the same time, it has been outlined how social scientists have paradoxically excluded the views of process participants from their own evaluations of EIA processes.

Vancouver International Airport EARP

Vancouver International Airport is located 13 kilometers south of downtown Vancouver on Sea Island, in the Fraser River delta. The airport was opened in 1931 and from 1962 to 1992 was under the jurisdiction of the federal government. It is now operated by the Local Airport Authority. There have been increasing traffic demands at Vancouver International Airport since the 1940s and the proposal to build a parallel runway to the main runway has a long and eventful history from its first proposal in 1946 to its opening in November, 1996. The part of this story in which EARP was involved spans a period of nearly twenty years.

In 1976, Transport Canada referred its runway proposal to the Minister of the Environment for public review under EARP. A panel was formed and Transport Canada submitted the environmental impact statement. However, the proposal was then temporarily withdrawn pending the results of a master planning exercise (Transport Canada, 1990). In 1983, the runway project was again referred to EARP. This time, public hearings were held, but due to the reduction in air traffic because of the economic recession in the early 1980s, Transport Canada again withdrew the proposal (FEARO, 1991). In November 1989, the Minister of Transport referred the proposal to the EARP a final time. The environmental impact statement was completed by Transport Canada in August 1990, and public hearings to review it were held in January and February 1991. In August 1991, the panel presented its recommendations to the Ministry of Transport advising that the runway proposal should go ahead, but attaching 22 conditions. The Minister of Transport responded in June 1992, declaring that the runway would proceed, while adopting twelve of the recommendations, and adapting eight. Two recommendations, pertaining to noise compensation and nearby commercial and urban development, were rejected outright.

Methods

In the spring of 1993, I interviewed all four panel members and 43 participants in the Vancouver Airport EARP, about one-third of the total number of participants. Those who were classed as participants had to have either submitted a letter to the panel or spoken at the public hearing, as no other public record of participation exists. Interviews lasted on average about 45 minutes and 92% of those approached agreed to be interviewed. Interviewees were asked open-ended questions about their views on the proposed runway, their participation in the Vancouver Airport EARP and whether they had participated in other similar processes. Interviewees were then asked their opinion of the Vancouver Airport EARP and how they thought the procedure needed improving, if at all. Although participants were asked their views of the whole process, their responses centred largely on the stage in which their involvement was concentrated - the public hearing.

Participants in an EIA process are not a unitary group with one voice or opinion. Instead they have multiple, often conflicting perspectives of the process. When considering which interviewees to approach for interview, I wanted to ensure that the broad spectrum of participants' opinions of the Vancouver International Airport EARP was covered. As a result, I selected two factors which I thought were likely to shape participants' views, namely position taken in relation to runway construction, whether they were for, against or neutral in relation to runway construction, and degree of embeddedness within the process. The latter was divided into 'high' and 'low' involvement and was based on the amount of time invested by participants in the process and the degree to which they became directly involved. Writing one letter to the panel was classed as 'low' involvement, whereas writing two or more letters, or giving a presentation at the public hearings, was considered to be a 'high' level of involvement. Participants who were variously situated in relation to these factors were then approached for an interview.

Participants were not approached randomly for interview as I was anxious to canvas the opinions of the key participants who were identified by the chair of the panel. They were likely to have formed considered opinions of the Vancouver Airport EARP, and I wanted to incorporate their views to acknowledge the enormous amount of time and energy they invested in the process - some had been involved for almost twenty years. In addition, the current addresses of several participants were not available. Although the aim was not to produce a statistically representative sample of participants' views, it was important that a broad range of opinion regarding the Vancouver Airport EARP was collected. Neglecting to do this could have resulted in various perspectives being ignored, which clearly would not result in a very open and inclusive EIA evaluation. It should be noted, however, that I chose the two factors that guided interviewee selection, and, therefore, it is possible that I have not captured the complete range of participant opinions.

Participants' Opinions of the Vancouver International Airport EARP

About one third of people interviewed thought the Vancouver International Airport EARP was good, and had no further comments about it. The vast majority of these people had campaigned for the runway. Given that the process served their interest, this result is perhaps not surprising, yet should not be dismissed. Space does not permit the documentation of all the views the other two thirds of interviewees had about the process, and instead, the five most common themes raised in interviews have been selected to illustrate the argument.

The most frequent issue (which was voiced by thirteen interviewees) regarding the Vancouver Airport EARP was that *the recommendations made by the panel were not binding*. Nine of whom were not in favour of the runway thought that this was a serious disadvantage of EARP, undermining the value of the public process. For example, the following comment made by an interviewee is fairly typical:

> Transport Canada ignored most of the panel's recommendations and this was the ultimate outrage and rendered the process a complete farce.

One of these people was a panel member who was very angry and distressed that Transport Canada should be allowed to reject the panel's recommendations. He commented that the 'bureaucrats completely manipulated the process', and blamed this on the British parliamentary model of Ministerial discretion. However, two other panel members declared that they were unconcerned about the non-binding nature of the panel's recommendations because it has been clear from the outset that this would be the case. One participant, who was in favour of the runway, actually considered Ministerial discretion to be beneficial. He was upset with some of the panel's recommendations, especially noise compensation for local residents, and was therefore pleased that this recommendation of the panel was overruled by our elected representatives.

The second most frequently voiced criticism of the Vancouver Airport EARP raised by interviewees was that *the decision to build the runway had been made* before the public hearings had begun. Nine individuals, all of whom opposed runway construction, commented that they believed this to be the case, although they had different interpretations as to whether this undermined the legitimacy of the process. One commented of the process, "it was OK, but the decision had already been made before we started". She was thus able to separate the fact that she perceived that the decision had already been made from the process itself. All the other interviewees who commented on this issue thought that the fact that the decision was already made totally undermined the process. For example, one commented with anger:

> I realized after a while, and this impression just strengthened until the end, that we were being co-opted. They wanted to give an illusion of a public process, of getting the public involved, but in fact it was always carefully managed, they were never listening. We were just tokenism, it was a way of saying look, we did include the public and yet this is what the panel came up with. I used to speak to people who I knew were sympathetic to [our anti-runway interest group] and opposed to the runway and begged them to turn out. Most simply told me that the decision had already been taken and to forget it.

Another issue raised by interviewees opposed to the runway was *resource inequity*. Frequently in EIA processes, there is a significant gap between the amount of resources controlled by the proponent and those of various opposition groups and individuals. This situation was no different in the Vancouver Airport EARP. One interviewee informed me that she asked Transport Canada what their budget was for the whole process. They replied 'as much as it takes'. In contrast, participants protesting the runway, despite being predominantly middle and upper-middle class professionals, obviously did not have access to the same level of resources. The Vancouver EARP panel was aware of such a potential resource inequity and set up a participant funding program to attempt to reduce the discrepancy. In total, $170,500 was provided for intervenor funding (FEARO, 1990). Nevertheless, the perception of resource inequity remained. One participant commented that the giant machine represented by Transport Canada felt like a 'Goliath' and those challenging them were 'David'. The public hearings were intense, lasting 11 days and continuing well into the night. One participant commented how exhausted his protest group was and that it was unfair that Transport Canada could keep bringing in 'paid fresh blood' when someone got tired.

However, as usual, not all participants in the Vancouver International EARP agreed with such sentiments. One participant who declared himself neutral in relation to the runway, commented:

> If you're not careful you wind up spending just a huge amount of money. The idea of giving protest groups money to protest what you're doing, I don't know, somehow doesn't seem right, it doesn't seem fair. To what extent do you want to go and make it more difficult? These guys [Transport Canada] went through a lot of effort to get this thing [the runway].

This interviewee has a very different notion of what is and is not fair. To him, Transport Canada had invested a lot of effort and taxpayer's money into the project and it did not make sense to use taxpayer's money to fund the opposition too.

The issue of *participant representativeness* was frequently raised in interviews. Obviously, the panel members only hear the views of those individuals and groups who are prepared to participate. This leaves open the possibility that there is a 'silent majority' or 'public interest' which is not being represented at the hearing, and that the process is being controlled by 'special interest groups'. Participants who mentioned this issue had very different opinions on the topic. Two individuals emphasized the importance that everyone in a democratic society should be able to speak at the public hearing. A participant who opposed the runway, realizing that participants in a public hearing are not representative of the general public, argued further that it was fair that participants' voices were given disproportional attention in deliberations:

> I think you have got to have a sense of what the general public thinks, but I think you have got to give value to groups of people who put the time in to become community informed people.

Two others, who had been in favour of runway construction, questioned this practice because it allows participants who may represent the views of a minority of the population to gain disproportional attention. For example, one of the participants criticized the process on the following grounds:

> Our point was that because it is a public process, and nothing against a public process, but because it works the way it does, the panel members bend over backwards to give equal time and equal voice to anyone, whatever view it may be. So if there is one person that represents friends of the longhorn sheep then they get equal time compared to a mayor that represents fifty municipalities across the

province.

Finally, a concern raised by four interviewees pertained to *the scope of* the Vancouver Airport EARP, although, as usual no consensus viewpoint was articulated. Two individuals, who were not in favour of runway construction, felt that the process was too narrow and would benefit from looking at the need of the runway within the context of the future development of Vancouver's Lower Mainland. They further noted the need to develop more creative solutions. However, two supporters of the runway thought EARP was currently too broad, one noting that it was too time-consuming, lengthy, and expensive for the tax-payer. The other suggested an alternate procedure to EARP which would involve two stages. The first stage would be dedicated to dealing with all the technical operational arguments, and if a proposal gained technical approval, then it would go to an environmental panel in order to determine the mitigation requirements. This proposed procedure is far more restrictive than EARP, and manages to avoid any public input at all.

Comparing EARP Evaluations

I want to highlight the differing views presented of EARP by participants and social scientists and to argue that the different critiques raised are related to individuals' situatedness in relation to the process. Unlike participants, social scientists are largely situated as onlookers rather than having participated in the process as stakeholders. In addition, social scientists tend to evaluate EARP as a whole rather than focusing on their experiences of a singular process as participants do (although there are several exceptions, for example King and Nelson, 1983; W. Rees, 1989; Sadler, 1990). As a result, it is likely that social scientists will have a very different perspective of EARP than participants. If this is the case, then clearly by incorporating the views of people who are differently situated in relation to EARP, social scientists would make their evaluations more inclusive as well as broadening and deepening the debate pertaining to the relative merits and demerits of EARP.

The foremost issue raised by participants relates to the fact that *the recommendations of the panel were not binding.* In addition, social scientists (for example; Rees, 1981; Jeffery, 1991; Smith, 1991; Gibson, 1993) have raised this as a concern, arguing it leaves EARP potentially open to political manipulation. Although this theme has been raised by both participants and social scientists, there is no consensus as to whether non-binding panel recommendations are desirable and, among those who consider them undesirable, why this is so. It is argued that these views are to a degree shaped by the situatedness of the evaluator. Those who opposed the runway were clearly upset that some of the panel's recommendations were overturned and considered much of their efforts participating in the process wasted. In contrast, social scientists ground their critique more technically. For example, Gibson (1993:18) has argued that ministerial discretion is undesirable because:

> the tendency in discretionary decisionmaking will almost always be to compromise the environmental assessment objectives in the face of other, immediate pressures.

Finally, from the perspective of the individual who was in favour of the runway, the final decision served his interests and he framed the issue not in terms of political manipulation or wasted participation, but simply that our elected decision makers should be the ones to make the final decision. Each perspective regarding the issue of the non-binding nature of the panel's recommendations is valid, and yet the views of participants have not so far been represented in debates on the topic. By pooling all these perspectives, the overall debate becomes multidimensional and therefore richer.

Another issue frequently raised by participants was that *the decision to build the runway had been made* before the public hearings began. Social scientists raised a similar point more generally with their argument that participation occurs too late in the process, namely after some irrevocable decisions have been made. However, the way the issue has been raised can be contrasted. Social scientists couch their criticism as a process fault that can be corrected, and raise it as a technical point, engaging with the accepted language of EIA. In contrast, for most participants, the view that the 'decision had already been made' undermined the legitimacy of the Vancouver Airport EARP process and was met with frustration and helplessness. Social scientists have therefore been able to represent their views as 'fact'; participants have only been able to frame their concerns as 'experience'. By incorporating the perspectives of participants, social scientists would be not only more inclusive, but their overall argument that participation occurs too late in the process would be strengthened.

As demonstrated, the condemnation of *resource inequity* in EARP was frequently raised by both social scientists and interviewees protesting the runway. Yet, two noticeable differences characterize the accounts. First, social science representations of resource inequity are often argued from the principle of fairness and justified in a logical, rational manner (for example Emond, 1983). In contrast, participants present a very different argument, basing it on graphic examples drawn from personal experiences of the process. Adjectives that were repeated over and over again included participants being 'exhausted' and 'overwhelmed'. Second, participants may suggest novel perspectives on an issue, for example, one participant who was not protesting the runway, voiced the opinion that resource inequity should not be challenged in EARP. Although this perspective may be considered unfair, it is still legitimate and comes from a 'taxpayer' who challenges the idea that government money is used to fight government projects. The only social scientist encountered who represents this perspective is Emond (1983). He was able to do this because to some degree he has departed from the scientific mode of EIA evaluation. As was outlined earlier, he has recognized that there are multiple possible legitimate evaluations of an EIA process. He is thus implicitly moving away from the scientific position that multiple perspectives can be reconciled and a singular, objective evaluation can be achieved.

Emond (1983); Parenteau (1988) and Smith (1993) discuss the issue of *participant representativeness* in EIA, recognizing that participants may not be representative of the views of the public at large. They have argued that, as a solution, the process should be as open and accessible as possible and that the panel should try to determine the representativeness of participants and the weight that should be afforded to the views of each on this basis. Social scientists largely agree with those participants who argue that everyone should be able to participate at the hearings and that over-representation of 'special interest groups' is undesirable. However, they differ in their suggested solution to participant representation. Social scientists argue that 'special interest groups' should be able to participate, but their views should be weighted. In contrast, the participants who commented on this issue argued that some people should have limited access to the process. I would suggest that again, the partiality of people's perspectives results in these differing viewpoints. Social scientists promoting inclusiveness are unlikely to recommend that certain people should not be allowed to participate, but participants advocated this because they were perhaps aware that, in practice, the weighting of arguments is very difficult once they are aired. Finally, one participant argued that disproportionate attention should be given to those who are committed enough to attend the hearings. Being aware of many structural barriers to participation, social scientists are unlikely to endorse this, yet from the perspective of a participant who has dedicated thousands of hours to the process, this interviewee is keenly aware of the personal tradeoffs involved in participation. Once again, participants have provided alternative, but equally legitimate, perspectives to social scientists.

The views of interviewees regarding *the scope of EARP* were very much tied to their particular perspectives as participants in the public hearings. The opinions of social scientists, while coinciding with those of participants who thought the process was too narrow, were expressed in a precise technical way. In contrast, two other participants who favoured the runway argued from a 'taxpayer' standpoint that the process was too broad and expensive. Because they consulted with the public, only Walsh et al. (1988) were able to represent the much broader debate on this issue, acknowledging the viewpoints of both those who find the process too narrow and too broad.

It is apparent that participants in the Vancouver Airport EARP and social scientists have raised similar issues in their analyses, yet they have dealt with them very differently. Participants have presented their views in experiential terms, outlining their frustrations and satisfactions with the process as stakeholders in the public hearing stage of a specific application of EARP. Social scientists, on the other hand, are frequently situated as 'expert' onlookers of the process as a whole and consequently used more dispassionate, scientifically rational language to present their views. Although participants and social scientists are differently situated in relation to EARP and consequently have different evaluations of the process, the perspectives of both groups are equally legitimate and by exploring these different perspectives, social scientists can challenge the knowledge/experience or fact/value hierarchy that is so disempowering to participants. Participants also tended to hold more diverse opinions than the more consensual body of social scientific analyses and by representing these views, social scientists as well as policy makers get a clearer picture of the multiple ways in which characteristics of EIA impact on people who are differentially situated in the process. The evidence also suggests that incorporation of participants' views in evaluations is likely to result in a more radical critique of EARP than has been provided by most social scientists to date. Not only does the incorporation of their views undermine the knowledge hierarchy which is currently so pervasive in society, but the comments of participants in the Vancouver Airport EARP have tended to challenge some of the foundations of EARP.

Towards Conducting Situated EIA Evaluations

The preceding discussion highlights a paradox inherent in the 'scientific' approach to EIA evaluations. On the one hand, social scientists are advocating an open and inclusive EIA process but on the other, there are exclusionary practices embedded in their own approaches. One way to avoid this political contradiction is to adopt a 'situated' approach to EIA process evaluations which attempts to demystify the evaluations of social scientists and elevate the concerns of process participants.

The 'situated' approach recognizes that everyone, including the social scientist, has a particular perspective of an EIA process and therefore, by implication, if social scientists wish to make evaluations more open and inclusive, they should solicit the views of participants. However, obtaining participants' views alone is only an aspect of the situated approach and issues of representation are also crucial. As discussed with regard to W. Rees' (1979) evaluation, social scientists need to be clear exactly whose views they are presenting in order to avoid universalizing them. Participants' opinions also need to be represented in a clear and fair fashion, and this involves a consideration of the social scientist's position in the evaluation. Recent approaches to representation have rejected the notion of the researcher being a transparent medium through which people's opinions are neutrally portrayed. Instead, as Duncan and Ley (1994:3) explain, an 'interpretive' account of representation has the following approach:

> Rather than setting up a model of a universal, value-neutral researcher whose task is to proceed in such a manner that s/he is converted into a cipher, this approach recognizes that interpretation is a dialogue between one's data - other places and people - and the researcher who is embedded within a particular intellectual and institutional context.

A recognition of the difficulties inherent in the presentation of other people's views is an integral part of a situated approach.

A situated approach would also involve searching for non-academic fora in which evaluations could be presented and discussed with participants and members of the public more broadly. Finally, a situated approach is not a relativist one in which the social scientist is unable to distinguish between the various perspectives presented. Once the social scientist has situated him/herself with regard to the process under evaluation and represented the views of participants, s/he should then engage with the debates that have been raised in order to make the case for a more open and inclusive EIA process. To attempt to remain 'neutral' perpetuates the image of the social scientist being a rational, value-neutral investigator.

This approach to evaluating EIA processes has several advantages. It avoids the paradox inherent in the scientific approach to EIA process appraisals by challenging the power relations embedded in the assumptions of scientific rationality and the cult of the expert. Through providing both a conceptual and a physical space for others to voice their opinions, social scientists and policy makers get a clearer picture of the multiple and complex ways in which aspects of EIA processes affect people. This in itself helps to broaden and deepen the debate on process as participants have raised many perspectives that have largely been ignored by social scientists. Even when participants have raised the same points as social scientists, they have often done so using alternative justifications and reasoning. Finally, a rejection of the notion that EIA evaluations are scientific places EIA into the political realm, which is where it belongs given that decisions as to the improvement of EIA processes are profoundly political; every scenario results in winners and losers.

I have been arguing that evaluations of EIA processes should be rendered more open and inclusive, and yet there are two important dimensions which, although not discussed here, would further promote the openness of evaluations. First, although the case for including participants is outlined here, I do not consider the views of the (even more marginalized) general public who did not participate in the process. It would be useful, in terms of enhancing the debate and being politically expedient, to solicit their views. Second, the notion of soliciting opinion could be developed further than has been done here. One-shot consultation in the form of an interview (as exemplified in this paper) is just one of many ways of including participants, and in terms of power sharing, is certainly not the best (see Arnstein, 1969). Other potential methods include an ongoing exchange between social scientists and participants. Alternatively, social scientist/participant workshop discussions could be held at which members jointly author the evaluation, noting points of congruence and departure. Further research along these lines would make EIA process evaluations more open and inclusive and would enhance the 'situated' approach outlined above.

Acknowledgments

I would like to thank Maureen Reed, Elizabeth Bronson, Martin Evans, Philip Kelly, John Sinclair and three anonymous referees for reading and commenting on earlier drafts of this paper.

Notes:
[1]The term 'social scientists' is used broadly and refers to researchers whose work would fall under the rubric of planning, environmental studies, policy analysis or other related fields. The term refers largely to academics, although consultants and government policy analysts are also included.

References

Arnstein, S.R. (1969) "A ladder of citizen participation," *Journal of the American Institute of Planners*, 35: 216-24.

Assembly of First Nations and the Inuit Circumpolar Conference of Canada (1993) "A preliminary research prospectus," in Sadler, B. and Boothroyd, P. (eds.), *Traditional Ecological Knowledge and Environmental Assessment*, Canadian Environmental Assessment Research Council, Ottawa, ON: Minister of Supply and Services, 84-93.

Boothroyd, P. (1978) "Issues in social impact assessment," *Plan Canada*, 18: 118-134.

Burdge, R.J. and Robertson, R.A. (1990) "Social impact assessment and the public involvement process," *Environmental Impact Assessment Review*, 10: 81-90.

Burdge, R.J. and Vanclay, F. (1996) "Social impact assessment: a contribution to the state of the art series," *Impact Assessment*, 14: 59-86.

Burr, V. (1995) *An Introduction to Social Constructionism*, London, UK and New York, NY: Routledge.

Canadian Gazette (1984) *Environmental Assessment and Review Process Guidelines Order*, 11th July, Ottawa.

CEARC (1985) *Social Impact Assessment: A Research Prospectus*, Ottawa, ON: Minister of Supply and Services.

_____ (1988) *Evaluating Environmental Impact Assessment: An Action Prospectus*, Ottawa, ON: Minister of Supply and Services Canada.

Code, L. (1988) "Credibility: a double standard," in Code, L., Mullett, S. and Overall, C. (eds.), *Feminist Perspectives: Philosophical Essays on Method and Morals*, Toronto, ON: University of Toronto Press, 64-88.

Corbett, R. (1986) *A Bargaining and Community Development Approach to SIA and Management*, Master's Thesis, Faculty of Environmental Design, Calgary, AB: University of Calgary.

Craig, D. (1990) "Social impact assessment: politically oriented approaches and applications," *Environmental Impact Assessment Review*, 10: 37-54.

Demeritt, D. (1994) "Ecology, objectivity and critique in writings on nature and human societies," *Journal of Historical Geography*, 20: 22-37.

Dene Cultural Institute (1995) "Traditional ecological knowledge and environmental assessment," in Gaffield, C. and Gaffield, P. (eds.), *Consuming Canada: Readings in Environmental History*, Toronto, ON: Copp Clark Ltd., 340-365.

Duncan, J. and Ley, D. (1994) *Place/ Culture/ Representation*, London, UK and New York, NY: Routledge.

Emond, D.P. (1983) "Fairness, efficiency and FEARO: an analysis of EARP," in Case, E.S., Finkle, P.Z.R. and Lucas, A.R. (eds.), *Fairness in Environmental and Social Impact Assessment Processes*, Canadian Institute of Resources Law, Calgary, AB: University of Calgary, 49-74.

Environmental Planning and Assessment Caucus (1988) *A Federal Environmental Assessment Process: The Core Elements*, Ottawa, ON: Canadian Environment Network's Environmental Planning and Assessment Caucus.

FEARO (1985) *Environmental Assessment Panels: Procedures and Rules for Public Meetings*, Ottawa, ON: Minister of Supply and Services.

_____ (1987) *Reforming Federal Environmental Assessment: A Discussion Paper*, Ottawa, ON: Minister of Supply and Services.

_____ (1988) *The National Consultation Workshop on Federal Environmental Assessment Reform: Report of Proceedings*, Ottawa, ON: Minister of Supply and Services.

_____ (1990) *Vancouver International Airport Environmental Assessment Review Participant Funding Program: List of Successful Applicants and Funded Work*, 1 page release, Ottawa, ON: FEARO.

_____ (1991) *Vancouver International Airport: Parallel Runway Project, Report of the Environmental Assessment Panel*, August 1991, Ottawa, ON: FEARO, 1-127.

Fenge, T. and Smith, L.G. (1986) "Reforming the federal environmental assessment and review process," *Canadian Public Policy*, 12: 596-605.

Finley, K.J. (1993) "A community based conservation strategy for the Bowhead Whale," in Sadler, B. and Boothroyd, P. (eds.), *Traditional Ecological Knowledge and Environmental Assessment*, Canadian Environmental Assessment Research Council, Ottawa, ON: Minister of Supply and Services, 28-40.

Freeman, M.M.R. (1975) "Assessing movement in an Arctic caribou population," *Journal of Environmental Management*, 3: 251-257.

_____ (1992) "The nature and utility of traditional ecological knowledge," *Northern Perspectives*, 20: 9-12.

Gibson, R.B. (1990) *Basic Requirements for Environmental Assessment Processes: A Framework for Evaluating Existing and Proposed Legislation*, Department of Environment and Resource Studies, Waterloo, ON: University of Waterloo.

Gibson, R.B. (1992) "The new Canadian Environmental Assessment Act: possible responses to its main differences," *Journal of Environmental Law and Practice*, 2: 223-255

Gibson, R.B. (1993) "Environmental assessment design: lessons from the Canadian experience," *The Environmental Professional*, 15: 12-24.

Haraway, D. (1991) "Situated knowledges: the science question and feminism and the privilege of partial perspective," in Haraway, D. (ed.), *Simians, Cyborgs and Women: The Reinvention of Nature*, New York, NY: Routledge, 183-201.

Hobson, G. (1992) "Traditional knowledge is science," *Northern Perspectives*, 20: 2.

Jeffery, M.I. (1991) "The new Canadian Environmental Assessment Act - Bill C-78: a disappointing response to promised reform," *McGill Law Journal*, 36: 1070-1088.

Johnson, M. (1992) "Dene traditional knowledge," *Northern Perspectives*, 20: 3-5.

King, J.E. and Nelson, J.G. (1983) "Evaluating the federal environmental assessment and review process with special reference to South Davis Strait, Northeastern Canada," *Environmental Conservation*, 10: 293-301.

Lang, R. and Armour, A. (1981) *The Assessment and Review of Social Impacts*, Ottawa, ON: Federal Environmental Assessment and Review Office.

Lawrence, D.P. (1994) "Designing and adapting the EIA planning process," *The Environmental Professional*, 16: 2-21.

Lawrence, D.P. (1997) "Integrating sustainability and environmental impact assessment," *Environmental Management*, 21: 23-42.

Lucas, A.R. and McCallum, S.K. (1975) "Looking at environmental impact assessment," in Elder, P.S. (ed.), *Environmental Management and Public Participation*, Toronto, ON: Canadian Environmental Law Association, 306-318.

Nakashima, D.J. (1990) *Application of Native Knowledge in EIA: Inuit, Eiders and Hudson Bay Oil*, Canadian Environmental Assessment Research Council, Ottawa, ON: Minister of Supply and Services.

Parenteau, R. (1988) *Public Participation in Environmental Decision Making*, Ottawa, ON: Federal Environmental Assessment Review Office.

Parkes, W. (1991) Reforming the Federal Environmental Assessment Process, Presentation to the Canadian Association of Geographers, 6th June, Kingston, ON: Queens University.

Pepper, D. (1984) *The Roots of Modern Environmentalism*, London, UK and New York, NY: Routledge.

Pinkerton, E. (1993) "Where do we go from here? The future of traditional ecological knowledge and resource management in native communities," in Sadler, B. and Boothroyd, P. (eds.), *Traditional Ecological Knowledge and Environmental Assessment*, Canadian Environmental Assessment Research Council, Ottawa, ON: Minister of Supply and Services, 70-83.

Racevskis, K. (1983) *Michel Foucault and the Subversion of Intellect*, Ithaca, NY and London, UK: Cornell University Press.

Reed, M.G. (1984) *Citizen Participation and Public Hearings: Evaluating Northern Experiences*, Cornett Occasional Papers No.4, Department of Geography, Victoria, BC: University of Victoria, 1-65.

_____ (1990) *Environmental Assessment and Aboriginal Claims: Implementation of the Inuvialuit Final Agreement*, Canadian Environmental Assessment Research Council, Ottawa, ON: Minister of Supply and Services.

Rees, J. (1990) *Natural Resources: Allocation, Economics and Policy*, Second Edition, London, UK: Routledge.

Rees, W.E. (1979) *Reflections on the Environmental Assessment and Review Process*, Ottawa, ON: Canadian

Arctic Resource Committee.

_____ (1981) "EARP at the crossroads: environmental assessment in Canada," *Environmental Impact Assessment Review,* 1: 355-377.

_____ (1989) "Norman Wells impact funding: boon or bust?," *Canadian Public Administration,* 32: 104-123.

Rees, W.E. and Boothroyd, P. (1987) *Reform of the EARP Process: Background Paper on Process and Structure,* Ottawa, ON: The Rawson Academy for the Canadian Environmental Assessment Research Council.

Sadler, B. (1990) *An Evaluation of the Beaufort Sea Environmental Assessment Panel Review,* Ottawa, ON: Federal Environmental Assessment Review Office, Canada.

Shapcott, C. (1989) "Environmental impact assessment and resource management, a Haida case study: implications for native people of the north," *Canadian Journal of Native Studies,* 11: 55-83.

Smith, D.E. (1990) *The Conceptual Practices of Power: A Feminist Sociology of Knowledge,* Boston, IL: North Eastern University Press.

Smith, L.G. (1987) "A performance rating for Canadian EIA," *The Operational Geographer,* 13: 12-14.

_____ (1991) "Canada's changing assessment provisions," *Environmental Impact Assessment Review,* 11: 5-9.
_____ (1993) *Impact Assessment and Sustainable Resource Management,* Harlow, UK: Longman.

Torgerson, D. (1981) "SIA as a social phenomenon: the problem of contextuality," in Tester, F.J. and Mykes, W.

(eds.), *Social Impact Assessment: Theory, Method and Practice*, Calgary, AB: Detselig Enterprises, 68-92.

Transport Canada (1990) *Vancouver International Airport Parallel Runway Project: Environmental Impact Statement Summary Report, August 1990*, Ottawa, ON: Transport Canada.

Walsh, A.A.M., Robertson, C.D., Riverin, G., Lachance, C., Dowling, M. and Duperron, J. (1988) *Public Review: Neither Judicial, nor Political, but an Essential Forum for the Future of the Environment*, Ottawa, ON: Minister of Supply and Services.

Weston, S.M.C. (1992) *The Canadian Federal Environmental Assessment and Review Process: An Analysis of the Initial Assessment Phase*, Canadian Environmental Assessment Review Office, Ottawa, ON: Minister of Supply and Services.

Wolf, C.P. (1983) "What is social impact assessment?," *Social Impact Assessment*, 83/84: 22-40.

Yearly, S. (1991) *The Green Case: A Sociology of Environmental Issues, Arguments and Politics*, London, UK: Harper Collins Academic.

Chapter 11

Contextualizing the Environmental Impact Assessment Process

Bryn Greer-Wootten
York University

... I know human relationships are not founded on reason any more than my roses are fertilized with debate. I know seeking asylum behind the wall of intellect and rationality is a selfish retreating into self-protectiveness at the expense of another's well being.

> Patricia D. Cornwell, Post-Mortem, 164.

In this chapter I contend that environmental impact assessment (EIA) is dead, but I also toast the long life of EIA - in a transformed state. The purpose of this paper is to examine the ways in which such a transformation might be achieved, through a critical evaluation of the process itself. My emphasis is on the process of knowledge construction evident in the practice of EIA, and I attempt to evaluate this process by placing it into different and competing socio-political contexts in which both the practice and the practitioners co-exist. In seeking to elucidate these contexts, I try to determine whether a greater awareness of them, largely but not exclusively on the part of practitioners, might lead to a transformation of EIA away from its present, overly positivistic tenor. Such a development would, I believe, change the nature of environmental decision making, while having the potential to impart new vigour into EIA.

Some definitions and elaboration of these concepts will help to make my purpose more explicit. The boundaries of

EIA are defined by legislation and the accompanying regulatory framework of government. They tend to be fixed for long periods of time, but they are constantly reviewed or contested every time a public hearing is held. If this were not the case, 'the public' would have no role to play in EIA. That which is mandated to lie outside these boundaries (temporally, spatially, or substantively) forms the context for EIA. As a form of environmental decision making, the EIA process is primarily concerned with the production of knowledge, a mechanism that produces information potentially of value for the political decision concerning some development proposal. Such knowledge can be represented in material documentary form (environmental impact statements (EIS), transcripts of public hearings, etc.), or, more implicit in form, as the outcomes of the learning process resulting for participants in the process.

Stepping outside of the EIA boundaries, into the context, distinctions can be made within the socio-political context, for analytical purposes. With respect to practice, for example, the administration of EIA responds to the legislation and regulatory framework, yet there is always an interpretation of these frameworks. Similarly, for practitioners - actors representing proponents, government agencies, independent consultants, public interest groups, etc. - interpretations of 'expected' roles are always in play. Awareness of such interpretations implies a self-reflection on one's role in the process and, since any actor does not act out his or her life on the EIA stage, awareness implies positioning or contextual orientation.

These two aspects of the EIA process - the institutionalized workings of the process and the socio-political context in which they exist - can be brought together, again for analytical purposes, by considering the construction of knowledge in a theoretical manner. Distinctions between technical knowledge, gained from a positivistic approach to EIA, and post-positivistic interpretations that relate to process, are important in this respect (Shadish, 1995). Such distinctions approximate the commonly-held categories of scientific assessments and planning-oriented evaluations, but these categories (of product) tend to simplify what is, in effect, a complex nexus of relations between all of the actors involved.

My contention here, then, is that attention to these relations between actors could lead to a re-invigorated EIA, but that such attention requires an appreciation of the context. The route to such a conclusion, if traced in depth, would be long, so I intend only to provide the signposts to the abundant literature that exists on the traditional status of EIA (see, for example: Sewell and Mitchell (1981), Smith (1993), Spaling et al. (1993) and Meredith (1995), for overviews).

The notion of 'transforming' EIA raises the question: "from what ... to what?" I believe that to attempt to answer such a question (and many others), while bounded by the present parameters established for the practice of EIA and the activities of its practitioners, is futile. From the perspective of practice, I believe that a re-evaluation of the administrative-bureaucratic mechanisms that contain EIA - legislation, regulatory frameworks, jurisdictional issues, etc., - is needed. Such structures, however, represent major obstacles to change in and of themselves: for an excellent overview of the problem of institutional inertia, see Gilmour (1993).

As noted above, the work of practitioners in the form of (EIS) reveals a broad distinction between scientific assessments and planning-oriented evaluations. Assuming some level of epistemic integrity (Guba and Lincoln, 1988), such a distinction constitutes a major problem, and a resolution of such separate and largely competing approaches to knowledge construction raise a second obstacle to changing EIA. The traditionally thorny territory of geographers could be encroached upon here: does the discipline encourage the "bridging" of the natural and human sciences, such that a geographical training would produce practitioners who could contribute to the transformation of EIA?

In order to lay the foundations for this examination, a retrospective overview of EIA , based largely on experience in Ontario, is presented. The various problems revealed in this overview are referenced to other jurisdictions as much as possible, and some relevant contexts in which it is useful to evaluate these problems are indicated. The potential for a more explicit contextual orientation of practitioners is treated in concluding remarks.

Assessing Environmental Impact Assessment: A Retrospective View

In theory, EIA procedures present an excellent test of the extent to which public participation in the environmental decision-making process is valued, and by implication, an evaluation of the role of localities and localism in achieving sustainable development in Canada (Greer-Wootten, 1990). In this chapter, the role of the public in EIA is of primary concern, given my position that EIA is essentially a socio-political process.

Ontario was the leading province in environmental legislation when it passed its Environmental Assessment (EA) Act in 1975. The EA process has been under review in Ontario, with the passage of new legislation (Bill 76: Environmental Assessment and Consultation Improvement Act) amending the 1975 Act. The outcome (regulations were in draft form in March, 1997) could be a signpost for environmental decision-making processes in Canada. The 1996 amendments should also be viewed in the context of a move to deregulate environmental protection measures (Ontario Ministry of Environment and Energy, 1996): the election of the neo-conservative Harris government in 1995 indicates the overriding importance of political context for any evaluation of EIA (Novek, 1993), but such has been the case since the 1960s (see Ditton and Goodale, 1972).

The Ground Rules for Assessment

The EA Act was in the planning stage for several years before it was passed in 1975, following the enactment of the US National Environmental Policy Act (NEPA) in 1969. The Act provided for the assessment of provincial public sector developments in Ontario, in order to ensure that the best alternative for implementing a project which caused least harm to the environment was chosen. Basically, a proponent prepared an environmental assessment of the proposed undertaking, submitting it to the Minister as the first stage of the approvals process. There is then a 'Government Review' of the EA, prepared by designated members of the various government ministries whose mandates may be affected by the project. The review and the EA are then released to the public for comment. After 30 days, the Minister decides whether or not to accept the EA. Once it is accepted, people who made submissions during the first review have 15 days in which to comment or to request a hearing. The Minister then decides whether to approve the undertaking, deny it, or refer the matter to the Environmental Assessment Board (an independent tribunal) for a public hearing and decision (Jeffery, 1990). The final decision must be agreed to by Cabinet and the Lieutenant Governor in Council.

The 1996 amendments (passed, November 4, 1996; proclaimed, January 1, 1997) change this approval process in significant ways. The new process requires the proponent to submit "Terms of Reference" that govern the preparation of the EA. If the Minister approves these terms, the EA must comply with them. Importantly, the proponent will be required to consult with interested members of the public when preparing the EA — and, by inference, in deriving the Terms of Reference. Further amendments include increased use of alternative dispute resolution (ADR) processes, such as mediation, for any concerns about a proponent's application at any time, before the Minister makes a decision to approve or deny the undertaking. Both of these types of changes appear to enhance the role of public participation in the process, but the opposite interpretation is equally reasonable (e.g., the reaction of the Canadian Environmental Law Association: Silcoff, 1996).

When the idea of public participation was first discussed in a policy proposal for EIA in 1972, the mechanisms were largely administrative in nature; there was little debate on why public involvement might be considered important. Also lacking at this time were issues such as the different types of "public interests" that might be affected by the proposal, whether these were provincial, local, or simply individual proprietary interests, etc. The focus on EIA as an administrative process means that it is a "partial emulation" of U.S. NEPA policy (Hoberg, 1991:125), without litigation as part of the process, although this may be changing following recent court decisions (e.g., the Rafferty-Alameda (Saskatchewan) and Oldman River (Alberta) dams cases: see Meredith, 1995, and Sundstrom, 1994). The 1996 amendments have institutionalized some of the recent changes to administrative aspects of the process, corresponding to the changing nature of public participation, particularly over the last ten years (Roberts, 1988). The Ministry of the Environment, for example, had provided guidelines to proponents in order to streamline the process, with an emphasis on prior consultation with affected parties. The 1996 changes, then, can be interpreted as an effort to make the planning process a cooperative venture

The original definition of EIA implied that it was to be an administrative process for contributing information about the likely environmental effects of proposed activities to the decision makers. The 1975 Act did not prescribe the way in which the information should be utilized and decisions taken, although most work is technocratic in nature (e.g., Bolton and Curtis, 1990). This aspect of the problem was amplified by a revision to the definition of 'environment'. Originally, impacts were defined as biophysical environmental effects. Then, in response to concerns that the Act should provide for a balancing of various interests, rather than having the consideration of biophysical impacts dominate decisions (as in many other jurisdictions today: see Glasson, 1994), the meaning of environment itself was expanded, to include economic, social and cultural considerations. With this change, the EA Act took on the unanticipated role of providing a process through which all of the various public interests in an undertaking would be assessed and weighed against each other. The 1975 Act made the Minister or a Board responsible for approving undertakings, and so by expanding the definition of "environment", the Minister and the Board were given authorities which up to then were those of the Cabinet as a whole.

In many ways, the 1975 Act and especially Section 5(3), ensured that a full EA would be carried out, as alternatives had to be considered and, over time, public participation became entrenched as part of the process. This "Jewel in the Crown" of the Ontario situation appears to be de-throned by the 1996 amendments. The minister now has discretionary powers to define what the Terms of Reference will be for the EA, and there is little doubt that the substantive requirements of Section 5(3) will be drastically reduced (Lindgren, 1996). The implications for public participation are also likely to be severe: any reduced emphasis on process will lead to increased emphasis on biophysical environmental impacts. The experience of some 20 years in working through what a "full" EA meant, aided by jurisprudence from public hearings and Board decisions (Brown, 1996), seems to have fallen by the wayside.

The EA Board and Public Hearings

Although the Minister, under the 1975 Act, retained control over the necessity of public hearings, on occasion the matter was referred to the Environmental Assessment Board, whose members were appointed by Cabinet but not employed by any Ministry: these provisions, too, have changed under the new legislation. The possibility of referral remains, however. Except in very rare circumstances, all Board meetings are open to the public. Critics of this process point out that although this means that the public has the opportunity to participate in the decision-making process, they are ultimately constrained by the fact that the proponents have most control of the information. Hearings may be conducted under Part III of the *Environmental Assessment Act*, or under the *Consolidated Hearings Act*. In the latter case, a proponent requires a hearing under more than one piece of legislation (e.g., Ontario Water Resources Act, Ontario Planning Act) to get approval. The hearings can be combined into one and are run by a joint board, usually composed of members of the EA Board and the Ontario Municipal Board (OMB). Under the new legislation, the Minister and the Board can refer the application to another tribunal, in circumstances they consider "appropriate". Regardless of the actual nature of the hearings, there are several problems in, for example, the handling of requests, facilitating conflict, and providing opportunity for effective participation in hearings, although Bill 76 attempted to deal with some of these operational and procedural issues, largely in the context of streamlining and clarifying rules, etc. For example, the Minister can direct the Board to hear testimony in respect only of matters specified by the government. In other words, scoping the issues (Lawrence, 1994) subject to EAB procedures should reduce the length and cost of hearings, although a fully-developed scoping process would also involve public inputs (Kennedy and Ross, 1992).

The hearings held by the EA Board are generally adversarial in nature. They operate with a trial-type format in which evidence is given by expert witnesses, who are then cross-examined. To some degree, the adversarial approach is unavoidable in any EA process, because the proponent is proposing an undertaking and the people requesting the hearing are challenging it. Furthermore, Ontario's *Statutory Powers and Procedures Act* lays down general court-like procedures for hearings by administrative bodies such as the EA Board. Although such proceedings produce juridical knowledge important for the EA process, the hearings often involve fundamental political choices about social policy and development strategies, as well as the more specific decisions on environmental tradeoffs and allocation of costs. On these policy/strategy matters, the adversarial approach tends to miss or reject relevant options or bases for analysis, because it favours evidence from narrowly qualified experts. It relies excessively on determination of "facts", when the issues at hand centre on social choices and policy decisions. Again, the 1996 legislation attempts to deal with this issue, in part by scoping but also because of new provisions enabling the Minister to issue policy guidelines that the Board must consider when making decisions. Clearly, "alternatives" can be made redundant by such discretionary powers. Minimally, the possibility of the EA Board serving as an independent voice representing the public interest in environmental decision making, has been compromised by the amendments.

Alternatives to the Adversarial Process

In the face of the time and cost of adversarial hearings, alternative dispute resolution strategies (ADR) for resolving environmental conflicts have been proposed, especially mediation, arbitration and community compensation. The 1996 legislation in Ontario has entrenched these processes in law, likely because they involve the active and voluntary participation of opposing parties in resolving differences through mutual agreement, with or without the help of a third party. The objectives are to mitigate the negative impacts of projects on the community, or to compensate for these disbenefits with amenities such as improved educational facilities, health and child care, and transportation.

Mediation, which is currently the most favoured alternative, is a specific and relatively formal technique of conflict resolution (Sadler, 1993). It is defined as a voluntary process in which those involved in a dispute jointly explore and reconcile their differences, with the help of a neutral third party or mediator. Agreements are reached by consensus, and the mediator is not authorized to select or impose a solution. The voluntary consensual and non-binding characteristics of mediation distinguish it from other formal means of settling disputes, such as arbitration and conciliation, giving it considerable apparent potential for use within the framework of EIA. Note, however, that since it is not binding on either party in any way, if a resolution is not found and a hearing is subsequently held, another step has been added to the process. Moreover, the use of such processes at the EAB has been primarily as a case management tool, with a mediocre record (Bozzo, 1996).

Besides the efficiency of the EIA process, however, there are important questions of equity for which most ADR mechanisms can only have a "wall-papering" effect, largely because they are used at a late stage in the process. There are very few examples of early interventions in the development process, because they would have to be in situ, perhaps as environmental planning organizations deliberately established at a local level. The experience of the Kativik Environmental Quality Commission (Mulvihill and Keith, 1989) in northern Québec is instructive in this respect. Legislating such proactive approaches to development is complicated, but the work of Local Assessment Committees in California under the Tanner Act (Craig, 1992) could provide evidence on the value of early intervention, with high levels of public input in terms of discussion of mitigation measures with a proponent. Perhaps inevitably, such community or organizational approaches to more cooperative and consensual EIA processes will be grounded in localities - at once a strength and a liability.

Moreover, the complexities, uncertainties and larger environmental implications of many undertakings addressed through public hearings mean that important issues cannot always be analyzed properly, or even delineated clearly, on the basis of adversarial testing of narrowly defined "facts". Boards and panels often need to see beyond immediate facts to the underlying values and unstated policy positions that will be confirmed or rejected through approval or non-approval of specific undertakings. Even with the 1996 changes in legislation with respect to scoping and policy guidelines for the EAB, there are some fundamental problems in resolving these issues: for example, to what extent can 'scientific explanation', 'legal inference', and 'value-based interpretation' be regarded as equivalent?

The Current Impasse in EA Process Reform

Notwithstanding the legislative changes in Ontario, the challenge for the EA process is to provide a means of clarifying the nature and implications of environmental policy choices, without denying their essentially value-laden character, as well as to ensure that decision making on these choices is open, well-informed, and fair. For most commentators on environmental issues, these challenges had been met in principle by the 1975 Ontario EA Act, but they criticized it as a process. In an adversarial hearing process, for example "relevant evidence" is often defined very narrowly, dependent upon established expertise. For EIA, however, interdisciplinary expertise is more relevant for the types of problems examined, and lay opinion is necessary for evaluation of the underlying social choice issues (Burdge and Robertson, 1990).

These problems had been well recognized in Ontario: for example, in 1987 the Environmental Assessment Program Improvement Project (EAPIP) was initiated with a comprehensive mandate to review all the existing legislation, building upon the extensive evaluation of the first decade of EA in Ontario by Gibson and Savan (1986). The review process evolved into a dominant concern with issues of efficiency in the existing process. Public input was elicited in the evaluation of nine components of the process, one of which dealt specifically with public participation. A major criticism is that only existing practices were subject to review. This assured an incremental approach to change, again reflecting a focus on administrative aspects of the process. It would also appear to set up barriers to dealing with the more fundamental questions of a policy nature.

Nonetheless, the work of process reform was thorough and consistent in its attention to fundamental questions raised earlier by Gibson and Savan: Is the EA process effective, fair and efficient? In 1990, the EAPIP mantle was passed to the Environmental Assessment Advisory Committee (EAAC), which held extensive public hearings and produced a well-grounded report containing 96 recommendations for reform of the process (EAAC, 1992). From then until June, 1996, when the Harris government released its Bill 76 draft amendments to the EA Act (ultimately passed with two minor changes), the reform movement was stymied. Now, it has received a major setback (see Brown, 1996, for a detailed analysis of the discrepancies between EAAC recommendations and Bill 76).

Many of the changes to the administration of the EA program should increase its efficiency, but critics of the 1996 legislation believe that too much attention has been given to bureaucratic details. They state, for example, that the idea of tracking all public consultation inputs is laudable, but extremely difficult to put into practice. Similarly, the long-term complaint about inequalities between proponents and public groups in terms of resources, which had been answered to some extent by the passing of the Intervenor Funding Project Act (1988), has been intensified since the Conservative government allowed this Act to lapse (April, 1996). When in operation, a noted difficulty was that funding was not distributed until after a hearing had been called. The preference of these critics would be that public interest groups be funded at the beginning of planning projects. The timing of funding is significant: this allows interested parties more time to conduct their own reviews. There are now requirements that regulations be drafted for proponents to carry out public consultation in the course of preparing their Terms of Reference for EA. Whether the legislation in Ontario results in this outcome is at present (March, 1997) unknown, of course. These administrative improvements had been proposed in the reform process (1986-1992), in the spirit of a more cooperative form of decision making. It remains unlikely, however, that these changes will be able to address the fundamental issues of EIA that relate more to the value-basis of social choice than to the specifics of a proposed facility.

The lessons to be taken from this abridged case study of the evolution of EIA processes in Ontario are many and varied. The institutional and regulatory frameworks emanating from the 1975 Act can now be seen as sufficiently open to increasing the role of the public in environmental decision making, that they reflected earlier promises for making EIA a stage for local democracy in action. The closing of such avenues appears to be one of the strongest implications of the 1996 amendments to the Act. Certainly, the fragility of public participation has been exposed. For environment non-governmental organizations, the amendments represent a triumph of the 'business agenda' of the Harris government of Ontario. In more general terms, the changes demonstrate a retreat from what Harvey (1996:373-383) describes as "ecological modernization" to the "standard view of environmental management". Placing these lessons from Ontario into a broader context is clearly necessary, but first I wish to consider another primary casualty of the 1996 amendments: the framing or representation of the problem to be resolved by EIA.

It is clear that the original broad definition of 'environment' engendered consideration of both biophysical and social impacts of a proposed development. Over the 20 years of public hearings and EA Board assessments, an appreciation of what was meant by a "full" EA had developed. Note that this implies two components of what can be regarded as a societal learning process: (1) the production of knowledge of environmental impacts, per se, (e.g., in the form of documentary evidence, transcripts, etc.); and (2) the actual involvement of participants in the process (i.e., major stakeholders such as proponents, government officials, consultants, public interest groups, etc.). These two components are strongly related to each other, and their co-evolution has been affected by the original framing of the problem to be resolved by the EA process. The 1996 amendments have likely changed this frame, since the Terms of Reference originate from the proponent, are subject to public consultation (likely minimal), and are determined by the Minister. Even the least skeptical observer may conclude that the problem to be resolved is likely to be quite narrowly focussed, in comparison to the earlier situation. The focus could be narrowed to consideration of biophysical environmental impacts at the expense of social impacts. In the next section, this question is subject to further exploration.

Re-Inventing EIA: More Complex Process or New Game?

Generally speaking, even in the relatively well-established process of environmental impact assessment, the specific impacts of a proposed project are often reduced to scientific or technological terms, with some rough evaluation (Glasson and Heaney, 1993) of economic factors (e.g., cost-benefit), to a greater extent than social impacts. Assumptions then appear to be taken forward into an assessment process which itself is largely technocratic in nature, because it is overly bounded. Limits are placed on the issues subject to debate, so that decisions reflect dominant values held largely by development proponents. As indicated at the outset, these problems can now be discussed with reference to the two primary types of outputs of the process: scientific assessments of biophysical impacts and planning-oriented evaluations (social impact assessments: SIA).

For many scientists, primarily ecologists, working in the applied area of EIA, their inputs have been less important than expected because of the emphasis placed on the administrative aspects of the process (Lemons, 1994). Most EIS documents lack sound scientific information, for several reasons: (1) the weak level of theoretical knowledge for prediction purposes; (2) the limited spatial and temporal scope of project-related EAs; and (3) the few, if any, possibilities for post-project auditing and monitoring of impacts, as discussed in Chapter 5. The audits are necessary both to estimate the quality of the scientific information used in prediction and to improve the EIA process itself (Lemons, 1994). Beanlands' (1985) proposal to establish "valued ecosystem components" for specific enquiry remains more rhetoric than reality, since the valuation is seen in relation to societal needs rather than the scientific objectives of understanding the structure and functioning of ecosystems. It seems that "the scientific community has such a low esteem for the EIA process" (Beanlands, 1985:10) because it is inundated in messy socio-political waters. More recently, for example, Policansky (1993:44) has argued that "... any definition of "ecosystem health" is an implicit value judgement. The challenge, therefore, is to arrive at an operational definition of the "something of value" that explicitly separates the value judgements from the scientific assessments". Little wonder, then, that the 1991 Ecological Society of

America proposal for a Sustainable Biosphere Initiative created such a controversy (Lemons, 1994) between 'pure' and 'applied' scientists.

At the same time, there have been concerted efforts in the last fifteen years or so, to break away from the constricting parameters imposed by project- and site-specific EIAs. Minimally, a regional scale allows consideration of global change issues more explicitly (Rees, 1995), as well as a first step in overcoming the mis-match between jurisdictional systems and ecosystems at a landscape level (Greer-Wootten, 1993). Scientific responses to these issues are seen in the burgeoning literature on cumulative effects assessment (CEA). Some valuable contributions have been made on the necessary theoretical foundations for CEA (e.g., Contant and Wiggins, 1991; Spaling and Smit, 1993). Some relevant methodological frameworks to deal with the complex impact problems resulting from changing scales (both spatial and temporal), and incorporating the interactions of ecosystem components in the analysis, have been identified by Smit and Spaling (1995). Much of this work remains strongly in the positivistic scientific tradition, a legitimate pursuit but one which does not answer the demands of EIA. Most commentators stress the need for complementarity in scientific assessments and planning evaluations (e.g., Spaling and Smit, 1993), but avoid the inevitable epistemological problems generated by a realization that all "facts" are, in fact, "value laden". As one example, Smit and Spaling (1995) argued for a distinction between 'CEAnalysis' and 'CEEvaluation' (i.e., scientific vs. planning-oriented approaches), rather than 'CEAssessment' as a generic term; in doing so, they repeat the epistemological errors that have plagued the risk assessment community for some twenty years or so (Greer-Wootten, 1988).

A common linkage between discussions of CEA that stress scientific inputs to the EIA process and those that are more strongly associated with planning concerns, is found in the assertion that post-project auditing and monitoring of impacts is essential because the complexity and uncertainty of impacts necessitates an adaptive management process (Geisler, 1993). This assertion follows the pioneering work of Holling (1978) in his approach to adaptive environmental assessment ('projects as experiments'), but Geisler (1993) demonstrates the equivalent value of research in the study of organizations in dealing with 'turbulent environments' of change. Similarly, the change in scales encompassed by scientifically-based CEA is matched by planning-oriented concerns, starting from projects (local, short-term) to programs (regional, medium-term) and to policy (national/global, long-term). As difficult as the scientific challenges are acknowledged to be, however, the complexities for social scientists are many times more problematic, especially at the policy level (Therivel, 1993), [sometimes referred to as strategic environmental assessment (SEA).] In fact, Bardecki (1994) argued that the nature of the question changes, and that many considerations relevant in project-based EIA lose their salience with scale change. The questions are unresolved: a relatively straightforward (EIA-based) methodology for national environmental policy analysis is overly simplistic (e.g., Wescott, 1992), because it would not include the impacts of lower levels in the jurisdictional hierarchy in order to devise integrated assessments (Bartlett, 1993), that might then be taken as constitutive of environmental policy.

Even at the project level, typical of most social scientific research on EIA, and especially for work on social impacts, however, the complexities of the issues are scarcely resolved. Two contradictory trends can be discerned: (1) greater concerns with micro-level responses to planning processes; and, (2) expression of the need to place project-specific findings into a broader social theoretic framework for the questions. At the micro-level, for example, attention has moved away from considering social impacts only at the project development stage, to include both before- and after-project construction effects (Gramling and Freudenberg, 1992). Empirical research has demonstrated the importance of anticipatory psychosocial impacts of the planning process (Taylor et al., 1991; Lowes, 1996) at individual, social network and community levels of analysis. As the research effort becomes more focussed, however, there is a danger that interpretation is based increasingly on disciplinary norms, to the detriment of the interdisciplinarity acknowledged as a necessity in EIA (Wildman, 1990).

There is an apparent contradiction seen in SIA research that calls for a broader social theoretic framing of the issues, but it can be resolved by noting the degree of explicit political orientation in such work. First, if SIA is regarded primarily as a technical process (like the scientific approach to EA), then it can be seen as contributing to the administrative mechanisms designed to integrate various publics into a pluralistic decision-making process (Rickson et al., 1990). As such, political orientations tend to be non-critical or implicit. On the other hand, if SIA is viewed as a critical socio-political process, the theoretical framing of pluralistic decision making (i.e., structural functionalism) is called into question, and greater emphasis is given to an explicit conflict formulation of the issues (Manring et al., 1990). Such contrasting theoretical frameworks clearly inform the research on questions such as whether SIA can empower local resource-based communities (Gagnon et al., 1993), whether co-management (between levels of jurisdiction) is a viable policy option for hinterland communities (Reed, 1995), or more generally, whether public participation in resource management can be regarded as effective (Gariepy, 1991).

In summary, both natural scientific and social scientific work within the established parameters of EIA have tended to become focussed on more specific impacts of the development process, and accordingly have become more complex. The tendency is clearly towards disciplinary value rather than work of an interdisciplinary nature that has more salience for EIA. Note that more focussed work is likely to emanate from a more narrowly focussed problem definition (or Terms of Reference?). Similarly, the producers of such work are likely to be more oriented to disciplinary norms (politically 'neutral'?). Changing the temporal and spatial boundaries to investigate CEA or SEA increases the complexity for both types of scientific pursuits. Importantly, for social scientists, such changes imply a different orientation to the theoretical frameworks guiding enquiry. Some indicators of these new orientations can be presented at this point. These changed contexts have important implications for the production of knowledge concerning environmental assessment, as well as for practitioners working in the EIA process.

Identifying New Contexts for EIA: Some Signposts

The various contextual framings of EIA are primarily defined by researchers working in the critical social sciences. Such questions are rarely found in the scientific literature per se, but are apparent in studies of science and technology as social processes (e.g., Yearley, 1995; Wynne, 1995), or more broadly in epistemological critiques of science (e.g., Ravetz, 1993). Even so, some scientific researchers, especially in the area of environmental risks to human health (Crawford-Brown and Arnold, 1993), have begun to consider the broader public policy implications of their work. As indicated earlier, the necessity of including social values in EIA such that the process itself is seen as primarily political in nature, is antithetical to most natural scientific research (with its claims of value neutrality), even though such work is, of course, consistent with its own (unwritten) set of values defined by its own practitioners. An appropriate label for this new context might be "Re-situating Science and Technology (i.e., Applied Science) in Society".

The positivistic nature of natural scientific research

continues to be equally present in the majority of social scientific inputs to the EIA process. Even with recent work to incorporate environmental goods and services into economic analysis, for example, the various attempts to improve on benefit-cost analysis (e.g., by using contingent valuation methods) are marginal at best, as an analytically closed system is created for purposes of predicting impacts. A more promising direction is indicated by organizational changes in the private sector itself, as both investments and insurance concerns redefine the limits of corporate responsibility for environmental degradation (Baram, 1991; Benidickson, 1994; Shrivastava, 1995). In effect, the globalization of economies has already changed the spatial and temporal parameters affecting the private sector; adding in environmental values (McCloskey and Smith, 1995) only increases the necessity of strategic assessments. In Canada, the importance of trade and competitiveness is reflected in various adjustments to EIA at the federal level (Morgan et al., 1992), and for some commentators similar processes have resulted in Ontario's revisions to its EIA processes. The response of the private sector is crucial in this respect, as much as the response of public interest groups to the new situation. It is possible that Canadian experience in multi-stakeholder decision-making processes (Greer-Wootten, 1994) can bear fruit in the more focussed situations of EIA. Generally, the signpost to this aspect of the contextual framing points to a greater concern with decision-making processes, especially the relationships between various stakeholders.

A similar movement away from positivist concerns can be inferred from work by social researchers generally outside EIA research community per se, i.e., in studies of the relationships between people and their environments. Although some such work remains clearly in a traditional framework (e.g., survey research on values: see Beatty, 1991), more innovative critiques of traditional models (Ungar, 1994) have shown that community social networks, and social movements generally (Yearley, 1994), are more meaningful for social impact assessment than the typical reliance on individual responses to development initiatives. Even some of the new technological innovations aimed at increasing public participation (Hughes and Schirmer, 1994) are more firmly rooted in a group-oriented perspective on local community involvement in decision-making processes (Campbell, 1996). Again, the direction appears to be toward the active involvement of workers in EIA with communities and groups facing potential impacts from development.

In a fairly consistent manner, risk assessment has been identified by many as a necessary component of EIA (e.g., Sewell and Mitchell, 1981; Dooley, 1985), yet the two areas of enquiry have largely developed in parallel. At a macro-social theoretical level, the case for urgent consideration of a necessary convergence has been made convincingly by Beck (1992). Methodologically, similar problems are realized in both areas of enquiry; for example, the limitations of quantitative approaches to risk estimation (Silbergeld, 1993) are reflected in the generally weak scientific inputs to EIA. Similarly, the problems engendered by public perceptions of risks (Renn et al., 1992) are indicative of the value differences between various stakeholders in evaluating the likely impacts of a proposed facility. Risk assessment, however, as a field of enquiry, has reached a more mature state than EIA research, perhaps because it is less conditioned by legislative and regulatory frameworks. The emphasis in this area for the last ten to fifteen years, for example, has increasingly focussed on risk management studies, i.e., on the policy and political aspects of risk assessment. Of particular interest for this discussion is the way in which the public has been incorporated into research interests, particularly with respect to risk communication (Kasperson and Stallen, 1991). Given the connections between human health and environmental risks, the work of Covello (1991), in particular, provides an important signpost for both the practice and practitioners of EIA.

The most important contextual framing for EIA identified here has developed in tandem with risk management studies, but it is more compelling - an explicit political analysis of the process. Interestingly, one of the first calls for more direct action in EIA originated from a practitioner (Craig, 1990) as a response to the technocratic constraints of the process. Much of the work in this area is intimately related to the ways in which public participation, in practice, does not match up to theoretical expectations - or even the levels at which it is legislated. As such, most researchers are involved with the process itself, in specifying the detailed levels of interaction between stakeholders as they become 'gridlocked' in conflict situations, or in examining variations in legislative and regulatory settings that appear to allow more voluntary, consensual decision-making processes to emerge and thus avoid conflict (Rabe, 1994). Much of the emphasis is on group conflict and the ways in which grassroots organizations can effectively participate in decisions that affect their community - even to the extent of effectively challenging scientific impact assessment (Fischer, 1995).

The theoretical framework for much of this important arena of contextualization is recent Critical Theory (Habermas, 1984, 1987). Habermas contends that the 'project of modernity' is not completed and that an ethical response to the problems of late capitalism is needed to re-insert democratic action into public policy mechanisms. Critical Theoretic approaches are based on a philosophy of communication that has a direct bearing on relations among actors in EIA. Like most philosophical models, a normative situation (the ideal speech act) is established, against which actual events (the discourse in a public hearing, for example) can be evaluated. Given the unequal position of proponents and intervenors in EIA, for example, it is highly likely that systematic bias in the process can be established. That much we know already, but Critical

Theory provides further aid in describing how bias occurred, and such knowledge can then be used to change the process.

The essential practical core of this approach is to examine relations among actors, particularly in terms of communicative competence (Renn et al., 1995a). The framework is proposed as a way of resolving the traditional social theoretic distinctions between consensus (i.e., structural functionalism) and conflict (i.e., Marxist) formulations, demonstrating the weaknesses of both in attempting to deal with problems surrounding public participation. The emphasis turns to the role of discourse in communications among stakeholders, especially important as both the degree of complexity of environmental problems increases and the potential for conflict escalates (Renn et al., 1995b). Establishing a set of normative rules (the ideal speech act), by which to judge the criteria of fairness and competence in public participation in environmental decision making, is a necessary foundation for this type of analysis. This has been achieved in Webler's (1995) detailed revision of Habermas' original formulation, and the first empirical test of these rules has been carried out successfully by Ward (1997) in his examination of a landfill siting EA in North Simcoe, Ontario.

The fact that Critical Theory has been employed to a greater extent in risk management studies, rather than EIA, is, in some ways, not surprising. Habermas' (1971) original work dealt with the problems of relations between technology and society, providing a conceptual framework for social research on nuclear power, for example (Kemp, 1992). Further, relatively limited attention was given to environmental issues in Critical Theory (White, 1988: 136-143) until recently (Vogel, 1996). In fact, a final contextual framing for EIA can be identified as a more explicit concern with philosophical analysis. For example, Satterthwaite (1997) employs models derived from Gadamer (1989) as well as

Habermas, in his analysis of the 1990 Northern Diseased Bison Environmental Assessment hearings in the Northwest Territories.

The changed emphasis to 'interpretation' rather than 'explanation' in critical social scientific research is not recent, of course, in general terms, but its application to empirical research on the socio-political processes inherent in environmental decision making does mark a new departure. Formerly a primary debate in policy analysis in the 1980s (Torgerson, 1986), the interpretive or 'argumentative turn' now has permeated discussions of planning (e.g., Dryzek, 1993; Forester, 1993; Healey, 1993). In analyzing the practice of stakeholders in the EIA process - for example, by discourse analysis of hearing transcripts or by actual participation in the process - the work of researchers in this contextual arena has some immediate and profound implications for practitioners.

Contextual Orientation and EIA Practitioners

The few EIA practitioners who comment on their roles in the process recognize their reliance on the rational or technocratic model of planning (e.g., Lawrence, 1992), the extent to which EIA professionals and planners have not merged in terms of methodological or institutional concerns (e.g., Armour, 1991), and the overarching influence of organizational situation or cultures on their work (e.g., Bronfman, 1991). The call for stronger theoretical frameworks is often heard, especially in terms of the sustainable development scenario (Spaling et al., 1993). A consistent underlying contention is that the voice of the public must be incorporated to a greater extent (e.g., Dirschl et al., 1993), in order to ensure social equity, community acceptance, etc.

Most of this commentary does not break out from the implicit epistemological bonds generated by working within an essentially administrative system. Stepping outside these explicit professional boundaries is essential if practitioners are to realize the strong influence of their epistemological and methodological perspectives on the task at hand (Serafin et al., 1992). The 'system' may require practitioners who are not reflexive in this manner, but as professionals there are too many post-positivistic critiques of the EIA process to be ignored. How, for example, do practitioners relate to Burningham's (1995) contention that we need to explore how social impacts are socially constructed? Unless the question is phrased in this way (among many other alternative framings), the technocratic imposition of methods such as using attitude surveys to estimate social impacts, will remain unquestioned. The role of participatory approaches to evaluating social impacts (Wildman, 1990) is a broadening of Burningham's contention.

Clearly, a post-positivist stance by the practitioner is 'necessary' to match the findings of critical social scientists with respect to the EIA process. It would also be 'sufficient' if the practitioner adopted a direct political approach to the task at hand. It is in this respect that Critical Theory provides a practical rationale for the politically-oriented practitioner, since the concern for communicative rationality requires a 'standpoint' epistemology. In this way, EIA can be changed, to avoid it being relegated to history as a "marginal managerial tool on the periphery of policy framing and budget allocation" (O'Riordan, 1990:155).

Conclusions

Recent changes to the EIA process in Ontario have been evaluated in this chapter in order to demonstrate the importance of contextualizing public participation in environmental decision making, primarily with reference to Critical Theory. Will the practical realization of the 1996 amendments lead to the more cooperative, consensual decision-making processes implicit in the sustainable development scenario (Smith, 1993)? Or, will the attention given to administrative mechanisms only serve to re-invent the conflict game and entrench the more traditional clashes between proponents and publics, affected or concerned (Greer-Wootten, 1990)? If so, then government could again be forced to take on its role of regulator, rather than the role most commentators would prefer it to have - as mediator or facilitator. An immediate implication is that there will be increased pressures for litigation in the future, and Critical Theory is also significant for research in this context (Blomley, 1994).

It is clear that ecological modernization (sustainable development) meets its greatest test at the local level. Yet, it is these same local impacted communities that are viewed as the 'front line' test cases for sustainable development by critics of the EIA process, concerned for a legitimate role for public participation. What they fear is that the cooptation of various publics into a decision-making process reflects their contention that "sustainable (economic) development is business-as-usual". In addition, a development proposal may have regional, provincial or national impacts, and these can hardly be considered only in the context of an impacted community (Lawrence, 1994). At present, too, it is still problematic as to which of the publics, affected or concerned, should be involved in any EIA, although this issue has been treated extensively for the broader question of policy design in May's (1991) theoretical framing of the problem.

In a pluralistic decision-making process, the extent of public involvement is of concern, but the record of public education in this respect is quite disappointing (Sinclair and Diduck, 1995 and Chapter 3). Intervenor groups stress that public involvement in EIA is important regardless of the power distributions involved, as it enables decision makers to become knowledgeable about the issues raised by the concerned publics, and to address their interests without resorting to adversarial means of resolving conflicts. Often the affected publics are the only ones aware of certain impacts, particularly where they affect community values. Public input and review supplements the government review by identifying concerns that may not be within the mandate of individual review agencies. The process itself is very important: those contributing must be allowed to present their views in an open and fair manner, and they should be able to see how their input has affected the decision made, particularly with respect to impact management (Zeiss, 1991). The government, then, would be acting as a facilitator of such processes, ensuring that the public sees how its involvement has been accounted for. In an ideal world, such processes would maximize cooperative decision-making processes, avoiding the conflicts that characterized many previous hearings.

The role of the public in EIA, especially following the 1996 amendments in Ontario, is not easy to predict, in part because the roles of the various actors are in flux (Greer-Wootten, 1994), but more importantly, because the resolution will be a political one. In fact, the politics of the environment at the scale of locality are extremely complicated (Reed, 1994). Adding sustainable development to the equation adds to the complexity. EIA has traditionally been more isolated from politics in Canada than in the US: the conflicts here have tended to be more technical, more bureaucratized, even with adversarial hearings and legalistic arguments. It is likely that this will change in the future, although much will depend on changes to the regulatory framework governing the EIA process, especially in the ways in which it can be interpreted and how practitioners respond to the changed situations. This is particularly true for social impacts; as Gramling and Freudenburg (1992:231) assert: "... the full range of social impacts have been not so much beyond our control as beyond our concepts", and it is but a short step to "... beyond our responsibilities as well".

Acknowledgements

The basic information used in this chapter was obtained from interviews with participants in the Opinion Leader Research Program, The Hay Group, Toronto, Ontario (see Greer-Wootten, 1994, for details), and I would like to thank Tom Atkinson and Gillian Gilmour for their continuing support and encouragement. I am particularly grateful to Antoinette Wells, Director of the Policy Development Branch of the Ontario Ministry of Environment and Energy, and to Rick Lindgren, Counsel to the Canadian Environmental Law Association, for their guidance in recent developments in EIA legislation in Ontario.

References

Armour, A. (1991) "Impact assessment and the planning process: a status report," *Impact Assessment Bulletin*, 9: 27-34.

Baram, M. (1991) "Rights and duties concerning the availability of environmental risk information to the public," in Kasperson, R.E. and Stallen, P.J.M. (eds.), *Communicating Risks to the Public, International Perspectives*, Boston, MA: Kluwer, 67-78.

Bardecki, M.J. (1994) "Policies and procedures for cumulative impact management," in Andrey, J. and Nelson, J.G. (eds.), *Public Issues: A Geographical Perspective*, Waterloo, ON: Department of Geography Publication Series No. 41, University of Waterloo, 355-368.

Bartlett, R.V. (1993) "Integrated impact assessments as environmental policy: the New Zealand experiment," *Policy Studies Review*, 12: 162-177.

Beanlands, G.E. (1985) "Ecology and impact assessment in Canada," in Maclaren, V.W. and Whitney, J.B. (eds.),

New Directions in Environmental Impact Assessment in Canada, Toronto, ON: Methuen, 1-20.

Beatty, K.M. (1991) "Public opinion data for environmental decision making: the case of Colorado Springs," *Environmental Impact Assessment Review*, 11: 29-51.

Beck, U. (1992) *Risk Society, Towards a New Modernity*, Newbury Park, CA: Sage.

Benidickson, J. (1994) "Canadian environmental law and policy: considerations from the investment perspective," in Benidickson, J., Doern, G.B. and Olewiler, N., *Getting the Green Light: Environmental Regulation and Investment in Canada*, Toronto, ON: C.D. Howe Institute, Policy Study 22, 1-52.

Blomley, N.K. (1994) *Law, Space and the Geographies of Power*, New York, NY: Guilford.

Bolton, K.F. and Curtis, F.A. (1990) "An environmental assessment procedure for siting solid waste disposal sites," *Environmental Impact Assessment Review*, 10: 285-296.

Bozzo, S.L. (1996) *A Conceptual Framework for the Evaluation of Alternative Dispute Resolution (ADR) Programs: The Ontario Environmental Assessment Board Experience*, unpublished M.E.S. Major Paper, North York, ON: Faculty of Environmental Studies, York University, 126 pp.

Bronfman, L.M. (1991) "Setting the social impact agenda: an organizational perspective," *Environmental Impact Assessment Review*, 11: 69-79.

Brown, L.C. (1996) *Waste Management EA: The Process is the Crisis*, unpublished M.E.S. Major Paper, North York,

ON: Faculty of Environmental Studies, York University, 136 pp.

Burdge, R.J. and Robertson, R.A. (1990) "Social impact assessment and the public involvement process," *Environmental Impact Assessment Review*, 10: 81-90.

Burningham, K. (1995) "Attitudes, accounts and impact assessment," *Sociological Review*, 43: 100- 122.

Campbell, H. (1996) "A social interactionist perspective on computer implementation," *Journal of the American Planning Association*, 62: 99-107.

Contant, C.K. and Wiggins, L.L. (1991) "Defining and analyzing cumulative environmental impacts," *Environmental Impact Assessment Review*, 11: 297-309.

Cornwell, P.D. (1990) *Post-Mortem*, New York, NY: Scribners.

Covello, V.T. (1991) "Risk comparisons and risk communications: issues and problems in comparing health and environmental risks," in Kasperson, R.E. and Stallen, P.J.M. (eds.), *Communicating Risks to the Public, International Perspectives*, Boston, MA: Kluwer, 79-124.

Craig, D. (1990) "Social impact assessment: politically oriented approaches and applications," *Environmental Impact Assessment Review*, 10: 37-54.

Craig, P.P. (1992) "Siting a liquid hazardous waste incinerator: experience with California's Tanner Act," *Environmental Impact Assessment Review*, 12: 363-386.

Crawford-Brown, D. and Arnold, J. (1993) "The role of evidential reason and epistemic discourse in establishing the risk of environmental carcinogens," in Cothern, C.R. (ed.), *Comparative Environmental Risk Assessment*,

Boca Raton, FL: Lewis, 261-278.

Dirschl, H.J., Novakowski, N.S. and Sadar, M.H. (1993) "Evolution of environmental impact assessment as applied to watershed modification projects in Canada," *Environmental Management*, 17: 545- 555.

Ditton, R.B. and Goodale, T.L. (eds.) (1972) *Environmental Impact Analysis: Philosophy and Methods*, Proceedings of the Conference on Environmental Impact Analysis, Green Bay, Wisconsin, January 4-5, Madison, WI: University of Wisconsin Sea Grant Program.

Dooley, J.E. (1985) "Risk and environmental management," in Maclaren, V.W. and Whitney, J.B. (eds.), *New Directions in Environmental Impact Assessment in Canada*, Toronto, ON: Methuen, 87-116.

Dryzek, J.S. (1993) "Policy analysis and planning: from science to argument," in Fischer, F. and Forester, J. (eds.), *The Argumentative Turn in Policy Analysis and Planning*, Durham, NC: Duke University Press, 213-232.

Environmental Assessment Advisory Committee (1992) *Environmental Assessment Reforms Part II: Summary of Recommendations by the Environmental Assessment Advisory Committee*, Toronto, ON: Queen's Publishing.

Fischer, F. (1995) "Hazardous waste policy, community movements and the politics of nimby: participatory risk assessment in the USA and Canada," in Fischer, F. and Black, M. (eds.), *Greening Environmental Policy. The Politics of a Sustainable Future*, New York, NY: St. Martin's Press, 165-182.

Forester, J. (1993) "Learning from practice stories: the priority of practical judgement," in Fischer, F. and Forester, J. (eds.), *The Argumentative Turn in Policy Analysis and*

Planning, Durham, NC: Duke University Press, 186-209.

Gadamer, H.G. (1989) *Truth and Method*, Second Edition, New York, NY: Crossroad Publishing Corporation.

Gagnon, C., Hirsch, P. and Howitt, R. (1993) "Can SIA empower communities?," *Environmental Impact Assessment Review*, 13: 229-253.

Gariepy, M. (1991) "Toward a dual-influence system: assessing the effects of public participation in environmental impact assessment for Hydro-Quebec projects," *Environmental Impact Assessment Review*, 11: 353-374.

Geisler, C.C. (1993) "Rethinking SIA: why ex ante research isn't enough," *Society and Natural Resources*, 6: 327-338.

Gibson, R.B. and Savan, B. (1986) *Environmental Assessment in Ontario*, Toronto, ON: Canadian Institute for Environmental Law and Policy.

Gilmour, G.M. (1993) *Changing Canada's Institutions: New Demands, Old Barriers*, Toronto, ON: Hay Opinion Leader Research Program, 55 pp.

Glasson, J. (1994) "EIA - Only the tip of the iceberg?," *Town and Country Planning*, 63: 42-45.

Glasson, J. and Heaney, D. (1993) "Socio-economic impacts: the poor relation in British environmental impact statements," *Journal of Environmental Planning and Management*, 36: 335-343.

Gramling, R. and Freudenburg, W.R. (1992) "Opportunity-threat, development, and adaptation: toward a comprehensive framework for social impact assessment," *Rural*

Sociology, 57: 216-234.

Greer-Wootten, B. (1988) "The science of locational risk or the risk of locational science?," in Massam, B.H. (ed.), *Complex Location Problems: Some Interdisciplinary Approaches*, North York, ON: York University Institute for Social Research Monograph Series, 98-132.

_____ (1990) *Canadian Environmental Issues and Localities: "Not In My Back Yard"*, Toronto, ON: Hay Opinion Leader Research Program, 41 pp.

_____ (1993) *Canadian Environmental Issues at the Regional Scale: "Not In Our Back Yard"*, Toronto, ON: Hay Opinion Leader Research Program, 38 pp.

_____ (1994) "The politics of interest groups in environmental decision making," in Andrey, J. and Nelson, J.G. (eds.), *Public Issues: A Geographical Perspective*, Waterloo, ON: Department of Geography Publication Series No. 41, University of Waterloo, 271-293.

Guba, E.G. and Lincoln, Y.S. (1988) "Do inquiry paradigms imply inquiry methodologies?," in Fetterman, D.M. (ed.), *Qualitative Approaches to Evaluation in Education*, New York, NY: Praeger, 89-115.

Habermas, J. (1971) *Knowledge and Human Interests*, Boston, MA: Beacon Press.

_____ (1984) *The Theory of Communicative Action: Volume 1, Reason and the Rationalization of Society*, Boston, MA: Beacon Press.

_____ (1987) *The Theory of Communicative Action: Volume 2, Lifeworld and System: A Critique of Functionalist Reason*, Boston, MA: Beacon Press.

Harvey, D. (1996) *Justice, Nature and the Geography of Difference*, Oxford, UK: Blackwell.

Healey, P. (1993) "Planning through debate: the communicative turn in planning theory," in Fischer, F. and Forester, J. (eds.), *Argumentative Turn in Policy Analysis and Planning*, Durham, NC: Duke University Press, 233-253.

Hoberg, G. (1991) "Sleeping with an elephant: the American influence on Canadian environmental regulation," *Journal of Public Policy*, 11: 107-132.

Holling, C.S. (ed.) (1978) *Adaptive Environmental Assessment and Modelling*, Chichester, UK: Wiley.

Hughes, G. and Schirmer, D. (1994) "Interactive multimedia, public participation and environmental assessment," *Town Planning Review*, 65: 399-414.

Jeffrey, M.I. (1990) "Environmental assessment processes in Canada and Australia: a comparative analysis," *Impact Assessment Bulletin*, 8: 289-307.

Kasperson, R.E., and Stallen, P.J.M. (1991) "Risk communication: the evolution of attempts," in Kasperson, R.E. and Stallen, P.J.M. (eds.), *Communicating Risks to the Public, International Perspectives*, Boston, MA: Kluwer, 1-12.

Kemp, R. (1992) *The Politics of Radioactive Waste Disposal*, Manchester, UK: Manchester University Press.

Kennedy, A.J. and Ross, W.A. (1992) "An approach to integrate impact scoping with environmental impact assessment," *Environmental Management*, 16: 475-484.

Lawrence, D.P. (1992) "Planning and environmental impact

assessment: never the twain shall meet?," *Plan Canada*, July: 22-26.

_____ (1994) "Designing and adapting the EIA planning process," *The Environmental Professional*, 16: 2-21.

Lemons, J. (1994) "The use of science in environmental impact assessment," *International Journal of Ecology and Environmental Sciences*, 20: 303-315.

Lindgren, R.D. (1996) *Submissions of the Canadian Environmental Law Association to the Standing Committee on Social Development Regarding Bill 76 - Environmental Assessment and Consultation Improvement Act,* Toronto, ON: C.E.L.A., 57 pp.

Lowes, P. (1996) *Pyschosocial Impacts of the Planning Process,* unpublished M.E.S. thesis, North York, ON: Faculty of Environmental Studies, York University, 266 pp.

Manring, N., West, P.C. and Bidol, P. (1990) "Social impact assessment and environmental conflict management: potential for integration and application," *Environmental Impact Assessment Review*, 10: 253-265.

May, P.J. (1991) "Reconsidering policy design: policies and publics," *Journal of Public Policy*, 11: 187-206.

McCloskey, J. and Smith, D. (1995) "Strategic management and business policy-making: bringing in environmental values," in Fischer, F. and Black, M. (eds.), *Greening Environmental Policy, The Politics of a Sustainable Future*, New York, NY: St. Martin's Press, 199-209.

Meredith, T. (1995) "Assessing environmental impacts in Canada," in Mitchell, B. (ed.), *Resource and Environmental Management in Canada, Addressing*

Conflict and Uncertainty, Toronto, ON: Oxford University Press, 360-383.

Morgan, N., Palleson, M. and Thompson, A.R. (1992) *Environmental Impact Assessment and Competitiveness*, Ottawa, ON: National Round Table on the Environment and the Economy, Working Paper Number 7, 47 pp. (mimeo).

Mulvihill, P.R. and Keith, R.F. (1989) "Institutional requirements for adaptive EIA: the kativik environmental quality commission," *Environmental Impact Assessment Review*, 9: 399-412.

Novek, J. (1993) "Environmental impact assessment in practice: exploring contradictions," *Great Plains Research*, 3: 337-357.

Ontario Ministry of Environment and Energy (1996) *Reforming Environment and Energy Regulation in Ontario, Responsive Environmental Protection*, Toronto, ON: OMEE, 72 pp.

O'Riordan, T. (1990) "An equilibrium not of this world," *Town and Country Planning*, 59: 154-156.

Policansky, D. (1993) "Application of ecological knowledge to environmental problems: ecological risk assessment," in Cothern, C.R. (ed.), *Comparative Environmental Risk Assessment*, Boca Raton, FL: Lewis, 35-51.

Rabe, B.G. (1994) *Beyond Nimby: Hazardous Waste Siting in Canada and the United States*, Washington, DC: The Brookings Institution.

Ravetz, J.R. (1993) "The sin of science, ignorance of ignorance," *Knowledge: Creation, Diffusion, Utilization*, 15: 157-165.

Reed, M.G. (1994) "Locally responsive environmental planning in the Canadian hinterland: a case study in Northern Ontario," *Environmental Impact Assessment Review*, 14: 245-269.

_____ (1995) "Cooperative management of environmental resources: a case study from Northern Ontario, Canada," *Economic Geography*, 71: 132-149.

Rees, W.E. (1995) "Cumulative environmental assessment and global change," *Environmental Impact Assessment Review*, 15: 295-309.

Renn, O., Webler, T. and Wiedemann, P. (1995a) *Fairness and Competence in Citizen Participation, Evaluating Models for Environmental Discourse*, Boston, MA: Kluwer.

_____ (1995b) "The pursuit of fair and competent citizen participation," in Renn, O., Webler, T. and Wiedemann, P. (eds.), *Fairness and Competence in Citizen Participation, Evaluating Models for Environmental Discourse*, Boston, MA: Kluwer, 339-367.

Renn, O., Burns, W.J., Kasperson, J.X., Kasperson, R.E., and Slovic, P. (1992) "The social amplification of risk: theoretical foundations and empirical applications," *Journal of Social Issues*, 48: 137-160.

Rickson, R.E., Western, J.S. and Burdge, R.J. (1990) "Social impact assessment: knowledge and development," *Environmental Impact Assessment Review*, 10: 1-10.

Roberts, R. (1988) "Public involvement: a Canadian government manual for planning and implementing public involvement programs," *Environmental Impact Assessment Review*, 8: 3-7.

Sadler, B. (1993) "Mediation provisions and options in Canadian environmental assessment," *Environmental Impact Assessment Review*, 13: 375-390.

Satterthwaite, A.J. (1997) *Public Voices and Wilderness in Environmental Assessment: A Philosophical Examination of Resource Policy Decisions*, unpublished Ph.D. dissertation, North York, ON: Faculty of Environmental Studies, York University, 390pp.

Serafin, R., Nelson, G. and Butler, R. (1992) "Post hoc assessment in resource management and environmental planning: a typology and three case studies," *Environmental Impact Assessment Review*, 12: 271-294.

Sewell, W.R.D. and Mitchell, B. (1981) "The way ahead," in Mitchell, B. and Sewell, W.R.D. (eds.), *Canadian Resource Policies: Problems and Prospects*, Toronto, ON: Methuen, 262-284.

Shadish, W.R. (1995) "Philosophy of science and the quantitative-qualitative debates: thirteen common errors," *Evaluation and Program Planning*, 18: 63-75.

Shrivastava, P. (1995) "Industrial and environmental crises: rethinking corporate social responsibility," in Fisher, F. and Black, M. (eds.), *Greening Environmental Policy, The Politics of a Sustainable Future*, New York, NY: St. Martin's Press, 183-198.

Silbergeld, E.K. (1993) "Revising the risk assessment paradigm: limits on the quantitative ranking of environmental problems," in Cothern, C.R. (ed.), *Comparative Environmental Risk Assessment*, Boca Raton, FL: Lewis, 73-77.

Silcoff, S. (1996) "Bill on landfills harmful, group warns," *The Globe and Mail*, 31 July, A5.

Sinclair, J. and Diduck, A. (1995) "Public education: an undervalued component of the environmental assessment public involvement process," *Environmental Impact Assessment Review*, 15: 219- 240.

Smit, B. and Spaling, H. (1995) "Methods for cumulative effects assessment," *Environmental Impact Assessment Review*, 15: 81-106.

Smith, L.G. (1993) *Impact Assessment and Sustainable Resource Management*, New York, NY: Wiley.

Spaling, H. and Smit, B. (1993) "Cumulative environmental change: conceptual frameworks, evaluation approaches, and institutional perspectives," *Environmental Management*, 17: 587-600.

Spaling, H., Smit, B. and Kreutzwiser, R. (1993) "Evaluating environmental impact assessment: approaches, lessons, and prospects," *Environments*, 22: 63-74.

Sundstrom, M. (1994) "Oldman river dam," in Andrey, J. and Nelson, J.G. (eds.), *Public Issues: A Geographical Perspective*, Waterloo, ON: Department of Geography Publication Series No. 41, University of Waterloo, 221-237.

Taylor, S.M., Elliott, S., Eyles, J., Frank, J., Haight, M., Streiner, D., Walter, S., White, N. and Willms, D. (1991) "Psychosocial impacts in populations exposed to solid waste facilities," *Social Science and Medicine*, 33: 441-447.

Therivel, R. (1993) "Systems of strategic environmental assessment," *Environmental Impact Assessment Review*, 13: 145-168.

Torgerson, D. (1986) "Between knowledge and politics: three

faces of policy analysis," *Policy Sciences*, 19: 33-59.

Ungar, S. (1994) "Apples and oranges: probing the attitude-behaviour relationship for the environment," *Canadian Review of Sociology and Anthropology*, 31: 288-304.

Vogel, S. (1996) *Against Nature. The Concept of Nature in Critical Theory*, Albany, NY: State University of New York Press.

Ward, S. (1997) *An Examination of Public Legitimacy: North Simcoe's Environmental Assessment Process*, unpublished M.A. Thesis, North York, ON: Geography, York University (in process).

Webler, T. (1995) "'Right' discourse in citizen participation: an evaluative yardstick," in Renn, O., Webler, T. and Wiedemann, P. (eds.), *Fairness and Competence in Citizen Participation, Evaluating Models for Environmental Discourse*, Boston, MA: Kluwer, 35-86.

Wescott, G. (1992) "A standard format for use in the analysis of environmental policy," *Journal of Environmental Management*, 35: 69-79.

White, S.K. (1988) *The Recent Work of Jurgen Habermas: Reason, Justice and Modernity*, Cambridge, UK: Cambridge University Press.

Wildman, P. (1990) "Methodological and social policy issues in social impact assessment," *Environmental Impact Assessment Review*, 10: 69-79.

Wynne, B. (1995) "Public understanding of science," in Jasanoff, S., Markle, G.E., Petersen, J.C. and Pinch, T. (eds.), *Handbook of Science and Technology Studies*, Thousand Oaks, CA: Sage, 361-388.

Yearley, S. (1994) "Social movements and environmental change," in Redclift, M. and Benton, T. (eds.), *Social Theory and the Global Environment*, London, UK: Routledge, 150-168.

_____ (1995) "The environmental challenge to science studies," in Jasanoff, S., Markle, G.E., Petersen, J.C. and Pinch, T. (eds.), *Handbook of Science and Technology Studies*, Thousand Oaks, CA: Sage, 457-479.

Zeiss, C. (1991) "Community decision-making and impact management priorities for siting waste facilities," *Environmental Impact Assessment Review*, 11: 231-255.

University of Waterloo

Department of Geography Publication Series

Available from Geography Publications
University of Waterloo
Waterloo, Ontario, Canada
N2L 3G1

Series

48 Mitchell, Clare and Dahms, Fred, editors (1997) Challenge and Opportunity: Managing Change in Canadian Towns and Villages, ISBN 0-921083-56-4, 298 pages.

47 Filion, P., Bunting, T.E. and Curtis, K., editors (1996) The Dynamics of the Dispersed City: Geographic and Planning Perspectives on Waterloo Region, ISBN 0-921083-55-6, 427 pages.

46 Sanderson, Marie (1996) Weather and Climate in Kitchener-Waterloo, Ontario, ISBN 0-921083-54-8, 122 pages.

45 Andrey, J., editor (1995) Transport Planning and Policy Issues: Geographical Perspectives, ISBN 0-921083-53-X, 261 pages.

44 Martopo, S. and Mitchell, B., editors (1995) Bali: Balancing Environment, Economy and Culture, ISBN 0-921083-52-1, 674 pages.

43 McLellan, A.G. (1995) The Consultant Geographer: Private Practice and Geography, ISBN 0-921083-51-3, 230 pages.

42 Shoemaker, Darryl (1994) Cumulative Environmental Assessment, ISBN 0-921083-50-5, 139 pages.

41 Andrey, Jean and Nelson, J. Gordon, editors (1994) Public Issues: A Geographical Perspective, ISBN 0-921083-49-1, 435 pages.

40 Sanderson, Marie, editor (1993) The Impact of Climate Change on Water in the Grand River Basin, Ontario, ISBN 0-

921083-48-3, 248 pages.

39 Lerner, Sally, editor (1993) Environmental Stewardship: Studies in Active Earthkeeping, ISBN 0-921083-46-7, 472 pages.

38 LeDrew, E., Hegyi, F. and Strome, M., editors (1995) The Canadian Remote Sensing Contribution to Understanding Global Change, ISBN 0-921083-45-9, 462 pages.

37 Nelson, J.G., Butler, R. and Wall, G., editors (1993) Tourism and Sustainable Development: Monitoring, Planning, Managing, ISBN 0-921083-44-0, 306 pages.

36 Day, J.C. and Quinn, Frank (1992) Water Diversion and Export: Learning From Canadian Experience, ISBN 0-921083-42-4, 236 pages.

35 Mitchell, Bruce and Shrubsole, Dan (1992) Ontario Conservation Authorities: Myth and Reality, ISBN 0-921083-41-6, 388 pages.

34 Mitchell, Bruce, editor (1991) Ontario: Geographical Perspectives on Economy and Environment, ISBN 0-921083-37-8, 311 pages.

32 Charette, Roxanne and Krueger, Ralph (1992) The Low-Temperature Hazard to the Quebec Orchard Industry, ISBN 0-921083-30-0, 166 pages.

30 Coppack, Philip M., Russwurm, Lorne H. and Bryant, Christopher R., editors (1988) The Urban Field, Essays on Canadian Urban Process and Form III, ISBN 0-921083-25-4, 249 pages.

29 Guelke, Leonard and Preston, Richard E., editors (1987) Abstract Thoughts: Concrete Solutions: Essays in Honour of Peter Nash, ISBN 0-921083-26-2, 332 pages.

28 Dufournaud, Christian and Dudycha, Douglas, editors (1987) Waterloo Lectures in Geography, Vol. 3, Quantitative Analysis in Geography, ISBN 0-921083-24-6, 140 pages.

27 Nelson, J. Gordon and Knight, K. Drew, editors (1987) Research, Resources and the Environment in Third World Development, ISBN 0-921083-23-8, 220 pages.

26 Walker, David F., editor (1987) Manufacturing in Kitchener-Waterloo: A Long-Term Perspective, ISBN 0-921083-22-X, 220 pages.

25 Guelke, Leonard, editor (1986) Waterloo Lectures in Geography, Vol. 2, Geography and Humanistic Knowledge, ISBN 0-921083-21-1, 101 pages.

24 Bastedo, Jamie, D. (1986) An ABC Resource Survey Method for Environmentally Significant Areas with Special Reference to Biotic Surveys in Canada's North, ISBN 0-921083-20-3, 135 pages.

23 Bryant, Christopher, R., editor (1984) Waterloo Lectures in Geography, Vol. 1, Regional Economic Development, ISBN 0-921083-19-X, 115 pages.

22 Knapper, Christopher, Gertler, Leonard and Wall, Geoffrey (1983) Energy, Recreation and the Urban Field, ISBN 0-921083-18-1, 89 pages.

21 Dudycha, Douglas J., Smith, Stephen, L.J., Stewart, Terry O. and McPherson, Barry D. (1983) The Canadian Atlas of Recreation and Exercise, ISBN 0-921083-17-3, 61 pages.

20 Mitchell, Bruce and Gardner, James S., editors (1983) River Basin Management: Canadian Experiences, ISBN 0-921083-16-5, 443 pages.

19 Gardner, James S., Smith, Daniel J. and Desloges, Joseph R. (1983) The Dynamic Geomorphology of the Mt. Rae Area: High Mountain Region in Southwestern Alberta, ISBN 0-921083-15-7, 237 pages.

17 Wall, Geoffrey and Knapper, Christopher (1981) Tutankhamun in Toronto, ISBN 0-921083-13-0, 113 pages.

16 Walker, David F., editor (1980) The Human Dimension in

Industrial Development, ISBN 0-921083-12-2, 124 pages.

13 Mitchell, Bruce, Gardner, James S., Cook, Robert and Veale, Barbara (1978) Physical Adjustments and Institutional Arrangements for the Urban Flood Hazard: Grand River Watershed, ISBN 0-921083-10-6, 142 pages.

12 Nelson, J. Gordon, Needham, Roger D. and Mann, Donald (1978) International Experience with National Parks and Related Reserves, ISBN 0-921083-09-2, 624 pages.

8   Walker, David F., editor (1977) Industrial Services, ISBN 0-921083-07-6, 107 pages.

6   Bullock, Ronald A. (1975) Ndeiya, Kikuyu Frontier: The Kenya Land Problem in Microcosm, ISBN 0-921083-06-8, 144 pages.

Occasional Papers

16 Wall, Geoff, editor (1993) Impacts of Climate Change on Resource Management of the North, ISBN 0-921083-47-5, 270 pages.

15 Wall, Geoff, editor (1992) Symposium on the Implications of Climate Change for Pacific Northwest Forest Management, ISBN 0-921083-43-2, 244 pages.

14 Hucal, Darlene and McBoyle, Geoff (1992) Job Opportunities for Geography Graduates, 8th edition, ISBN 0-921083-40-8, 178 pages.

13 Sanderson, Marie, editor (1991) Water Pipelines and Diversions in the Great Lakes Basin, ISBN 0-921083-39-4, 131 pages.

12 Wall, Geoffrey, editor (1991) Symposium on the Impacts of Climatic Change and Variability on the Great Plains, ISBN 0-921083-38-6, 376 pages.

11 Wall, Geoffrey and Sanderson, Marie, editors (1990) Climate Change: Implications for Water and Ecological Resources, An

International Symposium/Workshop, ISBN 0-921083-36-X, 342 pages.

10 Chalmers, Lex (University of Waikato), and MacLennan, Mark (State University at Buffalo, New York) (1990) Expert Systems in Geography and Environmental Studies: An Annotated View of Recent Work in the Field, ISBN 0-921083-35-1, 92 pages.

8 Adeniyi, Peter O. and Bullock, Ronald A., editors (1988) Seasonal Land Use and Land Cover in Northwest Nigeria: An Atlas of the Sokoto-Rima Basin, ISBN 0-921083-32-7, 32 pages.

7 Adeniyi, Peter O. (1988) Land Use and Land Cover in the Central Sokoto-Rima Basin, Northwest Nigeria (Map) ISBN 0-921083-31-9.

6 Bryant, Christopher, R., LeDrew, Ellsworth, F., Marois, Claude and Cavayas, Francois, editors (1989) Remote Sensing and Methodologies of Land Use Change Analysis, ISBN 0-921083-29-7, 178 pages.

5 Guelke, Leonard (1987) The Southwestern Cape Colony 1657-1750: Freehold Land Grants (Map) ISBN 0-921083-27-0.

3 Bunting, Trudi, E. (1984) Kitchener-Waterloo - The Geography of Mainstreet, ISBN 0-921083-02-5, 117 pages.

1 Diem, Aubrey, editor (1984) The Mont Blanc-Pennine Region, ISBN 0-921083-00-9, 186 pages.

DATE DUE